Hitler's Flemish Lions

HITLER'S
FLEMISH LIONS

THE HISTORY OF THE 27TH SS-FREIWILLIGEN GRENADIER DIVISION LANGEMARCK (FLÄMISCHE NR.1)

Book 2 in the *Hitler's Legions* series

by

Jonathan Trigg

The History Press

Front of jacket: *SS-Legion Flandern volunteers in the frontline outside Leningrad in the winter of 1941/1942. (Courtesy of Rene Chavez)*

Back of jacket: *Bert Degruytter, a freiwillige in the SS-Legion Flandern, carrying his Schmeisser MP40 submachine-gun and showing the strain of battle in the Volkhov Pocket in 1942. (Courtesy of Luc De Bast)*

First published in 2007 by Spellmount

This paperback edition published 2012

The History Press
97 St George's Place,
Cheltenham, Gloucestershire, GL50 3QB
www.thehistorypress.co.uk

British Library Cataloguing in Publication Data.
A catalogue record for this book is available from the British Library.

ISBN 978 0 7524 6730 6

Typesetting and origination by The History Press
Printed by TJ Books Limited, Padstow, Cornwall

Contents

	List of maps	7
	Acknowledgements	9
	Notes on the Text	11
	Introduction	13
I	A Tale of Two Peoples: The Flemish and the Walloons	17
II	Flanders: The Rise of Nationalism and the Extreme Right	25
III	1940: Blitzkrieg and Belgian Collapse	35
IV	The Waffen-SS and the Legionary Movement	45
V	Round One: Leningrad and the SS-Legion Flandern	65
VI	Round Two: Vlasov, the Volkhov Pocket and Krasny-Bor	73
VII	Rebirth: The SS-Sturmbrigade Langemarck	105
VIII	Dogged defence in the Ukraine	119
IX	The Legend of Narva: The Battle of the European SS	133
X	Last Throw of the Dice: The Formation of the SS-Langemarck Division	165
XI	The Ending: Pomerania	181
XII	Retribution	203
Appendix A	Waffen-SS Organisation	213
Appendix B	Waffen-SS Ranks	217
	Bibliography	219
	Index	221

List of Maps

1 Flanders and Walloonia, 1940, (page 22)
2 The Battle of the Volkhov Pocket, January–July 1942 (page 76)
3 SS-Sturmbrigade Langemarck Ukrainian Campaign, January–April 1944 (page 124)
4 SS-Kampfgruppe D'Haese, 25–29 July 1944, Battle of the European SS at Narva, Estonia (page 153)
5 The End – the 27th SS-Langemarck Division in northern Germany, 1945 (page 198)

Acknowledgements

I would like to express my thanks to a number of people, without whose help and support this book would never have been written. First to the Flemish veterans themselves, both from the SS-Legion Flandern and the Langemarck. As time marches on their numbers are dwindling – in recent years both Remy Schrijnen and Georg D'Haese have passed away – but, as ever, without the help and patience of the veterans in answering endless mind-numbing questions on obscure details of events that happened more than sixty years ago, this book would have been impossible to write. Thanks again to Frau Notzke at the Bundesarchiv; I think she is resigned to my constant correspondence from now until the series is finished or she gets another job!

Thanks to my publishers at Spellmount: to Jamie for starting me on this journey and to Shaun for his constant encouragement and chivvying. My thanks go yet again to my oldest and best friend Tim: you helping me has become a bit of a habit.

As any author writing military history will attest, one of the major challenges is to find photographs that are both interesting and illustrative of the text, and maybe even to find the 'Holy Grail' – photos that have never been previously published. This task was made so much easier for me with the help of some real stars from across the world, so thank you to Kris Simoens, Rene Chavez, Michel Breiz, Sébastian J. Bianchi and James Mcleod, and in particular thank you to Luc De Bast for allowing me access to his amazing private collection.

Thank you as well to everyone who has bought and read *Hitler's Gauls*. If no-one had then this book would never have seen the light of day.

Last but definitely not least I want to again thank my beautiful wife for putting up with me during the writing of this book and to my children, Maddy and Jack, who at least tried to stop yawning when Daddy was telling them what he was doing all this time.

Notes on the Text

Military ranks: Waffen-SS ranks are used for Waffen-SS personnel. A conversion chart has been provided as Appendix B. German Army (*Heer*) ranks and those of the Red Army are used for their respective soldiers.

Military terminology: As far as possible the military terminology used is that of the time and the army involved. On occasion an attempt has been made to 'translate' that terminology into modern British Army parlance in order to aid understanding.

Unit designation: All orders of battle use the German unit designation of the time and this is continued throughout except in certain circumstances where it is simplified to improve the flow of the text. Russian formations are numbered while German formations are written or use the original Roman numerals.

Foreign words: Where non-English words are used they are italicised unless in common usage and English translations are given immediately afterwards. If then used often in the text they are no longer italicised.

Measurements: Distances are given in miles but weapon calibres are given in their usual metric form.

Place names: Particularly as regards places in the Soviet Union I have stuck with one spelling if there are several but have also tried to include other derivations in brackets, the same goes for those cities/towns/villages in German Pomerania as was, that are now Polish.

Introduction

It was so damned hot! The young Flemish volunteer from Bruges wiped the sweat from his brow, but his eyes still stung from the salt in the perspiration that was pouring down his brick-red face. He risked a glance at the man on his right in the line and was pleased to see that he was also sweating freely and he looked damned nervous too – maybe it was alright to be scared. His comrade returned his look and suddenly they both grinned at each other, it was all they could manage not to burst into laughter. They had stood in the line since early that morning but hadn't had an opportunity to fight as yet. So far it had been a battle of missiles from both sides with death and injury claiming men seemingly by chance. As the morning had worn on the hot July sun had got fiercer and fiercer, and the men had had no chance to drink or seek shade. Behind them the young volunteers could hear the screaming of their wounded comrades and the laboured curses of the stretcher bearers nominated to carry the dead and injured from their ranks. But they didn't think about that; all their attention was suddenly focused out to their front again where they could see the massed lines of the enemy finally beginning to form up ready to attack. All along the line from left to right the enemy was beginning to move and get ready for what everyone knew would be the decisive charge. The Flemings settled their helmets more comfortably on their heads and gripped their weapons tighter. This was it. God, there were a lot of them out there in front! But the Flemings knew they had to hold. To hold was to live; to break was to be torn to bloody shreds in a panic-stricken mob, to be cut to pieces in the dust. The same thought went through many a Fleming's head: 'But there are so many of them, and they are so lavishly equipped with the very best, how can we stand?' There were no answers yet.

Then it began. The enemy line began to move forward, halting and jerky at first while they sorted themselves out. Then the pace picked up and the raucous cries and shouts of encouragement started. In contrast, the Flemings were silent. Only discipline held them now, that and the

13

proximity of their fellows. After all, running is easy when you're faceless but when you're surrounded by your neighbours from the street back home running is the hardest thing to do. If someone ran everyone would know it and the shame would be tremendous. So, held by fear of failure as much as iron discipline the young men of tiny Flanders stood their ground and waited with dry throats and bladders suddenly full.

The enemy was close now, the charge in full flow and the noise they made as they screamed their battle cries and pounded across the ground hit the Flemish line like a single living thing. The line seemed to shudder and the charging soldiers saw it and shouted for joy – they would break and be slaughtered! But the line didn't break: it steadied, and the charging Frenchmen saw that too. The French cavalry realised too late that the Flemish militia would hold, and those that tried to turn their horses away only succeeding in robbing their charge of momentum. But the vast majority of the first line hit the Flemish wall of pikes and spears head-on at full tilt. As the French cavalry stalled the Flemish foot soldiers swung their *goedendags*, bulky five-foot-long wooden staffs topped with vicious steel pikeheads (the name means 'hello' or 'good day'), into the melee of men and horses, cutting down the cream of French chivalry.

The result was military disaster for the French. Armoured cavalry, the acknowledged elite of the military world, had ruled the battlefields of Europe for the best part of 800 years but here in Flanders at Kortrijk (Courtrai in French) on the afternoon of 11 July 1302 that era was going to come to a bloody and inglorious end.

Kortrijk was a pivotal battle in the history of the Middle Ages in Europe and presaged the later victories of the Scots at Bannockburn in 1314 and the Swiss against the Austrians at Morgarten in 1315. It is more than coincidence that all three battles were not only won by previously subject peoples against their erstwhile imperial masters, but also that in all three battles it was steadfast infantry that humbled armies of mounted knights and men-at-arms.

This book, the second in the *Hitler's Legions* series, is about the men of Flanders who fought in their thousands alongside the Germans, firstly in the SS-Legion Flandern, then in the SS-Sturmbrigade Langemarck and finally, in their last incarnation, in the 27th SS-Freiwilligen Grenadier Division Langemarck (Flämische Nr.1). Although not a sovereign nation in themselves, and with their population totalling less than that of Birmingham in the UK, the Flemish were to supply the Third Reich with more volunteers than Great Britain, France, Sweden, Norway and Denmark combined. Indeed, along with their next-door neighbours and racial cousins the Dutch, the Flemish contributed more volunteers as a proportion of their population than any other Western European people. Not only would they supply large numbers of fighting men, but those same men would also earn glory for themselves in the bloody battles of the Eastern Front almost from the start of the war in the Soviet Union.

Of the thirty-eight nominal Waffen-SS divisions created by the end of the war over half were composed of either foreigners or the so-called *Volksdeutsche* (racial Germans born outside the borders of Germany at the outbreak of the war). But many of these formations contributed little if anything militarily to the Nazi war effort. This could not be said of the Flemings. From the bitter Siege of Leningrad in 1941 to the slaughter at the Battle of the Volkhov Pocket in 1942, the desperate defensive fighting in the Ukraine in 1943–44, to the famous 'Battle of the European SS' at Narva in Estonia in 1944, and finally to the snow-bound hell of Pomerania and the Oder in 1945, the Flemings made their mark in combat.

But who exactly are the Flemish? Flanders constitutes the northern half of Belgium, due northwest of Dover and a few hours' sailing time across the English Channel, so the Flemish are officially at least Belgians, but then why didn't they fight with that idol of the foreign legionary movement in World War II, Léon Degrelle and his Rexists? After all, he was Belgian. Were there differences between Degrelle and his men and the Flemings that made it impossible for them to serve together? Degrelle and his volunteers started out as as *Heer* volunteers, a German Army unit, and not Waffen-SS men, whereas the Flemings were a Waffen-SS Legion from the start.

What was the difference? The answer is complex, and as with so much else within the history of foreign volunteers in the Second World War, that complexity grows out of centuries of history and tradition. Any attempt to characterise the multiplicity of motives of Hitler's volunteers must begin with the climate of virulent anti-Bolshevik sentiment. Many at the time felt that Western European civilisation was under threat from the faceless hordes from the barbaric East. (Needless to say, volunteers from the Soviet Union shared the anti-communist part of this motivation, but without the same prejudice against people from the East!) But part of what makes the Flemish volunteers so interesting is that, unlike so many of their comrades in other volunteer formations, anti-communism was not the main motive for their participation in the war. Rather, it was the nationalism of the Flemish people, a long-standing determination that has yet to force a material result. The story of the Flemish Waffen-SS must be seen as a defining chapter in the history of a struggle that began centuries ago and continues even today, with the political machinations of the nationalist far-Right Flemish Vlaams Blok party and its successor, the Vlaams Belang.

In order to understand the Flemish SS volunteers in the Langemarck, one has to understand who the Flemings are. That identity includes the tumultuous events of the field of the 'Golden Spurs' at the climatic moments of the Battle of Kortrijk back in the hot summer of 1302.

I

A Tale of Two Peoples:
The Flemish and the Walloons

Belgium is a small country of around ten million inhabitants, and along-side its next-door neighbour, the Netherlands, it lies sandwiched between the twin giants of Germany to the east and France to the west. The southern half of Belgium is Walloonia, based on the medieval cities of Charleroi and Namur and containing about forty per cent of the population. The Walloons are Gallic in language, culture and outlook. French-speaking, they have always followed their southerly neighbours, the French. The northern half of Belgium, the provinces of West-Vlaanderen, East-Vlaanderen, Antwerpen, Brabant and Limburg, constitute the ancient territory of Flanders (*Vlaanderen* in Flemish and *Flandern* in German) and its inhabitants are called the Flemish. The Flemish make up the majority of the Belgian population, about sixty per cent, and speak their own language, which is closely related to Dutch and German. The country, like so much of the Low Countries, is still quite rural, with fertile, flat farmland stretching away in all directions. The countryside is dotted with prosperous and well-kept towns and villages and a few historic cities such as Bruges, Ghent and Antwerp which dominate the landscape, geographically, politically and culturally. The racial divide between these two peoples is the dominating issue in the history of Belgium and the most important factor in understanding the men who fought in the Langemarck and its predecessor units.

Rome and the Belgae

Present-day Belgium is named after its original Celtic inhabitants, the tribe of the Belgae. As with the rest of Celtic Europe (bar far-flung Scotland and Ireland), the Belgae were conquered by the Roman legions. Over nearly four centuries of the Pax Romana the local Celts in the fertile lands of the Belgae became thoroughly Romanised and integrated into the Empire. But finally, right at the beginning of the fifth century AD, the era of imperial Rome was coming to a bloody close (at least in the West) as a vast tide of barbarian Germanic tribes moved relentlessly over what was the imperial frontier – the mighty River Rhine.

The Germans are coming

Although at the time it was thought that the Empire was suffering from a series of invasions, we now know that it was actually the frontal edge of a huge migration that had started thousands of miles east on the borders of China. As nomadic peoples such as the Huns and Scythians moved west in search of fresh grazing and hunting grounds they displaced the tribes they met, who in turn pushed other tribes to move farther to the west, and so on. The net result was an irresistible wave that came crashing into the Western Roman Empire when it was at its weakest point in more than two centuries. For Roman Gaul (modern-day Belgium and parts of France, the Netherlands and Germany east of the Rhine) that meant a host of ferocious Teutons arriving in successive migrations over more than a century. Some of the barbarians moved through Gaul and onwards to other provinces: the Visigoths and Ostrogoths to Spain, the Asding and Gepid Vandals to North Africa and the Lombards to northern Italy. Some settled specific areas and gave them their names, for example the Burgundians and Suevi settled Burgundy and Swabia in southern Germany respectively. Others conquered territories and became the overlords of the people who already lived there.

One such tribe were the Franks, who, like all of the Teutonic peoples, were tall, blond haired and blue-eyed warriors. They moved into Gaul, seized land, built houses and began to farm and trade. In a few places they settled in large numbers, but in most they were fairly thinly spread, and overall they were greatly outnumbered by the existing Romano-Gallic inhabitants. Over time they intermarried and absorbed the language and customs of their new neighbours. In this manner, modern-day France began to establish its own identity, not Teutonic but Gallic. This meant that the true racial frontier between the invading mass of Germanic tribes and the settled Romano-Gauls lies not in France but in modern-day Belgium, or more accurately in its northern half, Flanders.

The Germanic Flemish

Flanders was the high water mark of mass migration westwards by the Teutons in Continental Europe. As it is with tectonic plates in the earth's crust – the pressures and cataclysms as the opposing masses strain against each other – so it is with human beings, and it is the eternal fate of the Flemish to lie at the northern end of the great curving 'racial' plates that separate the Germanic peoples of north and central Europe from their Latin and Celtic neighbours to the south and west. In the far south this line is anchored in Italy's Alto Adige region (the old Austrian South Tyrol), Italian in name and Germanic in blood, the curve then stretches north and west through the mixed peoples of Switzerland, up through the oft-disputed French provinces of Alsace-Lorraine, into Luxembourg and on into the Netherlands and finally Flanders.

The Dutch won their independence from Imperial Spain in 1581, and have hung onto it ever since, but the history of the Flemish is not of independence but of periodic conflict with their mighty French-speaking neighbours, and occasional disaster as they have suffered from either an expansionist German or French policy.

Medieval Flanders

The heyday of Flanders was in Medieval times. The entire Flemish population that now sits across modern Flanders, northern France and southern Holland came under the control of the ancient County of Flanders and its next-door neighbour the Duchy of Brabant. These two small but influential territories sat at the heart of western civilisation and were courted and fought over by successive monarchs from across Europe for their power, wealth and geographical position. The Flemish and their Dutch cousins were at the forefront of western European trade and burgeoning industries, particularly weaving, cloth making and metal working. For the English kings the Flemish were a gateway to mainland Europe, a maritime power in their own right and the destination for so much of England's 'white gold': sheep wool.

The huge flocks of sheep that covered England and much of Wales were harvested to supply massive amounts of wool to the workshops of Flanders, which turned the high-quality fleeces into clothes for much of Europe and even beyond. Such was the wealth that this trade generated for both sides, England in particular, that in the House of Lords the Lord High Chancellor of the United Kingdom still sits on a battered old scrap of woolsack.

Kortrijk – The Flemish Bannockburn

The trading strength of England was protected by its king, but the Flemish had no equivalent overlord to safeguard their interests. Instead, they formed themselves into powerful trade guilds with complex structures and strict codes to regulate their businesses and promote their growing wealth and influence. In time, the guilds came to dominate the cities of Flanders such as Bruges, Ghent and Antwerp, as well as the surrounding countryside. This type of organisation stood outside the feudal order of European society, as it did not rely on the countryside for its wealth and was controlled by a class of artisans and merchants rather than landed magnates.

This was, of course, anathema to Flanders' feudal neighbour France, who cast covetous eyes upon Flanders. In 1300 King Philip IV of France, Philip the Fair, attempted to annex the County by imprisoning the native Count of Flanders, Gwidje van Dampierre, and imposing his own governor, Jacques de Chatillon. Civil unrest broke out throughout the County, leading in 1302 to the infamous Good Friday massacre of every French citizen within the city walls of Bruges. The French response was to send a powerful army under Count Robert II of Artois to crush the uprising. After assembling at Arras in northern France the French host moved on to the city and castle of Kortrijk, the gateway to Flanders.

Robert of Artois' army was extremely impressive. It may have only totalled about 8,000 men, including 1,000 crossbowmen, 1,000 pikemen and 3,500 light infantrymen, but at its core lay over 2,500 heavy armoured cavalry. It was this force that made the French army truly dangerous. European warfare was still dominated by the aristocratic heavy horseman covered in full armour and wielding sword, lance and shield. Standard military methodology at the time equated one such cavalryman to ten foot soldiers in terms of effectiveness on the battlefield. By this calculation the French force stood at just over 30,000 strong in terms of combat power. In contrast to this feudal army of French chivalry, the Flemish force of just 9,000 men was composed wholly of infantrymen. The Flemish troops were composed overwhelmingly of urban guild militias. Willem Van Gullik (the deposed Count Gwidje's grandson) and Pieter De Coninck commanded 3,000 men from Bruges, Gwidje Van Namen (also called Guy of Namur - the son of Count Gwidje) led 2,500 men from coastal Flanders, and 2,500 men came from east Flanders including John Borluut's 700 men from Ghent and a further 500 from Ypres. In reserve for the Flemish sat John of Rennesse's 500 men. All of the militia were well equipped with pikes, infantry armour and shields, but they were considered no match for the might of the Capetian host.

The Flemish force also made for Kortrijk to seize the castle themselves and by a twist of fate the two armies arrived pretty much simultaneously. They spent 9 and 10 July manoeuvring for any advantage they could gain, but finally on the 11th the two hosts confronted each other in a large, fairly flat field east of the town to decide the issue. The French formed into their ten divisions called 'battles', and sent forward their crossbowmen, covered by infantry, to fire into the Flemish ranks, cause attrition and try to break up the enemy formation, itself organised in blocks eight men deep. The Flemings had no choice but to stand and take the punishment and wait for the inevitable French charge. The timing of that charge was critical to the outcome of the battle: the key was to launch it at just the right moment to either capitalise on a disintegrating Flemish line or to cause that break-up itself. Abiding strictly by the laws of warfare, the French had all the advantages and all they needed to do was be patient and maintain their discipline and cohesion. They failed to do either. With aristocratic arrogance they charged at the Flemish before their crossbowmen had inflicted enough casualties or broken up the ranks of pikemen. They fully expected them to turn and run; this the Flemings obstinately refused to do. The result was catastrophe for the French.

In a foretaste of what was to happen over the next century at Crécy, Poitiers and Agincourt the French nobility were dragged from their war-horses by their social inferiors and butchered in the mud. The greater part of the French army was annihilated, among them over a thousand of their heavy cavalry, including over sixty barons and lords. Among the dead lay the French commander, Robert II of Artois, plus the Constable of France, two Marshals of France, the Counts of Aumale, Dammartin, Eu and Ostrevant, the Duke of Brabant, the French-imposed Governor of Flanders Jacques de Chatillon and even King Philip IV's chief advisor, Pierre de Flotte. The Flemish dead amounted to just over 100. In commemoration of their famous victory the Flemings cut the golden spurs from the French knightly corpses and hung over 500 pairs of them in the Church of Our Lady in Kortrijk. It was this act that gave the battle its now famous name.

The effects of the battle were far reaching. At the time the result shocked all Europe – the Pope was even woken up in the middle of the night to be told the news – and an enraged Philip was stirred to send an even greater army to crush the uprising. In the longer term the Battle of the Golden Spurs set a precedent that would lead to the ending of the supremacy of the armoured knight and the death knell of the feudal system that sustained him. For the Flemish, it gave them a national identity based on an iconic victory against all the odds. Those who don't think such an event can really make much difference to a people should just ask any Scot about Bannockburn! Ever since the battle 11 July has been the Flemish national day and an official holiday in Flanders, and Pieter De Coninck's shield symbol of a black lion on a yellow background (the *Vlaanderen die Leu*) has become the national symbol of Flanders.

'Kissing Cousins': Flanders and Holland

The entire population of Flanders numbers just over six million, with maybe one hundred thousand or so Flemings in southern Holland, and

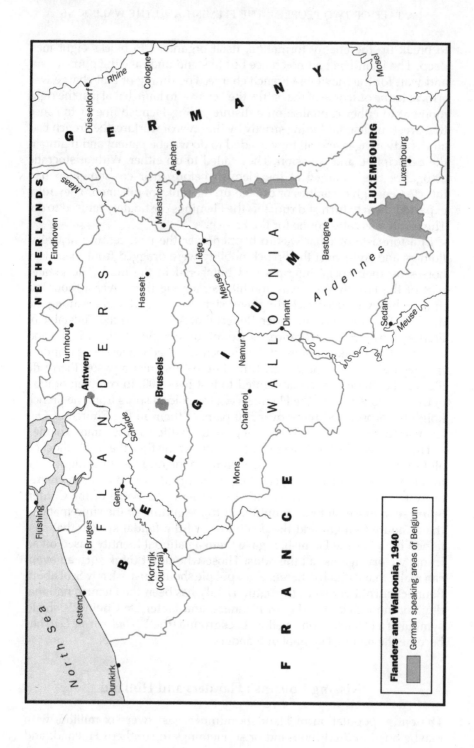

Flanders and Walloonia, 1940

German speaking areas of Belgium

another million of Flemish descent in the northern French *départments* of Nord and Pas de Calais (the so-called *Frans-Vlaanderen*). The Dutch population to the north are linguistically and culturally allied to the Flemish. However, and crucially, the Dutch are wedded to their Protestant faith. The Flemish are equally fiercely tied to the Church of Rome. Indeed, when the Congress of Vienna in 1815 created the Kingdom of the Netherlands, conjoining the provinces of Flanders and Walloonia with Holland, there was nothing but friction. The Catholics were treated as second-class citizens until the Flemings and Walloons overcame their traditional enmity, coming together in revolt against their Dutch overlords in 1830 and winning their independence.

The result was not as the Flemings intended. Under the influence of the British Prime Minister, Lord Palmerston, the European Powers convened a conference and recognised the new state of Belgium in December 1830. This decision set the fledgling country on a road that would be forever marked by internecine strife between its component 'tribes'. It would foment the rise of Flemish nationalism and was therefore a hugely important factor in the birth of the Langemarck and its predecessor Waffen-SS units. Coincidentally, it would also play a significant part in the story of Degrelle and his Walloon volunteers.

In the new state the minority Walloons soon came to dominate all aspects of government, commerce and culture. It was often said as a jibe against the Flemish that while the Walloons had culture, the Flemish had agriculture, and this Walloon sense of superiority translated into open contempt on their part for their Flemish fellow-countrymen and their way of life. French was made the official language of state and education, with Flemish marginalised. Entry and progress in the civil service, the armed forces and all the professions was dependant on speaking French, putting the Flemish at a huge disadvantage. Higher education was predominantly French-speaking. Indeed, it was not until 1930 that the University of Ghent – a city within Flanders – became the first Belgian university to accept Flemish as its first language.

The result was that Walloonia raced ahead economically to become the first continental European area to industrialise, and the Flemings fell even further behind in their own country. Even the new monarchy, the German Saxe-Coburgs, quickly became Gallicised and ignored their Flemish subjects. It was this tension at the very heart of Belgian life that would lead to the inevitable rise of Flemish nationalism.

II

Flanders: The Rise of Nationalism and the Extreme Right

Like so much else in the history of World War II, some of the reasons for the continuing rise of Flemish nationalism can be found in the mud and misery endured in the trenches of 'the war to end all wars'. When the Imperial German Army rolled over the borders of Belgium on its way to Paris in its doomed attempt to fulfil the strategy of the Schlieffen Plan in 1914, the mood in the country was the same as across all of Europe and volunteers flocked to the colours to defend their homeland from Prussian aggression. For the thousands of Flemings who joined up, what they found in the royal Belgian Army disillusioned them so completely that when the war was eventually over the survivors would become the driving force behind a strident new movement that pushed Flemish nationalism to the forefront and set the groundwork for the eventual birth of the Langemarck.

Much of Flanders, and indeed most of Belgium, was occupied and administered during the war as a conquered territory by the Germans, only a small strip of Flanders in the west, near the coast and centred on the town of Ypres, remained free. The rest of Belgium was governed by the German General von Bissing, and then following his death in 1917 by his successor General von Falkenhausen. (Interestingly, during the Second World War, when Belgium was once again overrun, she would be ruled by another von Falkenhausen, the son of the World War I general.) The portions of Flanders that weren't overrun by the Germans in 1914 then became the frontline of the titanic struggle fought in the west between the Great Powers.

References to 'Flanders fields' are well known to any reader of English literature of the First World War as the British faced the German Army across Flemish territory, and names such as Ypres, Menin and Passchendaele will forever link the area in the popular imagination to the muck and blood of the trenches.

The young Flemish farmhands and townsmen who either volunteered or were conscripted into the army found themselves in an alien environment where they were little more than cannon fodder. The mainstay of large parts of the army were Flemish infantrymen but the hierarchy was dominated by French-speaking Walloons who comprised the vast majority of the officer and NCO classes and who made little effort to hide their contempt for their Flemish soldiers. All orders were given in French and the Walloon officer corps showed little interest in learning the language of the men they commanded. The result was entirely predictable. Hordes of bewildered Fleming soldiers were led into battle by superiors that hadn't even bothered to explain what they were meant to be doing. Consequently they were swiftly mown down, achieving very little. At each failed attack and costly defence the resentment of the Flemish soldiery grew deeper.

The 'Council of Flanders'

Under von Bissing's governorship, occupied Flanders was encouraged to go its own way politically, and in February 1917 some two hundred nationalist activists came together and set up the rather grandly titled 'Council of Flanders'. Their initial intent was to provide Flanders with a new autonomous leadership, and over time to become a provisional government for a wholly independent country. The crowning act of this policy was a declaration of Flemish independence by the Council in December 1917.

This move was seen by their occupiers as a very large step too far – a reacton that should have been studied by every nationalist movement that allied itself with the Nazis in the Second World War. Von Bissing's successor von Falkenhausen reined in the Council and then suspended it all together. The German ideology in the two World Wars may have been very different in many respects, but what remained the same was their unwillingness even to contemplate a situation where they were not total masters of Europe. In the First World War this badly affected the ability of the Central Powers to combat the Allies; in the Second it was a deciding factor of the outcome of the conflict. Combined Allied efforts triumphed over Nazi Germany's refusal to do anything but attempt to crudely exploit its satellites and potential allies. This belief in the need for domination was Germany's Achilles heel in both World Wars.

The Frontpartij – the birth of modern Flemish nationalism

As with many other men engaged in the brutal slaughter of the Western Front, there began to develop a political consciousness among some of the Flemish soldiery that was hitherto unknown. So many young men who prior to the War had no political views came to think deeply about the politicians and political systems that had led them to a world that accepted the deaths of thousands of the best and bravest for the gain of a few yards of mud and little else. Given the circumstances, it was inevitable that the Flemish political awakening would be nationalistic in character, prompting a desire for self-rule or outright independence. The soldiers initially called their movement the *Frontbeweging* (the Front Movement), and they met together and produced crude leaflets and news sheets to discuss politics and how they wanted their country to change after the War was over. The *Frontbeweging* soon metamorphosed into the *Vlaamsche Front*, but that name also fell by the wayside very quickly, and it came to be called simply the *Frontpartij* (the Front Party). It was the tenets as well as the members of this party that were to set the tone for Flemish nationalism for the rest of the century.

The First World War ends

The ending of the War brought revolution and near civil war to much of Europe, including Belgium's eastern neighbour Germany. France was engulfed by severe political instability and sporadic street violence, but in the Low Countries of Luxembourg, Belgium and the Netherlands there was comparative calm. The Dutch had remained neutral in the War and possibly the biggest issue they faced was the fallout from having the former Imperial German Kaiser Wilhelm II take refuge in their country following his abdication. But the Belgians had to come to terms with huge changes from the pre-War status quo.

Firstly, large swathes of her territory had been fought over and were physically devastated. Although they had not suffered the truly monumental casualties that characterised the war efforts of Germany, France, Britain and Russia, the Belgians had lost over 58,000 men killed and wounded with several thousand more missing believed dead. Secondly, the genie of Flemish nationalism was now well and truly out of the bottle. The members of the collaborationist Council of Flanders were arrested, tried and convicted to loud acclaim by the Walloon population, with 112 receiving lengthy prison terms and forty-five ringleaders being sentenced to death. In Flanders the process only served to stir up unrest and resentment, so much so that the government moved to defuse tensions by commuting the death sentences.

However, even the shadow of collaboration hanging over Flemish nationalism didn't stop the *Frontpartij* from polling 57,422 votes in the 1919 elections and returning three members to the 202-seat Belgian parliament. By 1929 the party had gained significant strength and went on to triple its number of deputies on a popular vote of 132,962 in the election of that year. Although this was hardly a dominating political force, it must be remembered that the Socialists, the largest political party, only had some seventy seats in total. This steady growth in electoral support prompted an already jittery government to offer concessions and pass an amnesty law that released all the ex-Council members still being held in prison.

This time of growing success at the polls for Flemish nationalists saw the campaign to elect the former head of the Council, Dr August Borms, in a by-election for the Lower House in Antwerp in December 1928. Despite the fact that Dr Borms was still serving out his prison sentence at the time he was duly elected with a stunning majority of over 40,000!

Nationalism and the Extreme Right

Nationalism has a tendency to veer towards the Right of the political spectrum, and the more radical the nationalism the further right it seems to go. This is not true in every case – the IRA in both its Official and Provisional forms had long tied its nationalist goals to a socialist ethos – but more often than not the arena of nationalist activity embraces a love of order, traditional family values and quasi-military structure and ceremony. No nationalist gathering anywhere in the world would be complete without a sea of flags and devotees of the cause in bits and pieces of badly fitting, old cast-off uniforms, marching out of step. This outward devotion to order and discipline doesn't seem to hold, however, when it comes to their own unity, and again if there is another dominant characteristic for every extreme rightist nationalist movement in existence is its seeming predilection for internal wrangling, splits, political feuds and dissipation of strength through a multitude of often minuscule parties and organisations.

Such was the fate of Flemish nationalism. As support for the moderate Frontpartij began to wither in the early 1930s so the movement shifted to the far Right and splintered. Several dozen parties appeared to take up the mantle of nationalism in Flanders but in the years prior to the break-out of the Second World War the political landscape was increasingly dominated by three wildly differing organisations, each of whom would play a key role in the Langemarck and its predecessors.

No Flemish Quisling

The history of collaboration in the Second World War threw up an array of characters that came to symbolise their own peoples' alliance with the Germans. Vidkun Quisling in Norway, Joseph Darnand in France, Anton Mussert in the Netherlands and of course Léon Degrelle in Walloonia, were all leaders that embodied the collaboration of their respective countrymen. These men dominated their national agendas during the war, and the volunteers that their countries contributed to the Nazi war effort were heavily influenced by them.

Flemish collaboration could not be laid at the feet of one overarching figurehead; unlike all the other countries who collaborated with the Nazis, there were a plethora of leaders who more often than not competed amongst each other in the splintered politics of the nationalist Right. There was Joris Van Severen of Dinaso, Staf De Clercq of the VNV, Jef Van De Wiele of DeVlag and Reimond Tollenaere of the VNV's paramilitary Black Brigade, all of whom were prominent figures. In another departure from the norm, of all these leaders only Van De Wiele survived the war to be prosecuted. Elsewhere, the key figures were brought to justice at the end of hostilities and died before a firing squad or at the end of the hangman's rope. In the Flemish case Van Severen didn't even have a chance to collaborate as he was shot by French gendarmes during Hitler's 1940 invasion of France and the Low Countries, De Clercq died of a heart attack in 1942 and Tollenaere was killed in action on the Russian Front. There would be no single, reviled Quisling figure in the Flemish story.

The VNV, Dinaso and DeVlag

Without doubt the largest and most influential Flemish nationalist organisation was the *Vlaamsch Nationaal Verbond* (Flemish National Union), the VNV. Indeed, it would be from its party members and supporters that the lion's share of the Flemish wartime volunteers would come. This party, formed in October 1933 from the amalgamation of a host of smaller parties, became the standard bearer for Flemish hopes of self-rule. It set up female and youth wings alongside its mainstream adult male membership and was openly paramilitary in its appearance and style. Led by a burly school teacher and ex-founding member of the Frontpartij, Gustave 'Staf' De Clercq, the VNV became the mainstay of Flemish nationalism. Staf De Clercq himself was forty-nine when he founded the party. Jeroom Gustave Theophile De Clercq was born on 16 September 1884 into a solid middle-class family from Everbeek in Brabant. As 'De Leider' (the VNV's version of Nazi Germany's Führer), the VNV expounded a doctrine of a 'Greater Netherlands' where the combined peoples of Flanders, Holland and the Frans-Vlaanderen would unite into a new country. This land would be strongly pro-Catholic (it must be remembered that the Dutch are firmly attached to their Protestant faith) as well as authoritarian, the intent being to found a fascist state based on the VNV's motto of '*Alles voor Vlaanderen, Vlaanderen voor Kristus*' (All for Flanders, Flanders for Christ). The VNV was highly complimentary about Nazi Germany, indeed the party adopted the Nazi raised arm salute, and very antagonistic towards the Walloons and the French.

The VNV had its own uniformed militia, of course, the grey-shirted *Grijze Werfbrigade* (Grey Defence Brigade) and a party newspaper, the *Volk en Staat* (People and State) edited by the ex-Council of Flanders member Antoon Meremans. Both the militia and the paper, like the party in general, were fervently pro-Nazi but interestingly only mildly anti-Semitic. This religious tolerance was something that was shared across the Low Countries with anti-Semitism being a relatively minor issue for both Léon Degrelle's Walloon Rexists and Anton Mussert's Dutch *Nationaal-Socialistische Beweging,* as well as for De Clercq's Flemish nationalists.

The middle-aged Staf De Clercq was the most powerful of the nationalist Flemish leaders but he was not the most charismatic. That mantle went to the lawyer and ex-army officer Joris Van Severen. Born George Van Severen on 19 July 1894 in the village of Wakken in west Flanders, he was a bright student and won a place at Ghent University where he changed his Christian name to Joris, as he felt it was more 'Flemish', and became involved in nationalist student politics prior to the First World War. Having volunteered at the outbreak of hostilities, he served with distinction and was granted a commission as one of the very few Flemish officers in the army. He was an ardent supporter of the Frontpartij and when news of this reached his military superiors, it cost him his commission once the War was over . Undeterred, he went on to qualify as a lawyer and then stood for parliament, where he served as a deputy between 1921 and 1929. During that time Van Severen found that parliamentary democracy was not to his taste and he felt the Frontpartij's moderate stance had no chance of delivering any radical change for Flanders.

Impressed by the rise of the Nazis in neighbouring Germany, Van Severen left the Front in October 1931 and set up his own organisation, the cumbersomely named *Verbond van Dietsche Nationaal-Solidaristen* (the Union of 'Netherlandish' National Solidarity – *Dietsche* has a wider meaning than purely Dutch). Unsurprisingly the full title was seldom used and the organisation was commonly referred to as the abbreviated *Verdinaso,* and then the even shorter *Dinaso.* Dinaso was not a registered political party as Van Severen had no interest in elected politics. His platform was an overtly fascist one of independence from Belgium – a much used Dinaso slogan was 'Flemings, always remember that Belgium is not your fatherland' – and a union of all Dutch-speaking peoples across the globe including South African and Dutch East Indies communities. Unlike the VNV it was also strongly anti-clerical. Hitler's Nazis were openly cited as a model for Dinaso and, like the VNV, the raised-arm salute was adopted by the membership and huge emphasis was put on the organisation's paramilitary wing, the 3,000 or so members of the green-shirted *Dietsche Militanten Orden*, the DMO (initially called the *Dinaso Militie* before its reincarnation in 1934 as the DMO – the Netherlandish Military Order). The DMO had its own motto, '*Recht en Trouw*' – Right and Loyalty, which was also the name of its newspaper and they were led by Jozef 'Jef' François. He would later volunteer for the SS-Legion Flandern.

Dinaso was not a mass movement, but it was renowned for the discipline and devotion of its members. So much so that even after Van Severen announced a hugely significant political *volte face* in 1935, stating that Walloons and Flemings were of common Frankish descent and therefore Belgium was now indivisible as one nation, the movement didn't disintegrate. Perhaps a third of members resigned in disgust and confusion but the rest stayed with Van Severen until the outbreak of war dramatically intervened.

The last, and most extreme, of the three major Flemish nationalist organisations that influenced the Langemarck and its predecessors was the *Duitschen-Vlaamsche Arbeidsgemeenschap* – the German-Flemish Working Community, abbreviated to *DeVlag* (The Flag). Ostensibly a harmless 'cultural' body set up in 1935 and designed to promote cross-border artistic and linguistic fraternity and contacts between Flemish and German artists and luminaries, it was in reality an extremist pro-Nazi political pressure group. Its leader was the fanatical Jef Van De Wiele, who envisaged himself as nothing less than the Führer of an enlarged province of Flanders that sat within the borders of the German Reich. Very much like its rival Dinaso, DeVlag was not a political party but rather an 'order' of those nationalists dedicated to the overthrow of the Belgian state and its incorporation into a National Socialist Europe.

These three bodies dominated the landscape of Flemish nationalism before the Second World War. There were other fringe parties, most of them rabidly anti-Semitic as well as openly pro-Nazi or pro-fascist, but their numbers were tiny and their influence negligible. However, the major point is that Flemish nationalism was a genuine mass movement and not just the political home of a small number of malcontents. The VNV share of the Flemish vote in the last election before the war was approaching 10 per cent, to give some idea of relative popular strengths at the same time in neighbouring France the 250,000-strong far-right PPF was polling less than 5 per cent. Not only was the nationalist movement one of mass appeal in 'Germanic' Flanders but it was also veering steadily right. It was pro-German, paramilitary and authoritarian in nature, and in essence it was tailor-made to be used by the Waffen-SS for the recruitment of volunteers. In these fertile conditions the Langemarck had laid in gestation for a long time; only one defining event was required and it would be born. That event was the onset of war.

Two names to remember

The story of Langemarck is more than the story of hosts of competing Flemish nationalist parties and organisations and their struggle for power and recognition in a state that ignored them. It is also more than the phenomenon of the Waffen-SS legionary movement. It is at heart a story of many thousands of individual Flemings who made a conscious decision to join their erstwhile conquerors in wearing the uniform of a body that was to be later condemned at the Nuremburg War Crimes Tribunal as a 'criminal organisation', whose members of whatever nationality were to be denied the civil rights afforded to their defeated compatriots in the rest of the Wehrmacht.

But how did they make the momentous decision to join? The Langemarck came into being late in the War when the tide had already turned decisively against Nazi Germany, but the men at its heart had been in German uniform for years by that stage. The Flemish saw their country overrun by a military whirlwind that was epitomised by the dashing élan of the premier Waffen-SS formations, and when given the opportunity to join that same elite, they took it. The horrors of the concentration camps and the utter brutality of the Eastern Front were some way in the future when the seeds of the Langemarck were sown. Who were they then, these Flemings who flocked to a foreign flag, and what was their story?

When Remy Shrijnen made it onto Waffen-SS recruiting posters for his exceptional bravery at the front late on in the war, the figure that stared out at potential recruits was not the archetypal model of Teutonic manhood – a blue-eyed, blond haired giant he certainly was not! Indeed, Schrijnen stood only 5' 4" tall (approximately 164cm) in his stockinged feet, when the minimum required for the Waffen-SS at the beginning of the war was 5' 9" (Himmler's height). He was of fairly slight build and had an intense, serious air that never left him. Born into a working class family with strong nationalist roots in the town of Kemptich on Christmas Eve 1921, the young Remy was one of eight children. The Shrijnen's were a happy, close-knit family, intensely proud of their 'Flemishness' and their feeling of kinship with the Germans over the border. From the start young Remy was imbued with the politics of Flemish nationalism, indeed his railway worker father was an early member of the Frontpartij and then its successor the VNV. After completing his secondary education Remy's future before the war held out the prospect of nothing more dramatic than a lifetime of manual work and street-level political activism, but that was all to change in the summer of 1940.

Another young man destined to play a pivotal role in the Langemarck and the story of the Flemish volunteers was Georg D'Haese. Born in Lede in Flanders on 4 August 1922 the young D'Haese was also the offspring of Flemish nationalist parents. The well-educated D'Haese pursued German

Studies in his higher education, but the defining influence of his youth was his belief in the cause of Flemish nationalism and membership of the VNV, a membership which he continued throughout the War. His firm belief in the cause of Flemish nationalism was to remain with him throughout and was to have unexpected consequences years later in his service career. As an individual, D'Haese was artistic, intelligent and popular. A smiling figure, he was always ready with a joke, and though mature for his age he lacked the overtly serious air of Schrijnen.

III

1940: Blitzkrieg and Belgian Collapse

In Paris in 1932 a fifty-five-year-old ex-sergeant in the French Army dined out one evening and unknowingly ate a plate of oysters contaminated with typhoid. He fell ill that same night and very quickly died as a result. His name was André Maginot, and the line of fortifications that, as Minister for Defence, he had caused to be built along 195 miles (over 314 kilometres) of France's eastern border was still under construction. Costing around £2 million per mile the extensive defensive works were intended to protect France from any possible future German aggression and save her from reliving the horrors of the trenches of the First World War. The slaughter of Verdun was indeed never repeated but in terms of protecting *la belle France* from invasion the Maginot Line was a stunning failure, for two reasons. Firstly, its designers had failed to learn a basic strategic lesson of World War I: the Line did not extend to cover a German assault through Belgium. This was the essence of the plan to invade France devised back in 1906 by Graf Alfred von Schlieffen, the German Chief of the General Staff. Secondly, and far more crucially, it instilled in the French a false belief that behind its mechanical gun turrets, concrete emplacements, belts of mines and barbed wire they were safe – surely the Germans would not dare try to breach the greatest line of fortifications in history? But just like almost every wall in military history it bled the defenders of the very offensive spirit that without which you are doomed to defeat. In the words of Patton, 'Fixed fortifications are monuments to Man's stupidity.'

Operation Gelb

On 10 May 1940 the Germans decisively proved the impotence of the Maginot Line by beginning their blitzkrieg assault in the West with the invasions of the Netherlands and Belgium on their way through to France. This violated the non-aggression treaty that Germany had signed with

Belgium only some three years previously that had de-coupled Belgium from the Anglo-French alliance, but Hitler was never a man to let a treaty get in the way of a good invasion. At the time the French belief was that the line of armoured fortifications that the Belgians had also built inside their own territory would shield the gap between their own Maginot Line and the North Sea.

The greatest of these Belgian forts was the strategically vital Fort Eben-Emael. Shaped like a massive wedge 810 metres long on two sides and 700 metres across at its widest, Eben-Emael guarded both the three bridges leading from the north across the east–west running Albert Canal and the open land invasion route to the south, known as the Gap of Vise. To take the fort was to unlock Belgium, and the German plan was one of genius. It relied on military innovation, courage and audacity. The plan devised was to utilise the top of the fort itself as a landing strip and crash-land onto it a wave of gliders carrying a small force of elite para-engineers. These highly trained specialists would then use revolutionary, shaped charges to knock out the armoured gun turrets of the fort and seal its large garrison inside, rendering both them and the fort useless. The paras would then hold off all-comers until relieved by the swiftly advancing ground forces. That was the plan, but as the German First World War General von Moltke memorably said 'No plan survives contact with the enemy'. This was no different and from the start mishap dogged the venture. Some of the paras, including their commander Leutnant Witzig, didn't even reach the fort as their gliders came down early. However, this didn't stop the operation becoming a classic of its kind and as such setting a kind of benchmark for airborne *coup de main* operations ever since. Landing at first light on Friday 10 May those paras who did get through completely surprised the Belgian defenders. Within minutes several of the gun cupolas had been put out of action and over the next few hours the fort's ability to halt the incoming German ground offensive was smashed to pieces. Fort Eben-Emael, a supposedly impregnable barrier to an invasion, surrendered on Saturday 11 May after lasting little more than 24 hours of attack.

Massacre at Abbeville

Prior to the invasion the governments of most Western countries grew increasingly paranoid at the idea of Nazi infiltrators and sympathisers acting as an internal fifth column. Wild stories circulated after the conquests of Norway and Denmark that large numbers of home-grown fascists had played a pivotal role in undermining their countries' defences, and as a result police forces in Belgium, Holland and France had compiled lists of suspects who were to be rounded up in the event of invasion. Degrelle and his Rexists topped the list in Walloonia and in Flanders it was the Flemish nationalists who were targeted for arrest. As soon as the Germans attacked the Belgian police swooped and detained dozens of suspects deemed to be a threat to the State. Staf De Clercq and Joris Van Severen were among the most prominent arrests but inexplicably De Clercq was released after two days with no reasons given.

As the Wehrmacht advanced panic set in and the remaining prisoners were put on a makeshift fleet of buses and sent south over the border to France. Handed over to the French gendarmerie in the northern French town of Abbeville, the plan was to stick them in a local prison and await further instructions. However, the jail was full and the French police were at a loss what to do with these foreign detainees, who, it must be remembered, had committed no crime whatsoever and had not even had the opportunity to collaborate with the Germans as yet. Adopting an approach to problem solving that was more characteristic of the Nazis than the Allies, the French gendarmes decided to execute their captives. Twenty-two unarmed prisoners were marched to a local public park, lined up and shot. Joris Van Severen was among them, indeed he was meant to have been given the *coup de grace* by the French gendarme commander himself. In one stroke Van Severen was removed as a potential leader of Flemish collaboration and the militant and highly disciplined Dinaso organisation was beheaded, but at the same time the whole Flemish nationalist movement was provided with its very own martyr. De Clercq had survived by some twist of fate, as had other leading figures, but the first of Flanders' own possible 'Quislings' was dead before his country was even fully occupied.

Hold the Line!

With the line of forts over the Albert Canal breached, the outnumbered and ill-equipped Royal Belgian Army was no match for the Nazi blitzkrieg and was crushed. The Dutch Army was in equally dire straits as the French and the British struggled to form a cohesive defensive line from the sea to the Maginot Line. The key to the success of such a strategy was that all four allied armies had to hold their own sectors of the line; if just one failed the Germans could pour through and wheel either left or right to take the others in the rear. The Dutch were the first to break. After only three days Queen Wilhemina and her government left for England and the Dutch Army capitulated a day later. However, all was not lost for the Allied cause as the Germans would still have to advance through Belgium.

King Leopold III capitulates

The Belgians outlasted the Dutch by fourteen days. In the most controversial decision of his extremely controversial reign, King Leopold III signed a capitulation order in the early hours of the morning of the 28 May 1940 without properly consulting his allies or even his own military commanders or government. The immediate result was chaos as some Belgian units obeyed and surrendered while others fought on. The confusion enabled the Wehrmacht to rip through the front and sealed the speedy defeat of the Allies.

As both the Belgian Army and the front were disintegrating anyway, continued resistance probably would not have made a difference to the outcome of the battle. However, as any student of military history knows, very little is certain in combat and the most precious commodity on the battlefield is time. Given the respective strengths of the opposing forces, the Germans were almost bound to win the campaign in the West in 1940, but relatively minor events can have an impact on the future in completely unexpected ways. The British counter-attack at Arras a short time after the Belgian capitulation was localised, unsupported and badly coordinated, but it made Hitler so worried about the vulnerability of his precious armoured forces that he made his famous order that stopped his Panzer formations from attacking the evacuation at Dunkirk. If they had continued their advance the miracle of Operation Dynamo would not have happened and Britain would have been left without any army to defend her in the dark days of 1940. As it was, over 330,000 men, including Belgian soldiers, made it to Britain to continue the fight. That said, while the Belgian capitulation did not turn the tide of battle against the Allies – the surprise German assault at Sedan did that – it did drastically reduce the chances of Allied success.

On the ground, the majority of the Belgian armed forces dumped their weapons and marched dejectedly into German captivity. In the eighteen days of conflict several thousand soldiers had been killed, but the army that now found itself behind barbed wire was still largely intact. The Belgian government fled to England to set up in exile and the country was occupied for the second time in less than thirty years.

A revealing point on the Belgian Army's efforts was made by the architect of their destruction himself, Adolf Hitler. In a note written on 25 May, some three days before the Belgian capitulation, he outlined his views on the fighting qualities of his western opponents:

> The Belgian soldier, too, has generally fought very bravely. His experience of war was considerably greater than that of the Dutch. At the beginning his tenacity was astounding. This is now decreasing visibly as the Belgian soldier realises that his basic function is to cover the British retreat.

Bearing in mind that the majority of the Belgian Army was Flemish these martial characteristics were to be exhibited by those who went on to fight under the banner of the Langemarck and its predecessor formations.

Occupation

The Germans set the scene for their occupation by immediately recognising the separate identities of the Flemish and the Walloons. With the government in London, the king in self-imposed internal exile at his residence in Laeken outside Brussels and the army behind barbed wire, the country was bereft of most of its natural leadership. Indeed, the only major institution that remained more or less intact for the people to look to was the Roman Catholic Church, and the VNV in particular was well regarded by the Church. The Nazis responded to this vacuum by imposing a military administration headquartered in Brussels that briefly ran both Belgium and the Netherlands as one region. This was swiftly changed and the Dutch got their own Reichskommissar while the northern French *départments* of Nord and Pas de Calais were detached from France and incorporated into the new Belgian zone under the governorship of General Alexander von Falkenhausen. Belgium was not formally split into a separate Flanders and Walloonia but enough was done by the Germans to make both populations feel that they were sympathetic to their own cause and to sow considerable discontent between the two. This policy typified the Nazi love of intrigue and duplicity, and would be continued throughout the war.

At first the Flemings seemed to have the upper hand: bilingual Brussels was declared a Flemish city, only Flemish newspapers were allowed in Flanders and the Nazis decreed a 'cultural' separation between the two peoples while loudly trumpeting the achievements of Flemish artists such as Rembrandt. However, all of these moves were trumped by the issue of prisoners of war. The entire Belgian Army, with the exception of a few thousand diehards who had escaped to England from Dunkirk, was held by the Wehrmacht in prison camps awaiting their fate, and as such was a powerful guarantor for good behaviour back in Belgium. In a gesture designed to win over popular support for the invaders, the Flemish soldiery were released and sent home. Flemish officers were not repatriated, but since the officer corps was almost entirely Walloon this was of little import. Thousands of Flemish rankers left the prison camps and were reunited with their families and friends.

The effect in Flanders was exactly as the Germans hoped: much of the initial resentment towards their occupation was displaced by feelings of relief and gratitude. It was a master stroke and it was no coincidence that by the end of November 1940 a survey of Flanders found that 80 per cent of the population considered themselves friendly to the Germans. This was an amazing picture for an occupying power– compare for instance the position of the Coalition forces in present-day Iraq. The Germans reinforced this positive image of themselves by instituting rigorous discipline among their garrison troops, and this policy was replicated across occupied Western Europe. German soldiers were expected to be courteous and respectful to local populations. Any transgressions against civilians and their property were treated very harshly indeed, even to the extreme of Germans being publicly executed if their crimes were serious enough. Again, compare this to recent wars. This type of attitude to the populace and a zealous adherence to military discipline is always the basis for a successful occupation. The popular film image of desperately brave and widespread resistance facing the Teutonic brutality of the firing squad is not a reflection of reality. In Flanders, as elsewhere in the West, the vast majority of the populace did not take up arms against the invader but got on with life instead, and large numbers of them even looked on their new masters with approval.

Belgium's ethnic Germans

Some 65,000 'Belgians' looked on their occupiers with more than just approval – for them it was more of a homecoming. These were the ethnic Germans who had found themselves in Belgium as a result of the redrawing of the map of Europe carried out by the Treaty of Versailles. Now the map would be redrawn again, and the small region bordering Germany and centred on the quiet town of Eupen with its 17,000 inhabitants was declared 'free and liberated' and reincorporated back into the Reich. Luxembourg next door also became part of Nazi Germany, although the ethnic basis for that annexation was practically non-existent and the move was widely opposed by the populace. Nevertheless, the youth of Luxembourg was conscripted into the Wehrmacht and fought and died at the front alongside 'liberated' Germans from Eupen and St Vith.

The VNV in the ascendant

The newly appointed sixty-two-year-old German Military Governor, General Alexander Freiherr von Falkenhausen, did not throw the full authority of his office behind De Clercq and his VNV, but he did institute such legal changes as lowering the retirement age for state officials from sixty-five to sixty, which meant a host of government positions came up for grabs. VNV members were not shy in coming forward and hundreds of slots from burgomasters to town magistrates were filled by party appointees. A good slice of senior posts went the same way, with key governorships in Limburg, Antwerp, East and West Flanders all going to loyal VNV men, as well as the key ministries for Economic Affairs and the Interior. The latter, which controlled the police, was held from 4 April 1941 by the prominent Flemish nationalist Gerard Romsée. He would later flee to Germany with the retreating Wehrmacht at the beginning of September 1944.

The ascent of the VNV to power then went a huge step further on 11 May 1941 when von Falkenhausen announced that all existing Flemish parties had to merge with the VNV. Any party that was seen as anti-German had already been dissolved but this move in effect concentrated all parties with collaborationist tendencies into one organisation that the Germans could then more easily control. The pronouncement saw a host of minor parties come under the VNV banner, as did the Dinaso organisation, but in a move straight out of the handbook of Nazi intrigue the extreme DeVlag was exempted from the order as a 'cultural' body, and as a further warning sign to the VNV, the head of the SS-Hauptamt (the SS Main Office – responsible for enlisted SS men's personnel files as well as all Waffen-SS recruitment), Gottlob Berger, agreed to become DeVlag's President in November 1941. This infuriated De Clercq, but was typical of the Nazi approach in its occupied territories of always supporting more than one avenue of collaboration. However, De Clercq could not grumble too much – his movement was now more or less in power in Flanders and was growing steadily. At the party conference in June 1942 there were representatives from 860 party sections from Flanders and a further 40 from Flemish communities in Walloonia. The total membership was now above 100,000, with 10,000 of those being female and 12,000 in the party's youth wing. The inclusion of the ultra-disciplined Dinaso members had given a huge boost to the militancy of the party and the entire uniformed DMO was transferred wholesale into the VNV's Grey Defence Brigade. The militia was then reorganised into the newly established *Dietsche Militie*, the DM.

The DM was split into four sections based on the age and militancy of its members: the Guard and Auxiliary sections were made up of older men given limited, localised duties such as stewardship of meetings and guarding industrial property; the Motor section was a mobile unit equipped with a small number of miscellaneous trucks and cars; but by far the biggest and most influential section, particularly as regards the future creation of the SS-Legion Flandern and the Langemarck, was the *Zwarte Brigade* – the Black Brigade. The Black Brigade were the uniformed, though initially unarmed, stormtroopers of the VNV, and it was from among its members that the future strength of the SS-Legion Flandern, the Sturmbrigade and finally the Langemarck division was to be found. Dressed all in black, the Brigade members consciously aped their better-known cousins in the

German SS, although they used the 'wolf hook' emblem (a single line up and down with a hook at both ends turning opposite ways) rather than the double lightning flash of the *sig* runes. Like the sig, the wolf hook was a runic pagan symbol and was commonly used across the foreign volunteer movement outside Germany and especially in the Netherlands.

At its inception the Brigade had a membership totalling some 12,000 and was led by the charismatic Dr Reimond Tollenaere with the ex-Dinaso DMO leader Jef François as his deputy. Tollenaere was born in the Flemish village of Oostakker on 29 June 1909 into a well-to-do middle-class family with nationalist leanings. Growing up he became a fervent anti-communist and advocated the dissolution of the Belgian State and the formation of an independent Flanders. He went on to study law at the Flemish-speaking Ghent University while also becoming active in politics, rising up through the ranks of the VNV to become its Propaganda Leader in 1933, even before graduating from university in 1934. Through his position within the VNV he gained national prominence and was elected to the Belgian parliament in 1936, where he stridently spoke out in the cause of Flemish nationalism. Unsurprisingly, when the War came he was one of those detained by the Belgian police during the invasion. However, he did not suffer the fate of Van Severen and lived to be released by the Germans on 21 June 1940. He took up his place back in the VNV leadership and proceeded to find his true calling as head of the newly established Black Brigade. He, along with François and most of the Brigade leadership cadre, would go on to volunteer for the Waffen-SS, setting a crucial example to their men, who followed them in their droves. After volunteering Tollenaere was succeeded as the head of the DM by the far less charismatic Joris Van Steenlandt.

The Flemish SS

Strange as it may sound, the first SS men in Flanders were not part of Heinrich Himmler's empire but were local 'freelancers'! Two disillusioned former VNV men, René Lagrou and Ward Hermans, decided to launch their own organisation, the *Algemeene Schutscharen Vlaanderen* (the Flemish General SS), to create a local Praetorian Guard consciously mimicking Nazi Germany's SS. Initially successful, the organisation enrolled its first eighty volunteers in their headquarters town of Antwerp and then a further fifty in Ghent. The organisation went through an array of changes of name during its existence, such as the *Vlaamsche SS* and the *SS-Vlaanderen*, but was always distinct from the likes of the VNV and its Black Brigade. It adopted the customs and appearance of the German *Allgemeine-SS* (General SS) wholesale: its used the same motto '*Mijn Eer Heet Trouw*' (My honour is loyalty), it used the raised-arm salute and its uniform was almost indistinguishable from the German original, apart from some minor differences such as the use of an elongated swastika on the cap rather than a German eagle. Its structure was based on a single regimental model composed of area-based battalions as follows:

- Stormbaan I Antwerpen
- Stormbaan II Oost-Vlaanderen
- Stormbaan III West-Vlaanderen
- Stormbaan IV Braband
- Stormbaan V Limburg (also attached to this unit were the tiny number of French-speaking but ethnically-Flemish cells in Walloonia as well).

Commanders:

SS-Hoofdstormleider (SS-Hauptsturmführer) René Lagrou: 7 December 1940 – 10 May 1941

SS-Hoofdstormleider (SS-Hauptsturmführer) Jef De Langhe: 10 May 1941 – 1 September 1941

Jef De Langhe was replaced by first Raf Van Hulse, who went on to command the war reporters platoon in the Flemish SS-Sturmbrigade Langemarck in the middle of 1943, and then the waters were muddied further when Jef François was appointed commander as the organisation came more and more under the control of Himmler's SS. The Flemish SS was theoretically a non-party body like DeVlag, and the two organisations were avid supporters of each other with much mutual membership, including the DeVlag leader Jef Van De Wiele. But, as could perhaps be expected, there was serious antipathy between the Flemish SS and the VNV, as there was between DeVlag and the VNV. There would never be much love lost between a party that wanted at the very least Flemish self-rule and those who espoused a virtual annexation by the Third Reich. The end result of all these emerging structures, of course, was the further complication of the already congested collaborationist landscape. Now that there were three separate and often competing organisations that loudly proclaimed they were not only the true standard bearers of Flanders but that they were the favoured partners of the Germans, and two of them even had similar black-garbed militia, anyone could be forgiven for being confused.

The Flemish SS was never anything like a mass movement. It was in fact very small in number, indeed the nominal role of the organisation on 30 June 1944 contained only 3,499 names, but what it lacked in size it made up for in commitment. Out of that roster some 1,660 were serving at the time in the Waffen-SS with a further 939 in other German military formations, that is an astonishing 75 per cent of the total strength of the Flemish SS who were actively fighting for Nazi Germany. So many of these men were to become the hard core of the Flemish contribution to the German war effort.

Schrijnen and D'Haese

Young Remy Schrijnen wás just seventeen years old when the storm broke in the West and the Germans occupied Belgium, and so was too young for military service. His family survived the limited fighting intact and like the rest of Belgium they waited to see what occupation would bring. Considering his family background of Flemish nationalism and pro-German leanings, it is perhaps surprising that at first he was not an avid supporter of his land's new rulers. Indeed he was actually quite sceptical about the Nazis' willingness to deliver on their vague promises about the possible future position of Flanders after seeing the way they had abandoned the Baltic countries and Finland by signing the Nazi-Soviet Non-Aggression Pact in 1939. This streak of stubbornness and refusal to blindly follow the prevailing view was to be the hallmark of his later service in the Waffen-SS.

He did, however, want to see for himself what Nazi Germany had to offer. Along with 250,000 other Belgians, both Flemings and Walloons, Schrijnen volunteered to go to Germany as a foreign worker, first to follow in his father's footsteps on the railways and then later as a factory worker.

Georg D'Haese's life before the war was not too dissimilar from Schrijnen's. The cause of Flemish nationalism was the dominant topic of conversation in the family home and the young D'Haese had already moved on from words to deeds even before Nazi Germany's blitzkrieg:

> ... as 15 to 16-year-old sons of Flemish-nationalist parents, we were often on the prowl at night with paint, paintbrushes and hammers to paint over French street signs or other signs written in French or to smash them. ... under the conditions at the time we would have established a pact with the Devil himself to attain an independent administration or dissolve the Belgian State. (From Allen Brandt, *The Last Knight of Flanders*, Schiffer Publishing, 1998.)

IV

The Waffen-SS
and the Legionary Movement

By the end of the war an incredible total of 137,000 West Europeans had volunteered for, and served in, the Waffen-SS. This huge figure included, among others, 50,000 Dutchmen, 20,000 Italians, 15,000 Walloons, 11,000 Danes, 8,000 Frenchmen, 6,000 Norwegians and 1,000 Finns. For the Flemings the total was the unbelievably high number of 23,000! To give the reader some idea of scale the entire modern British Army is hovering around the 100,000 mark, and the offensive arm of the infantry number approximately 20,000. So for a nation of 60 million people with global interests and a history of military intervention and power projection, the United Kingdom just about musters the same number of fighting soldiers as a conquered Flemish populace that numbered less than five million souls in total contributed to the occupying power. And this specifically for an armed force that was highly selective about whom it admitted into the ranks, particularly early on in the War when the requirements were so stringent that only fifteen out of every hundred applicants were actually accepted.

The Nazis recruitment of foreign volunteers (*die freiwillige* as they were known), was chaotic and awesomely complicated. Regiments were raised and then disbanded, volunteers as individuals or groups were sent to serve in previously all-Reichsdeutsche divisions, and the elite foreign 5th SS Division Wiking was formed from among the first wave of volunteers from across Western Europe. However, what came out of this initial maelstrom of activity was the establishment of some nine national legions, five of which were under the aegis of the Waffen-SS as being from suitably Aryan countries (this includes a Finnish unit), with four being under *Heer* (German Army) control as non-Aryan formations. The Waffen-SS legions were the Legion Norwegen (Norwegian), Legion Flandern (Belgian Flemish), Legion Niederlande (Dutch), the Freikorps Danmark (Danish) and the Finnish Volunteer Battalion. The Heer units were the Légion des Volontaires Français contre le bolchevisme (French, see *Hitler's*

Gauls), the Legion Wallonie (Belgian Walloon), the Croatian Legion and the Spanish Legion. When war came in the East other legions were formed from the Baltic countries using the model already established in the West in 1940–41. These national legions were the basis for most of the foreign recruitment undertaken by the Nazis during the war, and they were the formations that would evolve to become firstly brigades and then later on divisions, and in so doing change utterly the face of the Waffen-SS.

The Waffen-SS were always portrayed by their creator Heinrich Himmler as an exclusively German elite, so why did they accept an influx of tens of thousands of foreigners? The answer lies firstly in the racial fantasy world that Himmler inhabited, and secondly in the vast bloodletting of the Russian Front. These two factors led directly to the recruitment of non-German European volunteers and to the legionary movement, and it was from this movement that the SS-Legion Flandern, and its successor the Langemarck, would spring.

Himmler and the Aryans

Heinrich Himmler, like so many mass murderers, was in many ways an entirely unremarkable man. A physically unimposing figure who suffered from poor eyesight and constant stomach cramps, he was, however, a gifted organiser and intriguer, and like so many of his bureaucratic type he had an enormous craving for intellectual respectability. When the Nazi Party rose to power and Himmler found himself in control of money and influence he used the opportunity to fund and direct a vast panoply of academic work into his favourite topics: racial theory and the history of the pagan Aryans.

Himmler's belief was that the Aryans were not only a historical fact but also a distinct global race from which the Germans and the other peoples of much of northern and western Europe were descended. The Nazi theory was that they were a bellicose people of warrior farmers who spoke an Indo-European language and had spread from their original homeland, wherever that was, to settle large regions of modern-day Europe. They were pagans who worshipped nature and a pantheon of bloodthirsty gods, and Norse and Teutonic belief in the likes of Odin and Thor were meant to be descended from this same foundation. Himmler further believed in the concept of 'racial struggle', that is the theory that seeks to explain human history as a never ending conflict between competing races where the prize for victory is world domination and the penalty for defeat is genetic extinction. Himmler believed that a thousand years of Christianity and population dispersal had severely weakened the Aryans and that it was his, and Nazi Germany's, sacred duty to act as a rallying point for all those of the true blood and bring them together under the political banner of Nazism so that they could stop fighting each other and focus on beating their inferior race enemies. This was the basis for Himmler's world view, and it was one that found a welcome home in the twisted visions of Hitler's state. The Nazi Party even had its own 'racial philosopher', Alfred Rosenberg, who championed the belief in the Nazis as the successors of the ancient Aryans as the 'master race'.

Eastern Slavs or Western Aryans?

The outcomes from this set of theories were to dominate the entire short-lived existence of Nazism. From it came the 'master race' belief, the so-called *herrenvolk*, where the Germans as true Aryans were destined to fight and defeat inferior races such as the Slavs and utterly exterminate the Jews. This was the origin of both the Holocaust and the invasion of Soviet Russia. This mixing of racial and political goals was the albatross round the neck of Hitler's Germany and consistently meant Nazi Germany was unable to take advantage of a broad church of anti-communist support in order to defeat Stalin. If the Nazis had been able to subordinate their racial fantasies to the overriding political objective of defeating communist Russia they could have ridden a huge swell of popular support that might have brought them victory and the domination they sought. The paradox for them would have been that final victory over Bolshevism would have only come through the military muscle of the very Slavic peoples that the Nazis so utterly despised. In the West, militant anti-communism was very much a minority pursuit, but in the East it was the preoccupation of the masses. This gargantuan blunder saw the Nazis turn to the relatively few adherents of their anti-communist crusade in the racially reliable West, rather than to the teeming hordes of Slavs who were only too willing to take up arms against the brutal repression of Stalin and his minions.

As ludicrous as it was, the Nazi theory of historical racial struggle was the pseudo-intellectual basis for the legionary movement from which the Langemarck was born. The second, and no less important, reason for the formation of the national legions was Himmler's overwhelming desire to break the Wehrmacht's stranglehold on recruitment in order to cope with the needs of an ever expanding war effort, particularly after 22 June 1941 and the invasion of Soviet Russia. The military process in Nazi Germany at the time was structured so that when a young man volunteered or was called up for military service he could express a preference to serve in the Waffen-SS, just as he could for service in the Luftwaffe, Heer or *Kriegsmarine* (German Navy), but there was no obligation whatsoever on the Wehrmacht authorities to abide by that wish. Indeed, the Wehrmacht hierarchy was keen to strictly limit the numbers of men going into the Waffen-SS to ensure it remained a minor force that in no way threatened the hegemony of the Wehrmacht as the main bearer of arms in the State. Himmler was desperate to overcome this barrier to his drive for further power, but the Wehrmacht was still the only force capable of deposing the Nazis from government and so had to be treated with caution.

The answer to the conundrum came from the head of the SS-Hauptamt, Himmler's trusted subordinate, and fellow believer in 'master race' theory, SS-Gruppenführer Gottlob Berger. Berger was born in Gorstetten, Swabia in 1896, an obsessive personality, intensely loyal to Himmler and his few friends, among which the vicious sadist Oskar Dirlewanger was one. He was imbued with an utter loathing of Germany's enemies that in large part resulted from his family's horrific experiences in the First World War when the young Gottlob was the only child to survive, having lost two brothers in the trenches and a third executed as a spy in the USA. Berger became a gymnastics teacher but soon found that his true talent was for organisation and detail and this, coupled with his interest in nationalist politics and racial theory, led him into the Nazi Party and the SS. He soon came to the attention of Himmler, who found his personal loyalty a refreshing counter-balance to the naked ambition of his other chief subordinate, Reinhard Heydrich. Berger himself had long been interested in the recruitment possibilities of the so-called *artverwandten Ländern* ('similarly related lands') such as Norway, Denmark, Sweden, Holland and Flanders, as well as Germanic communities abroad, the so-called *Volksdeutsche*. These *Volksdeutsche* were racial German populations that came about from mass German migration that had occurred since the Middle Ages and were often very large indeed, being spread all over eastern and south eastern Europe and into European Russia, particularly in Hungary, Romania, Yugoslavia and the Volga river region of Russia. This interest had found practical expression in Berger's chairmanship of both the *Deutsch-Kroatischen Gesellschaft* (the German-Croatian Society) and the *Deutsch-Flämischen Studiengruppe* (the German-Flemish Studies Group), both organisations seeming to be harmless cultural bodies but which in reality were fronts for the promotion of Nazi activity abroad. Learning from this experience, Berger came up with a simple and ingenious solution: if the Wehrmacht wouldn't let the Waffen-SS recruit inside Germany, then they would recruit from *outside* Germany! The Waffen-SS would not be a national force but would become a true army of empire, the Nazi Empire.

This option was, in many ways, a well trodden path. The military history of most empires has seen them recruit and deploy foreigners, mostly from peoples they have conquered in their rise to power. It is a historical phenomenon and not unique to the Waffen-SS. The Roman legions have some close parallels, being originally open only to Roman citizens, then to other Italian tribes, and over time metamorphosing into a truly international force composed of Celtic Gauls and Spaniards, Germanic tribesmen and men from the Balkans and North Africa, among others. Napoleon's armies had Dutch, Polish and German regiments, and of course the two greatest empires of the modern world, those of France and Great Britain, were sustained by huge polyglot armies controlled by a minority of commanders from the imperial homeland. These traditions are still alive today in Britain's Royal Gurkha Rifles and the French Foreign Legion. There were of course huge differences between the Waffen-SS and the imperial forces of Rome, Napoleonic or Imperial France and Great Britain, but there were also parallels. Where these imperial countries succeeded and Nazi Germany did not was in being flexible enough to utilise these foreign forces to win and maintain political power. This the Germans failed to do precisely because of their racial Aryan fantasies and the false sense of genetic superiority it gave them.

Berger's idea was exactly what Himmler wanted to hear. It was a perfect riposte to the Wehrmacht high command and offered huge possibilities for him to grow and deepen his personal power. No sooner had Scandinavia, the Low Countries and France fallen than Himmler and Berger put their expansionist plans into action, with Berger's SS-Hauptamt the perfect vehicle to carry out the task as it took on the role of all recruitment of personnel for the entire Waffen-SS.

The Westland and Nordland Regiments – the birth of SS Wiking

In May 1940 Himmler established the very first Waffen-SS units to be based on foreign volunteers, the *Standarten* (regiments) Westland and Nordland, although recruitment didn't start in earnest until the autumn after the fall of the West. Individual foreign enlistments had been allowed in the Waffen-SS as early as 1938 but never before had there been an attempt at this type of mass recruitment. After all, a German regiment was a very large military organisation of some 3,000 men, the equivalent of a British Army brigade. Berger's agents set up recruiting offices across occupied Western Europe, though not in the Gallic lands of France or Walloonia, and began to use all of Nazi Germany's mastery of propaganda and persuasion to draw suitable volunteers into the Waffen-SS. The idea was that suitable recruits from Norway, Denmark and neutral Sweden were to join the Nordland while those from the Netherlands and Flanders were to go to the Westland. Volunteers had to be between the ages of eighteen and twenty-five, in good physical condition and have no criminal record. All recruits were told that they were to train purely for 'police duties' in their respective homelands and nothing more – it must be remembered that the only unconquered enemy that Nazi Germany had left in Europe at that time was the British. Results were far better than Berger and Himmler had hoped, with the Westland in particular up to strength in a matter of weeks. This led to the momentous decision of November 1940, approved by Hitler directly, to raise an entire division based on suitable 'Aryan' foreign volunteers, the 5th SS Division Wiking.

Himmler appointed SS-Gruppenführer Felix Steiner, a tough storm-trooper from the First World War, its first divisional commander and allocated the Nordland and Westland regiments to the fledgling forma-tion along with the proven Germania Regiment, from the SS Division Das Reich, as its cadre. Every single one of these elements was an inspired choice. The foreign volunteers were among the very first, and very best, of their countrymen to join the Waffen-SS, while SS Germania was one of the original three elite regiments of the Waffen-SS, the others being the Austrian Der Führer Regiment and the elite of the elite, the legendary Leibstandarte. Steiner was, along with Paul Hausser, the co-architect of the Waffen-SS and an exceptional commander and leader of men, with a particular talent in welcoming his non-German soldiers into the fold and welding them all into a superb fighting machine. As such, Flemings were an integral element of this elite division from its inception, with 696 men in the Westland Regiment. These men were forever to be separate from the rest of their Flemish brethren at the front and did not serve in the Langemarck or any of its predecessor formations.

The 6. SS-Freiwilligen-Standarte Nordwest

The first wave of Flemish volunteers were now in the Wiking but still more were coming forward and this encouraged Himmler to order the estab-lishment of yet another foreign regiment, the 6. SS-Freiwilligen-Standarte Nordwest, on 3 April 1941. The regiment took recruits from Flanders, Denmark and the Netherlands and a total of 920 volunteers had enlisted by 25 May, with the Flemish being concentrated in the 1st, 6th and 8th Companies. The enlistees were concentrated in the Hamburg-Langenhorn barracks, to be joined by over 560 more Dutch, Flemish, and Danish volunteers over the next three months. As was the original intention for both the Westland and its sister regiment the Nordland, the new unit was designated a 'security' formation, although the imminence of Barbarossa weighed heavily on Himmler's mind as he contemplated its possible future use. After initial orientation in Hamburg they were then shipped out to the new SS training grounds at Radom and Debica in conquered Poland in the newly established General Government region. This was a hallmark of Waffen-SS training throughout the war, with their depots and training infrastructure being mainly outside the borders of Germany itself, the SS officer academies at Bad Tölz and Braunschweig were exceptions. The main reason for this rather unusual feature of Waffen-SS organisation was that the Wehrmacht owned almost every available training ground in Germany and it wasn't about to let the upstart Waffen-SS use its facilities. As ever, improvisation was the order of the day for the black guards, and the old Polish Army cavalry grounds at Debica became a major centre for Waffen-SS training throughout the war.

Barbarossa and the coming of the SS-Legion Flandern

On 22 June 1941 the largest army the world had ever seen carried out the biggest military operation of the entire war and invaded Soviet Russia, beginning the cataclysmic conflict that was to utterly dominate the Second World War. This event was to change the Flemish contribution to the war immeasurably. Added to the nascent belief in Nazi Germany's willingness to deliver some sort of Flemish independence, there was now the powerful cry of the anti-Bolshevik crusade that was to become the dominant theme in the rise of the legionary movement and all of the successor formations that came out of it.

In Flanders the locals celebrated the commemoration of the Battle of the Golden Spurs as ever on 11 July, and the Nazis then announced that a new Flemish national unit would be set up to fight on the Russian Front and volunteers were called for to serve 'for the duration' or for twelve months minimum if they were below the age of twenty-three. Recruiting standards were much the same as they were for the Westland and the Nordwest Regiments previously, the only big difference being the raising of the upper age limit from twenty-five to forty years old. The reason for this was the desire to attract ex-Royal Belgian Army soldiers, particularly officers and NCOs who, it was planned, would form the bulk of the command staff of the Legion with only a relative handful of German cadre personnel. This was a distinct departure from the SS-Westland and Nordland where it was always envisaged that Germans would form a major part of the order of battle, particularly at command levels. Former soldiers were promised a range of inducements to encourage them to enlist including retention of their previous rank, and all recruits received SS pay and allowances with the promise of farms in the conquered East when the War was won. Volunteers' families also received rations on the higher German scale than the normal Belgian one. However, even with these incentives, relatively few ex-soldiers came forward. This was unusual in the legionary movement across Europe with the majority of the national legions, both Heer and Waffen-SS sponsored, attracting a strong cadre of ex-regulars from their home armies. Career soldiers like Edgar Puaud and Pierre Rostaing in the French LVF, or Henri Derricks in the Legion Wallonie and Count Christian von Schalburg in the Freikorps Danmark are all examples of this trend. One explanation for this apparent anomaly is the fact that there were still very few Flemish officers and NCOs in the Royal Belgian Army at the start of the war, and so a Flemish national legion was fishing in a very small pool for trained and experienced leaders. The result was that even though around half of the Legion's original officers were ex-Belgian Army Flemings, there were very few Flemish NCOs indeed and the unit had much more of a 'German' feel to it than its French, Walloon or Scandinavian counterparts.

The unit was initially christened the *Verband Flandern*, then it became the *Landesverband Flandern* and then in another change the *Bataillon Flandern;* this was entirely typical of the pattern at the time and of Nazi Germany's love of ever-shifting nomenclature and the minutiae of organisational detail that it entailed. Finally, in September 1941 the name was settled on as the *SS-Freiwilligen Legion Flandern*, or more commonly the SS-Legion Flandern.

The formation of a national legion for the Flemish was mirrored in Denmark and the Netherlands, as well as Norway, and the men of the Nordwest Regiment clamoured to be allowed to join their own Legions. Himmler agreed and the Nordwest was duly disbanded on 24 September 1941 after a bare six months of existence, although some of its elements were kept on to provide depot and reserve functions at home while the Legions were on active service. The vast majority of its ranks were split up between the three national Legions of Flanders, Denmark and the Netherlands, with the Flemish 1st, 6th and 8th Companies transferring en masse and being renamed the 1st, 2nd and 3rd Companies of the SS-Legion Flandern. Of the 420 Flemings who transferred from the Nordwest to the Legion at this time, some 160 would be killed in action during the war, a further thirty-six would die in captivity in the East, and almost every single survivor would be wounded in combat. The Legion's original establishment was set at a battalion of five motorised companies in total, with the 4th and 5th Companies drawn from the new wave of recruits sparked into action by the formation of the Legion. This fresh batch of applicants was an impressive twelve hundred, but as ever the fastidiousness of the Waffen-SS selection process began its cull and only some 405 were enlisted on the enrolment day of 6 August 1941. No doubt poor dental health disqualified many a would-be volunteer, as was the case throughout Waffen-SS recruitment continent-wide.

The successful applicants were not only the best available but included a host of big names from across the Flemish collaborationist spectrum. The VNV's Black Brigade in particular was well represented in this new intake with the Brigade Commander himself, Dr Reimond Tollenaere, volunteering along with his deputy and second-in-command the ex-Dinaso DMO leader Jef François. With them came a cohort from the VNV's rival, the Flemish SS, led by its first commander SS-Hoofdstormleider (SS-Hauptsturmführer) René Lagrou. Lagrou, like so many of his Flemish SS comrades, would be killed in action on the Eastern Front.

Rex in Flanders

Just as there was a small VNV organisation in Walloonia, there was a corresponding mini-Rex set-up in Flanders, called *Rex-Vlaanderen*. Their leading light was a 33-year-old member from Antwerp called Paul Suys who had a fascinating wartime career, at first joining the Dutch SS-Legion Niederlande on 6 August 1941 before transferring to the SS-Legion Flandern in November of the same year. He stayed in the Legion and signed on again to join the newly-created SS-Sturmbrigade Langemarck in 1943 before becoming the *Fürsorgeoffizier* (welfare officer) for both the Flemish and Walloon communities representing the Waffen-SS *Dienstelle Fürsorgeoffizier Flandern und Wallonien* (the welfare service for Flemish and Walloon volunteers), and then finally he would join the Walloon SS division in September 1944.

Almost nowhere else in occupied Europe did so many key leaders of the collaborationist movement put their money where their mouth was and volunteer so quickly and so wholeheartedly for service at the front. They were to pay a very heavy price for this idealism. But in the flush of that summer of 1941 the horrors of the Russian Front were still far away and recruitment was brisk, so that by the end of August there were a total of 875 Flemings enlisted in the Legion, including the ex-Nordwest men.

Uniform and insignia

As suitably Aryan volunteers the Flemish legionnaires were allowed to wear standard Waffen-SS uniform just like their German comrades. To denote their Flemish nationality they wore a black and silver cuff title on their lower left sleeve as did all Waffen-SS units. In their case it read *Frw. Legion Flandern* (the German spelling of the Legion's title) on the common machine-embroidered version, but it was written as *Freiw. Legion Flandern* on the far rarer machine-woven version. Both cuff titles were of aluminium wire. To demonstrate a clear lineage that tied the SS-Legion Flandern to centuries of Flemish nationalism reaching all the way back to Kortrijk and the Battle of the Golden Spurs the volunteers also wore a national arm shield; again, this was common practice among the foreign volunteer formations. For the Flemish the shield was yellow, black-bordered, and emblazoned with a black lion rampant of Flanders. It was worn just above the cuff title on the left arm. There were at least five variants of the lion emblem.

Confusion is sometimes caused as well by the use of the *trifos* symbol by the Flemings. The trifos is a three-legged mobile swastika, also called a sun-wheel swastika, and was worn instead of the usual double *sig* runes on the right collar patch. The trifos was originally issued for the Nordwest

Regiment but when the Nordwest members left for the SS-Legion Flandern many of them took it with them even though the double sig runes were designated as the proper form of dress. To make matters even more complex, when the Sturmbrigade Langemarck was instituted the trifos was again officially authorised as the new unit's collar patch, and this was reaffirmed when the Brigade was upgraded to become a division. As can be imagined, this has often led to confusion among uniform scholars.

Broken promises

Not for the first time in history the promises of the recruiting posters did not live up to the reality for the Flemish recruits. The Flemings soon found that 'their' Legion was German in all but name. The language of command was German, there was no modification of German SS discipline or training to adjust to Flemish sensibilities and the practical promises of equivalent ranks for ex-Belgian Army personnel did not materialise. René Lagrou and his Flemish SS men were not overly concerned by these circumstances as they saw them as the realisation of their wish to become a full part of the Third Reich, but for the bulk of the volunteers who were ex-VNV men the situation was unacceptable. The Waffen-SS's constant attacks on established religion and aping of a pagan past flew directly in the face of the faith of the staunchly Catholic VNV personnel; and even worse, several of the German cadre instructors looked upon their new recruits with barely concealed contempt. 'The Flemish were maltreated as "filthy people", a "nation of idiots" and "a race of gypsies".'(Rupert Butler, *The Black Angels*, Arrow, 1989.)

This attitude was diametrically opposed to the pan-European Aryanism that Himmler espoused in his view of the Waffen-SS as a potential future European army, albeit under German control, and is a subject that remains anathema to those who wish to unduly romanticise the legionary movement. It was also an almost inevitable consequence of the decisive shift from a wholly-German Waffen-SS to an international model. The Flemings were not the only ones to suffer in the transition, much the same issue was reported by volunteers from almost all nationalities and to a large extent by the *volksdeutsche* recruits who were wooed, sometimes with conscription, into the ranks of the Waffen-SS only to be ridiculed for their lack of fluency in German and the differences in their culture and attitudes from their comrades from Saxony or the Saar.

For Gottlob Berger the direct result was a significant fall-off of recruiting for the Legions. With expected levels of attrition at the front this would mean that the Legions would become combat ineffective in a relatively short period of time and the whole experiment in which both he and his boss, the Reichsführer-SS, had placed so much political capital would come crashing down. This could not be allowed to happen, so ironically in essence the legionary movement was in danger of failing because of the same German bigotry (not a strong enough word) that Himmler and the SS had espoused for years. Berger's answer was to propose a series of sweeping changes to the way foreigners were treated. In his report to Himmler he highlighted a series of practical blunders such as problems with the field post service and lack of communication to next-of-kin back home, but by far the most damning indictments were lack of training time for volunteers and insufficient foreign nationals being promoted to non-commissioned officer and commissioned officer ranks, sometimes despite good prior service records. For example, in the original SS-Legion Flandern there were indeed 14 Flemish junior officers alongside 11 Germans, but for NCOs the disparity was huge with 77 German NCOs to just the one Fleming. The result was that Berger recommended to Himmler that he intervene personally and state categorically the importance of the *freiwillige,* and that positive steps be made both to promote foreign nationals as well as educate German commanders about how best to treat them.

This was a fundamental battle within the Waffen-SS itself; the black guards were created, and perceived by the early members at least, as an incredibly exclusive elite of the very best of German manhood, with years of Nazi propaganda in the past decrying all those who were not German as inferior and degenerate. This went for Western European peoples as well as the usual Jewish and Slavic targets. These early German recruits had to prove a 'pure' Aryan genealogy, dating back to 1800 for enlisted men and 1750 for officers, and now in their eyes they saw this purity being diluted by an influx of foreigners who were not subject to the same hurdles to entry, and some of them were unhappy with this new situation.

But the reality of war finally forced this exclusivity to be discarded and for many it was a very big leap to make. Things did not always go the way of the old traditionalists, as related by the Dutch *freiwillige* SS-Standartenoberjunker Jan Munk of SS-Panzergrenadier Regiment Westland, 5th SS Panzer Division Wiking:

> We liked the great majority of our superiors, the squad leader, the platoon commander and the company commander, and not just liked but respected them. If we were wet, cold and tired we knew they would be as well. I only know of one case of an NCO being disliked, a corporal, because of his treatment of the Flemish in particular. One Christmas night, when he was stoned out of his mind, we wrapped him in a blanket, dragged him feet-first down the stairs into the cellar, threw him into one of the long washing troughs and turned on the cold water. He got a sound beating, his colleagues turning a blind eye. He behaved much better afterwards. (From Gordon Williamson, *Loyalty is my Honor*, Brown, 1995)

In Flanders complaints flooded into the VNV headquarters and De Clercq himself made a formal protest to the SS authorities about the treatment of the volunteers.

The Reichsführer reacts

Himmler himself got wind of the situation very quickly and was absolutely furious, railing at the 'iniquitous and psychologically mistaken treatment' some of his instructors were meting out. What would become of his cherished anti-bolshevik crusade if this was allowed to continue! He moved swiftly and issued a direct edict to all SS personnel involved with the legionary movement that they were to treat *die freiwillige* with respect and sensitivity and in particular refrain from jokes or comments that could be construed as offensive. These edicts centred on the twin themes of *Erziehung und Umsorgung* – instruction and care – and were binding on all Waffen-SS personnel.

In more practical terms an effort was made to honour the promises made for equivalent ranks and promote Flemings into command positions in the Legion. All German instructors were also sent on 'cultural sensitivity' courses to learn about Flemish history and traditions, although they were not required to learn the language. Bizarrely, with these policies Heinrich Himmler was proving himself to be an early proponent of political correctness! (Although it would be irresponsible to suggest a link between an architect of death like Himmler and modern officials and politicians.)

Another move to placate the criticism was to institute the Dienstelle Fürsorgeoffizier Flandern und Wallonien, which, as a specific section of the *Dienstelle Fürsorge und Versorgungsamt der Waffen-SS Ausland* (the welfare and benefits agency for foreign SS men) provided financial and material assitance to Flemish and Walloon Waffen-SS volunteers and their families. The ex-head of Rex-Vlaanderen and Legion Flandern veteran, Paul Suys, would later head it up in 1943. Chief mover behind the strenuous efforts made to respond to the outcry about maltreatment was Robert Ozswald (1883-1945) of Gottlob Berger's SS-Hauptamt. Ozswald was a German archivist and historian and a well-known architect of 'Flamenpolitik' (nationalist Flemish politics) during World War I, and who then worked in Goebbels' Propaganda Ministry and the Wehrmacht's intelligence service, the Abwehr, before the war. He tirelessly worked behind the scenes to promote German-Flemish relations and ultimately keep the stream of volunteers flowing to the Legion and its successor units.

Combat ready

As ever with the Waffen-SS the training regime for the Flemings was intense and comprehensive. They underwent the same basic training as their German comrades focusing on physical fitness, weapons training and character development. (For further details on Waffen-SS training, see Hitler's Legions Book 1, *Hitler's Gauls*.)

Sport was heavily utilised to promote physical fitness and build the team ethic, while familiarity with all the units weapons systems came about through the innovative use of live firing exercises and inculcated the legionnaires with the German doctrine of an all-arms battle dominated by aggression and attack. All the while, emphasis was placed on the elite nature of the volunteers' position and his status as a Waffen-SS grenadier and the responsibilities that came with that role. Individuals selected for specialist functions within the Legion went to learn their trades at the various schools such as assault pioneers at the SS Pioneer School at Hradischko in Bohemia-Moravia, and Signallers to the SS Signals School at Sterzing-Vipiteno in the South Tyrol. For the Flemish officers it was a different approach, all of them had seen service in the old Royal Belgian Army but to ensure they were trained in German tactics they were surprisingly dispatched not to the Waffen-SS officer academies of Bad Tölz or Braunschweig, but to the Heer officer school at Lauenberg in Pomerania for a two month refresher course.

By October 1941 the SS-Legion Flandern was going through its final paces on the Arys training grounds in East Prussia, alongside its sister unit the Dutch SS-Legion Niederlande, under the joint command of the German SS-Standartenführer Otto Reich, who had previously commanded the Nordwest Regiment during its short life. At the end of the training package Reich declared both formations 'combat ready', the Flandern was going to war!

SS-Legion Flandern Order of Battle

Recruitment had continued throughout the Legion's work-up period so that by the beginning of November 1941 there were a further 75 Flemings on the roll, taking the total to some 950 trained Flemings out of a total Legion strength of 1,112 men. Of that total the Legion's NCOs were almost exclusively German but 14 of the officers, just under half of the total complement, were Flemish, and over ninety per cent of the enlisted men were Flemings.

The Legion had a battalion headquarters staff and supporting elements, with No.s 1–3 Companies being rifle companies. The 4th Company was a heavy infantry sub-unit with two platoons armed with machine-guns and a third platoon equipped with heavy mortars. The 5th Company was the PAK (*Panzer-Abwehr-Kanone*, anti-tank cannon) anti-tank company. Initially established with two platoons of the small and increasingly obsolete 37mm PAK guns, and a further platoon of heavy mortars, this would later be supplemented by the addition of three of the far more powerful 75mm PAK 97/38's, which were captured French Army gun barrels on German gun chassis. The size of the Legion made it far stronger than a comparable Heer battalion, with each company numbering in excess of 200 men (except for the 5th Company which was slightly smaller) and this would enable it to survive significant attrition at the front without becoming combat ineffective. For comparison, a modern British Army infantry company is lucky if it consists of 90–95 men.

The Legion order of battle, its orbat, was as follows:

Legion Commander	SS-Sturmbannführer Michael Lippert (German – no relation to the Legion Wallonie commander Lucien Lippert)
Adjutant	SS-Untersturmführer Günther Steffen (German)
Ordnance Officer	SS-Sturmbannführer Bohez (German)
Intelligence Officer	SS-Obersturmführer Seipold (German)
Medical Officer	SS-Obersturmführer Dr Prix (German)
Medic aid	SS-Obersturmführer Michel
Paymaster	SS-Hauptscharführer Odoj (German)
Dentist	SS-Untersturmführer Hepburn (German)
Feldpost Number	44853A

1. Schützen-Kompanie (1st rifle company – 220 men)

Commander:	SS-Obersturmführer Peter Nussbaum (German– killed in action on 2 March 1942 while a com pany commander in the Dutch SS-Legion Niederlande)

Company Officers:

SS-Untersturmführer Kurt Mahrenholz (German – later a company commander in the Sturmbrigade Langemarck)

SS-Untersturmführer Jozef 'Jef' François (Flemish – ex-head of Dinaso DMO and second in command of the VNV Black Brigade)

SS-Obersturmführer Van Der Smissen (Flemish)

SS-Obersturmführer Deicke

SS-Untersturmführer Harder

Feldpost Number 44853B

2. Schützen-Kompanie (2nd rifle company – 218 men)
Commander: SS-Untersturmführer Helmut Breymann
                             (Austrian – killed in action in July 1944 at Narva
                             while a battalion commander in the Dutch
                             SS-Panzergrenadier Regiment 48 General
                             Seyffardt)

This Company became renowned throughout the Legion for its esprit de corps and close-knit nature, being referred to as the 'Circus Breymann' after its charismatic commander.

Company Officers:

SS-Untersturmführer Friedrich Ritzau (German – later commanded the 1st Battery of the 7th self-propelled gun company in the Sturmbrigade Langemarck)

SS-Untersturmführer Sven Marteson (German – later commanded the 2nd Company in the Sturmbrigade Langemarck)

SS-Untersturmführer Dr Reimond Tollenaere (Flemish – ex-VNV Black Brigade leader)

SS-Untersturmführer Müller (German)

SS-Untersturmführer Hoffmann (German)

SS-Untersturmführer Tupuchies

SS-Untersturmführer Vieweger

Feldpost Number 44853C

3. Schützen-Kompanie (3rd rifle company – 219 men)
Commander: SS-Untersturmführer Hans Moyen (German
                             – died of cancer in 1942)

Company Officers:

SS-Untersturmführer Herbert Kahrl (German – killed in action while commanding the 1st Platoon of the 3rd Company of the Sturmbrigade Langemarck)

SS-Untersturmführer Willi Köhn (German – later commanded the 5th Company in the Sturmbrigade Langemarck)

SS-Untersturmführer Vogel (German – later commanded the 3rd Company in the Sturmbrigade Langemarck)

SS-Untersturmführer Paul Suys (Flemish – ex-head of Rex Vlaanderen)

SS-Untersturmführer Kühlbach (German)

Feldpost Number 44853D

4. Granatwerfer-Kompanie (4th heavy weapons company – 223 men)
Commander: SS-Untersturmführer Karl Neuhäuser (Austrian)
Company Officers:

SS-Untersturmführer Jack Delbaere (Flemish)

SS-Untersturmführer Jan De Wilde (Flemish)

SS-Untersturmführer Karel Lagast (Flemish)

SS-Untersturmführer Polsterer
Feldpost Number 44853E

5. Panzerjäger-Kompanie (5th anti-tank gun company – 159 men)
Commander: Initially SS-Untersturmführer Karl Weingärtner
                              (Austrian – killed in action on 3 January 1944 in
                              the Ukraine while commanding the 7th self-
                              propelled gun company in the Sturmbrigade
                              Langemarck), from March 20 1942
                              SS-Hauptsturmführer Willi Dethier (German)
Company Officers:
SS-Untersturmführer Johannes Gläser (German)
SS-Untersturmführer Fürst (German)
Feldpost Number 44853F

Lippert as Commander

Who was the Legion's first commander, the man who would set the tone
for the unit, who would mould it during its tough SS training and then
lead it into combat on the killing grounds of the Eastern Front? Michael
Lippert was an early convert to Nazism who joined the SS, as so many
did, through the regionally-based Totenkopf organisation, Lippert himself
joining Totenkopf-Infanterieregiment 2. He rose swiftly through the ranks
until becoming the commander of the SS guard unit at the newly-created
concentration camp at Dachau. This brought him firmly into the world of
the head of the Totenkopf, the brutal Theodor Eicke.

Eicke was an ardent disciple of Hitler and in Lippert he saw a reflection of
his own fanatical beliefs. Lippert became Eicke's Adjutant and it was in this
capacity that he went with his superior on 1 July 1934 to Stadelheim Prison
just outside Munich. Imprisoned in a small, dank cell all by himself was a man
who a few scant hours before had wielded almost as much power as Hitler
himself within the Nazi Party as head of the brownshirted stormtroopers of
the SA (Sturmabteilung), Ernst Röhm. But now the decision had been made
to purge the SA of any elements that could threaten Hitler's supremacy
or challenge the Army. Head of the list to be executed was the SA's leader
himself. Röhm was given a loaded pistol by Eicke who told him that suicide
was an honourable way out. Röhm disagreed and refused to shoot himself.
Who then went into the cell and actually shot Röhm point blank in the head
is open to question. At the time most believed it was Lippert, but at his subsequent trial after the war Lippert claimed he stood outside the cell while
Eicke went in and shot his former comrade. It was difficult to disprove as
Eicke himself died on the Russian Front in 1943. Whatever the truth, the fact
is that Lippert went on to be selected to command the SS-Legion Flandern

as an SS-Sturmbannführer. His appointment was not an effective one as he lacked that vital empathy with his foreign volunteers that was so necessary to create an elite from their ranks, a character trait that the most successful Waffen-SS commanders of foreign volunteers, such as the legendary Felix Steiner, had in spades. Indeed many Flemish veterans still speak of Lippert's open disdain for them and their homeland, but then this was an all-too common view in the Waffen-SS in the early years and one that did huge damage to relations in the unit and recruitment back home, as we have seen.

After being severely wounded in Russia leading the Legion he spent time convalescing in Germany before returning to active service. He never returned to the Flandern, instead filling a number of miscellaneous command appointments in a pretty unremarkable military career. After disappearing off the radar for a while he surfaced again as the first commander of the mixed Reichsdeutsche and volksdeutsche 10th SS Panzer Division Frundsberg, for the very short period of January to 15 February 1943, when it was first being formed in the Saintes area of Poitou-Charente in western France. He then left that post as the division moved towards combat readiness and again disappeared, before finally ending the war commanding yet another foreign volunteer formation, the Dutch SS-Freiwilligen Grenadier Regiment 83 of the 34th SS-Freiwilligen Division Landstorm Nederland. This less than elite unit was a last-ditch attempt by Himmler and Berger to replicate the combat success of the more widely-known Dutch SS Nederland Brigade and later Division. The Landstorm Nederland Divison itself was formed from various Dutch SS and other collaborationist organisations in the Netherlands and was placed under the command of SS-Oberführer Martin Kohlroser. The unit saw no significant fighting before it, and Lippert, surrendered to Canadian troops at Veenendaal in the Netherlands in May 1945.

Eastward

With official confirmation of their combat-ready status the SS-Legion Flandern left their training grounds for the Eastern Front at 0700hrs on 10 November 1941, their destination the town of Tossno in the Soviet Union. The horrors of Nazi Germany's first winter in Russia awaited them as they headed to their post as part of Army Group North, east of the Baltic States and surrounding Russia's second city, Leningrad.

Names to remember

Schrijnen had moved to Nazi Germany for work and had settled in deepest Bavaria in the town of Kempten-Allgäu where, as was customary, he lived with a local family, the Eberle's, who sponsored his employment, provided accommodation and generally looked after him. Bavaria was the birthplace of Nazism but it was also, and still is, the heartland of German Catholicism, and this suited Schrijnen's own Flemish Catholic heritage. It was during this time that his opinions of the Nazis began to change dramatically. As a staunch member of the working-class he viewed with approval the conditions of Germans workers and the social benefits they received, things like free universal health insurance and paid holidays were the norm and he compared this with the misery he had heard was commonplace in the Soviet Union. The end result was that he turned decisively against communism at the same time that Himmler's 'anti-bolshevik crusade' was gathering steam.

On 22 June 1941 when the Wehrmacht launched Operation Barbarossa and invaded Soviet Russia Schrijnen's world changed forever. That same day the 19-year-old Fleming marched into his local Waffen-SS recruiting office to volunteer. The recruiters took one look at his lack of height and rejected him. Undeterred, Schrijnen made a further six applications over the following year but was rejected each time for the same reason. Finally admitting defeat he volunteered instead for the Gebirgsjäger, Germany's famed mountain troops, whose home base was in Kempten-Allgäu. He was accepted and sent to basic training in July 1942, only to mysteriously receive a transfer straight away, on 1 August 1942, to the Waffen-SS. Schrijnen himself said of this time:

> As a Flemish nationalist, with a great admiration for the Germans, and as an anti-communist, I volunteered to work in Germany in early July 1940, to learn more about the country and its people. On the very day that war with the Soviet Union broke out, I reported to the Waffen-SS to offer myself as a 'Germanic volunteer'. Unfortunately, because I was only 1.64m (5ft 4in) tall and the minimum height requirement was 1.78m (5ft 9in), I was rejected. This didn't put me off though. I continued trying to enlist. In the end, in the summer of 1942, I was accepted into the Flemish Volunteer Legion. I served on the northern sector of the Eastern Front, in the swampy terrain around Leningrad, as a company runner. (From Gordon Williamson, *Loyalty is my Honor*, Brown, 1995)

Like Schrijnen, D'Haese had been too young to participate in the fighting against the invading Germans, but unlike Schrijnen, he had few qualms about supporting them afterwards:

> ...after many decades of repression, (we) could finally achieve an independent administration as a state within the greater Belgian state. We wanted to achieve this required reformation, not as a 'charity case' and we were ready to fight on the side of the German troops. (From Allen Brandt, *The Last Knight of Flanders*, Schiffer Publishing, 1998)

For D'Haese this could mean only one thing and so on 23 May 1941, shortly before his nineteenth birthday he went into the recruiting office and volunteered for the Waffen-SS. He was one of the first Flemings to join up. He would not be the last. He became a private soldier in the 8th Company of the Nordwest Regiment under the command of SS-Hauptsturmführer Kaiser. After several months preliminary training he, like all his fellow Flemings in the Nordwest, was transferred to the newly forming SS-Legion Flandern. On arrival he was assigned to SS-Untersturmführer Hans Moyen's 3rd Company where he was quickly picked out as a soldier with potential. As such he was sent for specialist training to the Assault Pioneer School in Dresden where he learnt the techniques of Germany's combat engineers, including explosives, hasty bridge building and bunker busting. This was not a common set-up across Europes' armies at the time, usually the term 'pioneer' denoted inferiority and most forces, including Britain's, used pioneers for menial labour such as road and ditch maintenace as well as trench digging. In the Wehrmacht, by contrast, 'pioneer' was a term used to describe highly trained and capable combat engineers able to fight as infantry but also to utilise specialised skills. On completion of his course in Dresden, D'Haese headed back northeast to rejoin his Company on the training grounds of Arys as a newly-promoted Gruppenführer, a non-commissioned section commander. He was ready for his baptism of fire on the Russian Front.

V

Round One:
Leningrad and the SS-Legion Flandern

The single most critical factor determining the nature of battles and campaigns is without doubt, terrain. Any commander worth their pay will tell you that it is the very first thing they take into account when entering or planning operations. Every modern British Army officer and NCO is trained that when they deliver their formal orders to the men they will lead into combat the first heading in that set of commands is entitled 'Ground'. Only when the terrain has been considered and everyone is familiar with it does the commander turn his attention to that other critical factor, the enemy. The war on the Eastern Front is almost universally viewed in the popular imagination as one characterised by titanic battles involving millions of men in huge, sweeping armoured movements covering vast expanses of the open steppe such as was the case at Kiev, Uman or Kursk; either that or the utter savagery of urban warfare in the dust and smoke of Stalingrad. The campaign fought from late June 1941 to May 1945 in the northern sector of the Russian Front encompassing the Baltic countries, Leningrad and the north-eastern German coast was a world away from that picture.

The overriding reason for this popular misconception is ignorance of the landscape itself. The region was, and is, criss-crossed by fast flowing rivers such as the Narva, the Luga, the Plyussa and the Schelon all the way west to the Vistula and the Oder. Many of these rivers are also bordered by wide swathes of marsh and swamp such as the truly huge Pripet Marshes, interconnected with large inland lakes, such as Lakes Peipus and Pskovkoye. More often than not the land between these various watery obstacles is covered with almost trackless forests. Add to that the lack of major roads and otherwise poor communications and it becomes clear that this was not a land destined to see fleets of tanks engaged in daring pincer movements.

This meant that the campaign in the north was fought primarily by the infantry, the footsloggers, the workhorses of any army. It was to be a war characterised on both sides by dogged defence and horrendous attrition of men and equipment in a land that winter bit hard, and where spring and autumn brought the cloying reek of mud, Russia's infamous *rasputitsa*, and summer meant endless clouds of flies and mosquitoes. It was the junior and least resourced of the three sectors that the Wehrmacht divided the Eastern Front into, with the aristocratic Prussian Field Marshal Wilhelm Ritter von Leeb's Army Group A (later changed to Army Group North) fielding just 29 divisions on the day of invasion. The Army Group was composed of two infantry armies, the Sixteenth and the Eighteenth Armies, with over 20 divisions of infantry relying for movement on boot leather and horses, and the smallest of Germany's panzer strike forces, Panzergruppe IV, comprising three panzer and three motorised infantry divisions as well as the powerful motorised 3rd SS Division Totenkopf. The comparatively weak 4th SS Division SS-Polizei was in Army Group reserve. This was in comparison to the 50 divisions of Fedor von Bock's Army Group B (later Centre) and the 42 divisions of Gerd von Runstedt's Army Group C (later South).

If the truth be told the northern sector was a front that lacked 'glamour'. The terrain discounted huge battles of envelopment carried out by waves of steel monsters, there were no natural resources to aim for, no oil wells or coalfields, and little in the way of iconic place names apart from, of course, Leningrad. In short, this was not the front where the War in the East would be decided. But it was here that the Flemish volunteers would spend the majority of their wartime service. From the first time the SS-Legion Flandern went up to the front in November 1941 the Flemish were in combat in the northern sector of the eastern Front for 21 of the next 42 months until their final surrender in northern Germany in May 1945.

Situation Report: Barbarossa in the north

Von Leeb's forces had swept out of East Prussia on 22 June 1941 heading north-east towards Novgorod and Leningrad. Just as with the soldiers of Army Group C down south in the Ukraine the invading Germans were first hailed as welcome liberators by most of the population in the northern sector as the Wehrmacht swept through the previously briefly independent countries of first Lithuania, then Latvia and on into Estonia. These Baltic peoples had suffered dreadfully under Stalinist repression with thousands murdered or deported to gulags, and the Germans were seen by them as their deliverers.

It was a different story further east in Russia proper when the German advance neared its goal, the old capital of Imperial Russia, Leningrad. Here resistance stiffened considerably and the headlong march came to a grinding halt as autumn came in September. The city of St Petersburg, built 300 years earlier by Tsar Peter the Great, had transformed itself in World War I into Petrograd to sound 'less German', and was again rebranded after the Bolshevik Revolution as Leningrad. In 1941 it was Russia's second city and a centre of industry and culture. The Wehrmacht pushed to the very gates of the city in the west, taking the suburbs of Slutsk and Pushkin and even the old Tsarist summer palace at Krasnoye Selo, before they swung south and east to cut the city off from mainland Russia by reaching the shores of Lake Ladoga to the east; but this complete encirclement was never quite achieved. Army Group A then lost its main attacking punch when Panzergruppe IV was detached and sent to reinforce Army Group B to take part in the failed offensive on Moscow, Operation Typhoon. Lacking sufficient offensive strength to take the city outright and with its divisions seriously worn down by three months of constant fighting, the decision was made by von Leeb to invest the city. Unlike Stalingrad over a year later, the German strategy for taking Leningrad was now not to conquer it by force of arms but rather to starve and bombard it into submission. They would also seek to completely isolate the city by pushing east and southeast towards the north-south running River Volkhov and the city of Tikhvin in an attempt to link up with the allied Finnish Army advancing south to the River Svir.

To achieve the necessary encirclement the Germans then proceeded to build a massive set of entrenchments and fortifications that almost surrounded the entire city both north and south on the Karelian Isthmus. The aim was 'no-one in and no-one out'. Over the next 900 days something like one million of Leningrad's citizens and defenders would die – some estimate as many as 1.5 million – mostly from starvation and exposure, many thousands from artillery fire, and much of the city would be reduced to rubble and ash by the Germans in the longest military siege seen since the Middle Ages and the deadliest city siege in history. The Wehrmacht would never have it all their own way though, as from the start the Soviets did manage to maintain a wafer-thin channel into the city from the east for resupply and reinforcement. Their main military effort was focused on relieving the siege by offensive action and the destruction of the Wehrmacht forces besieging it. Into this maelstrom of trench warfare, defence and counter-offensives the Flemish were sent to begin their war.

Struggle to the Front

Lack of vehicles meant that when the order for deployment east came on 27 October 1941 the SS-Legion Flandern was looking at a foot march and horse-drawn slog of some 2,300 kilometres to even reach the front. Unsurprisingly this news was not met with overwhelming joy by either the Flemings or their German cadre. Hurriedly the Legion was issued with about 150 vehicles, and drivers were hastily trained before finally setting out on 10 November. As the column headed east they received a grim taste of what they could expect that winter when on the morning of 14 November not a single engine could be started as the temperature had dropped in the night to a breathtaking minus 28 degrees Celsius. But despite the problems the Legion struggled on and began to arrive in its deployment area south of Tossno 10 days later, on 24 November.

The 2. SS-Infanterie Brigade (mot.)

At this time the Waffen-SS was still a small organisation with only five frontline combat divisions; the Leibstandarte, Das Reich, Totenkopf, SS-Polizei and the still-forming Wiking. Alongside these formations were three SS brigades, the 1. and 2. motorised infantry brigades and the SS Cavalry Brigade, originally established to act as rear area security troops but who were increasingly being used at the front due to the terrible attrition suffered by the Wehrmacht during the invasion. A flavour of a typical action by these brigades was that undertaken on 26 October by the 2. SS-Infanterie Brigade, when it was put on readiness after intercepted Soviet signal traffic indicated a potential assault through the Skajadub Novka bridgehead. The Brigade drove off two Red airforce overflights above Krasny-Bor and went on to capture 'fifteen suspected terrorists and saboteurs from Tossno', who were swiftly sentenced to death and shot. The war behind the lines in Russia was often even more brutal than at the front and the 2. SS-Infanterie Brigade played its full part in that. It was to this brigade that the SS-Legion Flandern was attached in November 1941.

The 2. SS-Infanterie Brigade (mot.) itself was, as the name denotes, a motorised formation originally created in May 1941 from the Totenkopf's SS-Infanterie Regimenter 4 and 14 along with the SS-Flak-Abteilung 'Ost' (anti-aircraft battalion 'East') and the Begleit-Battalion Reichsführer-SS, Himmler's own reinforced Escort Battalion, although the 14. Regiment never actually served with the Brigade. Originally authorised to a strength of 7,301 men, by 14 November 1941 the actual ration roll was reduced by casualties down to some 4,189, but it was hoped that the addition of the Flandern would help bring it back up to strength. It was this Brigade that would have the the accolade of being the first ever German formation to have a wholly foreign volunteer unit under its command, the thousand-plus strong SS-Legion Flandern, and it would continue to act as a 'home' for many of Nazi Germany's first wave of foreign volunteer formations including the Dutch and Norwegian Legions.

As it was this baptism of fire proved a bit of a damp, or rather frozen, squib for the Flemings. Arriving in their designated billets south of Tossno in the Tarrassovo region in late November several Flemish platoons saw some minor action as early as 24 November but it was nothing more than a few shots fired and desultory artillery fire. The biggest shock to the Flemish came not from the Red Army but the Russians' friend and traditional ally, 'General Winter'. In the coldest winter in living memory the effect on the ill-equipped Germans and their allies was truly horrific. General Heinz Guderian, one of Germany's greatest generals and the architect of blitzkrieg, said of that first winter in the Soviet Union:

> There is nothing more dramatic in military history than the stunning assault of the cold on the German Army. The men had great coats and jackboots. The only additional clothing they had received consisted of a scarf and a pair of gloves. In the rear, the locomotives had seized up with cold. In the line, weapons were unserviceable and, according to General Schaal, the tank motors had to be warmed up for 12 hours before the machines could get going. One hideous detail is that many men, while satisfying the calls of nature, died when their anuses froze.

There was good reason why the campaign medal awarded for serving at the front during the winter of 1941-1942 was referred to by the troops themselves as the 'Frozen Meat Order'.

Low level action for the SS-Legion Flandern continued for two weeks from 24 November to 6 December with protection of the rail line from Mga to Kirischi and south to the Maluska swamps. During this time the Flemings settled into a routine of classic infantry activity with dug-in static defence and proactive patrolling.

Patrolling against the partisans

The aim of infantry patrols was then, and still is today, to dominate the area of ground a unit is operating in without having to physically occupy all of it. In such a programme each company would act pretty much independently, but conforming to an overall unit plan, the first task being the gathering of intelligence on the enemy; their strength, equipment, intentions, behaviour and locations. Local people would be questioned and a series of small reconnaissance, 'recce', patrols would be sent out. Typically of section strength under a junior NCO, these recce patrols would hopefully find and target enemy positions, supply dumps or troop concentrations. They would not seek to engage the enemy, not having the strength or equipment to win a firefight. The aim of each patrol would be to get as much information as possible without the enemy becoming aware of their presence.

Standard British Army practice is for the recce patrol to establish a safe point, called the Final Rendezvous – the FRV for short, where most of the patrol members would lie up in an all-round defensive formation near to the suspected enemy location. Leaving his second-in-command in charge of the FRV the patrol commander and one other patrol member would then move forward and carry out a close target recce of the area noting all relevant information and even sketching the position if at all possible. They would then silently return to the FRV, pick up their patrol mates and head back to their own lines. On reaching base the patrol commander would de-brief his men and write down all the information they picked up as well as critiquing their general performance. He would then report to the company patrol master, typically the company second-in-command, or senior commander, briefing him on the results of the recce. If the patrol had identified a suitable target then plans would be made to destroy the position. This would be carried out very shortly afterwards, to ensure the enemy hadn't moved, by a much larger patrol, called a fighting patrol. These fighting patrols would typically be at least of platoon strength if not larger and the recce patrol commander would act as guide for this force to bring it right on top of the target. With advances in the technology of modern weapon sights and night vision aids, it is again standard UK practice to carry out all patrols at night to utilise the advantages of superior technology and thorough training, but back then in the forests and swamps of northern Russia most patrols were daylight operations.

First blood to the Flandern

The official Wehrmacht unit diaries, the *Kriegstagebücher*, that each formation in the field had to keep updated as a record of their activity, states that on 20 November the SS-Legion Flandern killed its first two enemy partisans on a patrol sweep, but that its fighting patrols of 25 November met with no further success. On 27 November parts of the Legion and the RF-SS Escort Battalion were strafed and bombed by ground attack aircraft but suffered no losses. Over the next couple of weeks the partisans stepped up their activities, often coming together in large formations of several hundred men to attack and overwhelm isolated German positions. On the evening of 1-2 December 1941 the SS brigade strongpoint at Podberesje was overrun and destroyed by about 150 partisans, followed by the loss of the village of Orivnovka the following night to another similar-sized partisan force. The SS troopers fought back throughout their sector and powerful Flandern patrols spent five days trying to sweep the area clear of enemy, but this was only partially successful. The fighting was reaching a crescendo and on 4 December a general attack was launched on the RF-SS Escort Battalion by a substantial force of partisans and regular Red Army men stranded behind the German lines. The former members of Himmler's bodyguard grimly held onto their positions against the onslaught until the Flandern led a counter-attack on the Soviets that resulted in several hours of fierce fighting in the freezing waist-deep snow. Six Flemish legionnaires were killed and a further three were wounded, but the Soviets were thrown back and dipersed and the sector stabilised. By now the weather was making operations incredibly hard to maintain with weapons jamming in the cold and men simply being worn down by the freezing temperatures. With the failure of their latest offensive even the extremely hardy partisans were concentrating on settling into winter quarters in the forests to wait out the season with minimal activity.

Into winter quarters

Finally on 14 December the 2. SS-Infanterie Brigade (mot.) was ordered into winter quarters near Tukkums, 70 kilometers west of Riga in Latvia, the Flandern itself being billeted in the Talsen region with the headquarters staff and 1st Company in the village of Kandau, and the 2nd, 3rd and 4th Companies five kilometers south in Adsern. Casualties had not been light but neither had they been debilitating. On the roster there were still some 23 out of the original 26 officers, 72 NCOs out of 81 and 559 legionnaires from an original complement of 898. There were even some 125 vehicles still running, a triumph given the conditions.

Overall the Legion's first engagement had been brief but successful. Frans Coulombier had become the first Flemish volunteer to earn a bravery award, the Iron Cross 2nd Class, and the unit itself had held up well in a campaign that was both bloody and unglamorous. In fighting the partisans there were no frontlines or safe areas, and everywhere was vulnerable to attack at any time. Even without the partisans, life would have been a struggle against the bitter cold that plummeted to 40 degrees centigrade below zero. It is truly impossible to understand cold of that depth without experiencing it, but to give some sort of example of what that meant physically, a cup of boiling water left out in the open would be a frozen block of ice in 60 seconds. Such cold is truly horrific, and even with warm clothing and regular hot meals and drinks a soldier is only able to operate effectively for short periods without needing to take a break, but in that winter in Russia hot meals were the exception rather than the rule and there were no rest breaks. To try and fight against an enemy on their home ground in such conditions was a daunting prospect to say the least, but the Legion had played its part well and had had valuable time to learn its trade at the front.

Names to remember

Remy Schrijnen was still working in Bavaria desperately trying to enlist in the Waffen-SS when the Legion was undergoing its baptism of fire in northern Russia, his time would come later.

For Georg D'Haese the incredibly harsh winter of 1941-1942 was his first taste of combat. Starting off as a section commander in Hans Moyen's 3rd Company he began his war fighting Soviet partisans in the forests and snows outside Leningrad. While the fighting was hard, it was the cold that was especially brutal and like the rest of the Wehrmacht in that horrendous winter D'Haese and his comrades suffered terribly, with a shocking lack of equipment and clothing. He survived the fighting and was awarded the much-prized 'Frozen Meat Order' (East Medal for the winter of 1941-42). As casualties mounted he had often stepped in to command one or more platoons as well as his original section and he was marked out by his superiors as future officer material.

VI

Round Two:
Vlasov, the Volkhov Pocket and Krasny-Bor

In the early 1930s, under the leadership of the now almost forgotten Marshal Mikhail Tuchashevsky, the Red Army was a world leader in armoured warfare and the all-arms battle. Tuchashevsky, the so-called 'Red Napoleon', had created a doctrine combining mobility and firepower on a grand scale and built an army that could deliver that strategy with huge fleets of tanks operating in conjunction with masses of mobile infantry, artillery and waves of aircraft. Many of these advanced ideas were adopted and adapted by the Wehrmacht during its years of secret cooperation with the Russians leading up to the War and were the very essence of blitzkrieg. The execution of Tuchashevsky and generations of Soviet officers by a violently paranoid Stalin during the 1930s purges effectively wiped out this advantage and condemned the Soviets to fighting the Wehrmacht with what amounted to World War I tactics until all the lessons had been learned again. The direct result was a string of catastrophic defeats for the Soviets in the summer and autumn of 1941.

The loss of the Baltic States, Belorussia, the Ukraine, and the encirclement battles of Uman and Kiev were all hammer blows to an already weakened Soviet military. By the time the Germans launched their belated offensive, Operation Typhoon, to capture Moscow towards the end of the year, more than three million Soviet soldiers had already surrendered to the Wehrmacht. The majority of the Red Airforce and the existing pre-war tank fleet had been utterly destroyed, but still Soviet Russia would not lie down. In fact, the talk at STAVKA, the Soviet High Command, was not of impending defeat but of actually going over to the offensive. Most of the Soviet General Staff favoured a limited offensive to take advantage of the winter cold and the recent reinforcement from the Soviet Far East Army. Those well-equipped and well-trained troops were now released from guarding the far eastern border against a possible Japanese attack following the German communist spy Richard Sorges' revelations that the Japanese had no intention of attacking the Russians and were instead focusing on the Pacific.

The Red Army counter-attacks!

Stalin had come closer to losing his power, and his life, than at any other time in his bloody dictatorship and he wanted swift revenge. Brushing aside all opposition Stalin demanded large-scale counter-offensives on all three major fronts to throw the Wehrmacht back towards Nazi Germany. The result was a general offensive against all three Wehrmacht Army Groups launched on 6 December by over one and a half million Soviet soldiers grouped in 17 Armies, the equivalent of some 40 German divisions. On the central front the Soviet counter-attack against the halted and weary German troops trying to capture Moscow caused confusion and chaos. The previously mobile German forces had been worn down by cold and constant combat, they were spread out over the limitless Russian steppe and had been brought to a shuddering halt by the weather and fierce Russian resistance. The Soviet counter-offensive hit them like a steamroller and ground them into the snow. Whole regiments and then divisions disappeared off the German order of battle as they became isolated in the white wasteland and fought losing battles against fresh Red Army divisions. Moscow was saved.

Destroy Army Group North

In the northern sector the Soviet intention was nothing less than the relief of Leningrad and the destruction of von Leeb's entire, renamed Army Group North. Concentrated as the Wehrmacht forces were in front of Leningrad with little armour and few reserves, the Soviet intent was twofold; firstly to strike at the southern end of Army Group North and eliminate the German Sixteenth Army, and then in their second phase to strike west from the Volkhov River and head for the Baltic. The farther west the Russians could then hit the sea the more German and Axis-allied troops would be caught in the net. It was an audacious plan, and the Red Army of 1944 would probably have been able to carry it off successfully, but this was not 1944, this was the dawn of 1942 and the days of Soviet superiority had not yet arrived.

The Soviets' intent was first signalled by a short attack on 24 September against the Eighteenth Army in the north of the sector that caused the Germans to give up some ground on the east bank of the River Neva and laid the foundation for a further offensive. Secondly, German intelligence identified a Soviet build-up on the east side of the River Volkhov and the Valdai Hills to the south which, in their view, was aimed at the thinly held junction of the Sixteenth and Eighteenth Armies. Junctions between formations are often the weakest spots in a line and for the Red Army this smelt of opportunity. The Wehrmacht's response was typically decisive. The German

High Command, OKW – *Oberkommando der Wehrmacht* – ordered that von Leeb be reinforced by an infantry regiment from Army Group Centre and two parachute regiments from the central front reserve, and the scheduled transfer to Army Group Centre of one of von Leeb's four motorized divisions was cancelled. The reinforcement operation was meant to be completed by air but the Luftwaffe was unable to fulfil the task and so the railway was used, and the decision was made to increase the infantry reinforcement contingent from a single regiment to an entire division, the volunteer Spanish *Azul* (Azul meaning Blue after the colour of the shirts the Spanish volunteers wore, its proper Wehrmacht name the 250th Infantry) Division.

The intelligence turned out to be accurate and the Red Army attacked. The first phase of the Soviet counter-offensive against the Sixteenth Army led to the misery and heroism of the Demyansk Pocket, where Eicke's 3rd SS Division Totenkopf in particular fought itself to near extinction over the following few months.

West from the Volkhov

The second phase was then unleashed. This phase was designed as the hammer blow that would crush Army Group North when its attention and reserves were focused on Demyansk to the south. To lead this daring assault the Russians had General Klykov commanding the crack 2nd Shock Army, supported by the 59th Army to his north and the 52nd Army to the south. Klykov chose to begin the offensive with a narrow break-in at the junction of the German 126th and 215th Infantry Divisions. These formations had seen constant Soviet patrols and feints for weeks but on the misty morning of 13 January 1942, with the temperature showing at a truly eyeball-freezing 50 degrees centigrade below zero, their forward units were deluged by an artillery firestorm from 0800 hours onwards. At 0930 hours the call came over the German radio net, 'The Russians are coming!' The Volkhov offensive had begun.

Initially comprising some six infantry divisions, plus supporting formations, Klykov's Army was tasked with advancing north-west from the Volkhov River to first cut the Leningrad-Novgorod road, then the railway line, and then push on to the Baltic, encircling the whole of the Wehrmacht's Eighteenth Army. At the same time the Soviet 54th Army to Klykov's north was to attack from Petrokrepost, pinning the Wehrmacht forces besieging Leningrad in place and allowing the 2nd Shock Army to sweep up from the south unhindered. This assault was crucial to the success of the combined operation, but having succeeded in its opening stages when Klykov reached and then overran the Leningrad-Novgorod road on 17 January, the whole plan was jeopardised when the German I Corps refused to follow the Soviet script and stubbornly held the 54th Army right on its start line.

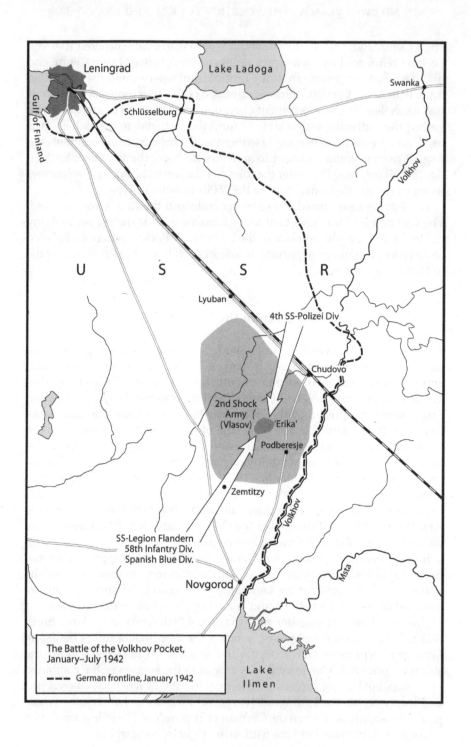

The Battle of the Volkhov Pocket,
January–July 1942

- - - German frontline, January 1942

Von Leeb replaced

At this time an exhausted von Leeb had had enough of Hitler's interference in military decisions and asked to be replaced as Commander of Army Group North. Hitler accepted von Leeb's resignation on 15 January and promoted Eighteenth Army's Commander, von Küchler, to overall Army Group command.

The fighting at the front was fierce and confused. Lines of German strongpoints and scattered units were bypassed by the Soviet spearheads but held out against follow-up assaults. The battered Westphalians in the 422nd and 424th regiments of the 126th Infantry Division took heavy criticism for letting the Soviets break their line but that was little comfort to the 15,000 dead Russians lying in front of the Division's trenches. But despite their usual horrific losses the Red Army offensive was succeeding in its drive to the west. STAVKA followed the von Clausewitzian principle of war in reinforcing success and they rushed a further three infantry divisions, the 13th Cavalry Corps, six light infantry brigades and three armoured brigades into the line to support Klykov. It was hoped that this now very significant force, basically two entire Soviet Armies with 130,000 men in total, would be able to carry out its original mission as planned even against the opposition from the Eighteenth Army to the north now under the command of General of Cavalry Georg Lindemann. Klykov's spearheads were now a full 55 miles west of their start line on the Volkhov River and his troops were spreading out over the forests and swamps in the area behind the broken German frontline.

The offensive was, however, vulnerable. The Soviet penetration now resembled a fan in the German lines with the base being only 13 miles wide at the point of break-in. If the Wehrmacht could attack from north or south, or both, and close that gap it would mean that the entire Soviet offensive force would be cut off from its own lines and effectively be surrounded. In such circumstances supplies would no longer be able to reach the Soviet troops and without a constant stream of hundreds of tonnes of ammunition, fuel, food, weapons and the other paraphanelia of modern war they would very quickly cease to be able to offer resistance and would either die or go into captivity.

SS-Legion Flandern returns to the front

For the Flemings their winter rest in Latvia was cut short on 9 January by the call to return to the front to try and halt the Soviet counter-offensive. On arrival the 2nd Infantry 'Circus Breymann' and 4th Heavy Weapons Companies were thrown into battle immediately to retake the tactically important villages of Koptsy and Krutik on the southern flank of the

Russian penetration in support of the 126th Infantry Division. The snow was very deep round the villages and the temperature was achingly low but even in these seemingly winter wonderland conditions the fighting quickly became savage.

> In certain positions along the lines we would pile the dead bodies of Russian soldiers on top of each other and cover them with snow so that we could lay in some kind of protection since we couldn't dig trenches. (From Allen Brandt, *The Last Knight of Flanders*, Schiffer Publishing, 1998)

Against strong Soviet resistance the Flemings took Krutik and then stormed the burnt-out village of Koptsy and flung the Red Army back in hand-to-hand fighting. With Koptsy secure the Flemings dug in to protect themselves from the inevitable Soviet shelling and also to try and get at least a little shelter from the horrendous weather. Every day the Russians delayed before counter-attacking allowed the legionnaires more time to strengthen their positions and, as so often, the watchword in the life of the infantryman was 'dig'. Surprisingly the expected assault did not materialise until over a week later when following an artillery barrage the Soviet infantry threw themselves at Koptsy, on January 20. As usual the Russians were almost suicidal in attack, flinging themselves in masses onto the Flemings's guns screaming their 'Urrahs!' But the Legion companies held and hundreds of Russians died in the snow.

Tollenaere killed in a 'blue on blue'

The day after the Red Army was repulsed at Koptsy the Legion was reminded of exactly why the deadly mix of shrapnel and high explosive was by far the biggest killer weapon in all the wars of the twentieth century. SS-Untersturmführer Reimond Tollenaere of the Legion's 2nd Company, and ex-head of the VNV's paramilitary Black Brigade the DM-ZB, was in the forward trenches with his comrade, the 4th Company's SS-Untersturmführer Jan de Wilde, when a mistake was made by the Legion's neighbouring unit, the Spanish Blue Division. This highly praised formation from Franco's Spain would see a lot of service at the front with the SS-Legion Flandern in the months to come, but on this day it just got it wrong. While the Spaniards were shelling the Russian positions to their front and at the juncture of their lines with the Flemings, some of the shells landed short and hit the Flemings' trenches. Tollenaere died in the blasts. (These friendly fire incidents, called 'blue on blues' in modern NATO parlance, have been a depressing fact of conflict for centuries and are still with us in modern times. Despite the use of incredibly sophisticated technology soldiers are still being killed by their own side in Iraq and Afghanistan today.) In the far less technologically advanced Second World War it was not uncommon to be bombed or strafed by your own airforce or shelled by your own artillery. The only, horrifyingly glib response is that in war mistakes are made. And in this case it was the idol of the VNV that paid for that mistake. Tollenaere was an icon to his Black Brigade comrades and had the potential to become the Degrelle of the Flemings, but it was not to be and his career and life ended in Koptsy on 21 January 1942. Buried by his comrades at the front a funeral service was held for him in Brussels in the second week of February 1942 at which his brother Leo pledged to volunteer for the Legion to take his brother's place. Flemish nationalism had now lost its two youngest and most charismatic proponents with the deaths of Joris Van Severen and Reimond Tollenaere.

Plug the gaps

The fighting around Koptsy continued but on the 4 February the 2nd Company was pulled out of the line for a rest in nearby Podberesje. By that time the Legion had its first Flemish company commander in Jan de Wilde, who had taken over the 4th Company from SS-Untersturmführer Karl Neuhäuser as the casualty lists mounted. In total the two Legion companies involved had suffered over 200 casualties, roughly half their strength, but the Soviets had lost more than 700 dead in their battles with the Flemings. The 4th Company was joined in the line by the 3rd and 5th Companies forming battlegroups with the II and III Battalions of their neighboring Heer unit, the 424th Infantry Regiment, to fight around the village of Zemtitzy just to the north of Koptsy. The 1st Company meanwhile was building a defensive line at Ossiya to stop any further Soviet advances westwards or south-westwards. For the rest of February the pattern remained the same, with companies from the Legion being used up and down the southern flank of the Soviet penetration to try and contain it and build a solid defensive line. The villages of Koptsy, Krutik, Zemtitzy and Lyubsty were fought over repeatedly by the two sides, taken and then lost and then retaken in quick succession. Very quickly they became nothing more than piles of blackened rubble and timber.

Finally, exhausted, the Legion was again brought out of the line on 27 February and rested once more at the strongpoint at Podberesje that had temporarily fallen to the partisans in the earlier winter fighting. Here it was reunited with the detached 1st Company and prepared for the next phase in German operations. This next stage was clear to the Germans. Having established firm flanks at both the northern and southern ends of the Red Army penetration it was time to launch a counter-strike and seal off the 2nd Shock Army. The orders were given on 1 March 1942. The plan was for the 58th Infantry Division, with assorted units subordinated to it including the Spanish Blue Division and the SS-Legion Flandern, to attack the break-in point from the south and the 4th SS-Polizei Division to lead the attack from the north. The two thrusts would then meet at a wide clearing marked on the map. This was nothing more than a patch of land of a few hundred metres square that was relatively clear of scrub and swamp. The German planners nicknamed it 'Erika'. It was to go down in the annals of every unit that fought there that spring, including the SS-Legion Flandern.

With the orders given the Legion was called upon to move up to the front once more and launch a preliminary attack on 2 March to force the Russians behind an important road that ran between the villages of Vyeshki (Wishiki) and Zemtitzy, which was once again in Russian hands. With support from the Spanish Blue Division on its flank, the Legion attacked with its 1st Platoon up and after being initially pinned down by defensive fire took its objectives on both that and the subsequent day's fighting. This attack was made by the entire Legion bar the 2nd Company, which stayed in reserve. Over the next few days the Legion continued to be used to press in on Zemtitzy, finally re-taking it on March 7 after heavy fighting in atrocious conditions. Although battle casualties were fairly low the extreme temperatures meant that many legionnaires went down with frostbite and of 388 effectives on March 2 there were only 101 left in the line by March 9 just one week later. But the attack was successful and Zemtitzy was now firmly in Flemish hands. After a week of defensive fighting the Legion went into reserve for XXVIII Corps, before being placed formally under the command of General Friedrich Altrichter's 58th Infantry Division on 12 March, in preparation for the planned counter-offensive.

In recognition of the staunch fighting qualities that the Legion had already exhibited the Wehrmacht mentioned them not once but three times in their daily combat bulletins. These bulletins were widely circulated at the front and even back home, in Germany and Flanders. The first of these in January 1942 stated: 'During the heated battles in the northern sector of the front, the Legion Flandern inflicted the heaviest casualties on the storming Russian troops.'

February's mention was much the same; the one in March stated the Flemish had 'among other things managed to overtake 25 enemy pill-boxes in heavy close combat.' Another result of the laudable combat performance of the Flemings was the promotion of their commander, SS-Obersturmbannführer Michael Lippert, to SS-Standartenführer. Though relatively few in number, the Flemings' presence and impact was deemed worthy of note.

Zip the bag

You see what the situation is: the enemy has already driven deep into our lines, and in strength. Frontal engagement can no longer lead to success since we don't have the inexhaustible reserves that would be necessary for that kind of operation. Our only chance is to strike at the Russians at the basis of their operation, at the breakthrough point ... The regiments of 126th Infantry Division and all other formations employed there, including the battalions of the Spanish Blue Division, which have fought splendidly so far, will be subordinated to us. With these forces we should be able to manage it. And we've got to manage it – otherwise Eighteenth Army is lost.

This was the sombre briefing given by General Friedrich Altrichter, commanding officer of 58th Infantry Division, to his assembled divisional officers prior to the launching of the Wehrmacht counter-offensive on the Volkhov front. (Altrichter was a doctor of philosophy and a former teacher at the prestigious Dresden Military College. He was to die in Soviet captivity in 1949.) No-one was under any illusions as to how difficult the operation was going to be, or how big the prize was. Defeat would mean annihilation for an entire Wehrmacht Army, but success would mean the bulk of two Soviet Armies going into the bag. This was the enormity of the battle the SS-Legion Flandern was about to embark on.

With preparations hastily completed the scratch Wehrmacht formations swung into the attack on 15 March right at the very break-in point of the original Red Army offensive. The distance between the northern and southern jaws of the counter-offensive was short, but although not impassable, it was pretty close to it. The ground the Flemings were going to have to fight over was heavily forested and cloaked in up to four feet of snow, even in March. When the snow did go it was replaced by mud and swamp and the only roads in the area, crucial to both sides, were corduroy ones made up of endless mats of tree trunks tied together. As can be imagined they needed constant repair to remain passable but without them no vehicles could hope to move. The one factor that remains forever in the minds of the men who fought there was of course the energy sapping cold. With spring well underway across almost all of Europe and Russia, here in the dark forests of northern Russia it was still a numbing 50 degrees below zero. Machine-guns froze up, mortar barrels kept filling with ice, and artillery gun barrels kept exploding as the rifling held the shells fast. This then was to be a close-quarters battle. A fight of rifles, pistols, grenades and entrenching tools. Many histories of the Second World War comment negatively on the ability of the ordinary Wehrmacht soldier, the *Landser* and his foreign comrades, to compete against the Russian *Ivan*, the peasant soldier, without the benefits of their superior technology. Well on the Volkhov in the frozen spring of 1942 this theory was to be tested; and with the Ivans holding the advantage of being the defenders against the attacking Landsers. This battle was going to be decided, not by superior firepower and the application of technology, but by the willingness of ordinary soldiers to go forward in horrendous terrain and meet and kill the enemy on their own ground. (For a recent comparison, the hill battles in the Falklands have some clear parallels, with the Scots Guards and the Paras in particular having to win with the bayonet in shocking weather and terrain on the slopes of Mounts Tumbledown and Longdon.)

Back on the Volkhov front, from the very first crash of German supporting artillery the Soviets were alert to the danger. However, being alert to an attack and being able to stop it are often two different things, and in this case the Soviets had neither the reinforcements nor the tactical know-how to stop the impending encirclement. In essence, the Soviets were defending a T-junction, with a north-south corduroy road section in their hands and the bisecting main highway running to the northwest towards to Lyuban. The German intention was to advance along the road from both north and south and meet at the T-junction, the clearing 'Erika'. Concentrated, well-coordinated infantry assaults with strong artillery and air support battered the Red Army units providing flank protection to the 2nd Shock Army. Exhorted by their commanders and their commissars as to the importance of their task the defending Russians fought with particular ferocity, and many of their units only gave up their ground when they had been wiped out. They had had time to build significant defences and thick belts of mines shielded their positions in which they had concentrated infantry guns, machine-guns and even that most dreaded of infantry weapons, flame-throwers. But the Germans and their allies would not be denied and eventually, at 1645 hours on 19 March, Major Materne led the men of his 2nd Battalion, 209th Infantry Regiment, across 'Erika' and met up with the forward assault units of the SS-Polizei. The pincers had closed and the Soviets were now trapped.

Someone had put up a crudely painted sign in the middle of the clearing reading 'Here begins the asshole of the world', and for both sides this was to be a premonition of the hell to come as the Wehrmacht raced to reinforce the encirclement and trap the Soviets inside it, while the Russians hurled themselves bodily at their enemies to break out and reach the safety of their own lines. The lifeline of supplies that brought ammunition, fuel, food, weapons and reinforcements to the hitherto advancing Russians was now severed, and for the Red Army wounded there was nowhere to go. In such a critical situation the deterioration of the ability to resist was rapid. The Soviets needed either a miracle or something close to it.

Enter Andrei Andreivich Vlasov

With the capriciousness that only dictators seem able to master, the decision made by Klykov to avoid the mistakes of other Soviet broad fronted counter-offensives, and focus instead on a narrow break-in battle, was now thrown back at him by his political overlord far away in the Kremlin. Klykov was roundly pilloried for not establishing a wide front for his attack and therefore preventing any attempt at his offensive being 'pinched off' at the base. Disgraced, Klykov was sacked by STAVKA and relieved of command of the troops in the newly-created Volkhov Pocket. Stalin and STAVKA already had their saviour lined up to take over from Klykov and rescue the situation on the Volkhov front. The man they chose was one of their relatively few senior commanders who had distinguished himself in the battles of the previous summer and autumn, Lieutenant-General Andrei Andreivich Vlasov.

Knowing the part Vlasov was to play in future Russian collaboration with the Nazis it is easy to forget that at the time in early 1942 he was a rising star in the Red Army firmament and a favourite of Stalin himself. Vlasov had been lauded in the state-controlled Soviet press in 1941 and early 1942 and was well-known to the head of German intelligence in the East, Reinhard Gehlen, as a Red Army leader to watch in the future. If events had been different it was probable that Vlasov would be remembered alongside the likes of Zhukov, Rokossovsky, Chuikov and Koniev in the pantheon of Soviet military leaders of the Second World War. As it was he ended up on a very different path.

Born in September 1900 to a peasant family, Andrei Andreivich Vlasov had started his education in a priests' seminary before becoming a communist during his teenage years, which coincided with the horrors of the First World War and the Bolshevik Revolution. On finishing his schooling he had decided to pursue a career as a professional army officer, a calling in which he excelled. He had quickly risen through the ranks on account of his distinguished record and obvious ability, and then survived the Stalinist purges of the thirties by the great good fortune of being posted as an advisor to Generalissimo Chiang Kai-Shek in China. A tall, thin figure who wore thick-rimmed round spectacles at all times, he had the air more of a university professor than a leader of fighting men, and unlike many of his contemporaries in the Soviet military he spurned the garish affectations of senior rank and always wore a simple, unadorned uniform. A holder of the Order of Lenin, he had been involved in the defences first of Kiev and then Moscow before his promotion to Lieutenant-General and his decoration with the coveted Order of the Red Banner on 2 January 1942. In the History of the Great Patriotic War the historian A. M. Samsonov speaks of the 13 army commanders who led the Soviets to final victory and talks of them all specifically by name, all except the leader of the

Soviet 20th Army, where he wrote: 'The forces whose Chief-of-Staff was General Sandalov, in pursuit of the 2nd Panzer Division and the 106th Division, took Solnechnogorsk.' The original text broadcast by Stalin himself on 11 December 1941 actually read: 'Lieutenant-General A.A. Vlasov defeated the 2nd Panzer Division and the 106th Infantry Division and took Solnechogorsk.' This was expunged from the official record and from Soviet history, as was Vlasov himself. However in spring 1942 his then-meteoric rise in the Red Army was confirmed by his appointment to replace General Klykov and command the massively-reinforced 2nd Shock Army in the Volkhov Pocket.

That Pocket had grown and now contained no less than 14 infantry divisions, three cavalry divisions, seven rifle brigades and one tank brigade, with in excess of 200,000 men and huge amounts of materiel crammed into a lozenge-shaped area centred on the main highway between Chudovo in the southeast and Lyuban in the northwest. Vlasov was already the deputy commander of the sector and so was close at hand to be flown in past the roving Luftwaffe air patrols to land at an improvised airstrip in the middle of his beleaguered forces and brief his commanders in a forester's cabin east of Finev-Lug. The situation he faced on disembarking from his plane was critical indeed.

Break out or die!

The trapped Soviet units were bewildered and disorganised. With regular supplies cut off there were already signs of ammunition shortages in particular, and the fuel and food situations were not looking much better. The Red Airforce was able to airlift in some ammunition and vital supplies but without a substantial heavy lift capacity it was a drop in the ocean. There were only really two alternatives for the encircled soldiers, either to break out east and regain the Soviet lines or else have their entrapment ended by a swift relief offensive from their comrades. In military terms the latter is always the better option as it allows the vital supply line to be opened again to the trapped units and thus they can operate more effectively, whilst avoiding the 'hedgehog' effect, a situation in which a trapped force has to fight its way back to its own lines while facing attacks from all angles. Its leading units are battering through enemy lines while its rearguard is desperately trying to hold off the enemy assault and maintain contact with the rest of the formation, at the same time that its vulnerable flanks are being hit. If anyone is in doubt about how difficult such an operation really is then they should study the battle of Cherkassy and the epic struggle of the 5th SS Panzergrenadier Division Wiking and Degrelle's SS-Sturmbrigade Wallonien.

In a relief attempt, speed of assault is critical as the encircling forces will be naturally weak at the point where they join up. It is a race as to who can act first. The besiegers must consolidate and reinforce their positions, and the besieged must break out before that happens. Accordingly, Vlasov assessed his position swiftly and asked STAVKA to authorise a relief attempt while he rallied his troops to break out east. While he waited for a response from STAVKA, a formality as far as he was concerned, the energetic Vlasov began to concentrate his forces at the eastern end of the Pocket nearest the Russian lines and launch preliminary attacks to support the relief column he fully expected to see coming to his aid. Then the scarcely credible happened. Stalin refused point blank to authorise an offensive and ordered Vlasov to break out with what he had. When Vlasov protested that this was a virtual death warrant for his Army his arguments were met with complete indifference. For the general who had so recently been feted by his military peers and the Soviet press, as well as being praised by Stalin himself, it was indeed a bitter pill to swallow.

The Russians rally

All was not lost for the trapped Red Army formations. Vlasov may well have been shocked by Stalin's orders but he was a professional soldier and a committed communist and for him his duty was clear – break out of the Pocket! The snow and ice that had held the front in a vice-like grip for so long finally began to disappear in the last few days of March and Vlasov used this as a spur to launch a powerful assault to recapture 'Erika' and re-open his supply route back to his own lines. As the men of the SS-Polizei and the 58th Infantry Divisions rushed to try and prepare their defences against the inevitable counter-attack, the Soviets too concentrated their very best to burst through the still-weak German lines. Vlasov brought all his armour and his Siberian assault brigades up and flung them headlong at the Germans on 27 March. The Germans desperately defended the clearing but had no reserves and precious few men to try and stem the tide and were elbowed out of the way. 'Erika' was once more in Soviet hands and a tenuous link was established with the main Russian front. The gap now held by Vlasov was less than a mile wide and subject to constant German harassing artillery fire, but it allowed him to move his wounded back and receive much-needed supplies, particularly of ammunition. No reinforcements were forthcoming though, and Stalin and the STAVKA would not contemplate a general withdrawal from the Pocket. Their view was that Vlasov should widen his link with the main Red Army, continue to tie down significant Wehrmacht forces, while preparing for a resumption of offensive operations in the campaigning season of the summer.

SS-Legion Flandern is worn away

The Flemish had played a not-insignificant part in 58th Infantry Divisions push in the south. Alongside its stable mates of the 2. SS-Infanterie Brigade (mot.), especially the Dutchmen of the SS-Legion Niederlande, they had advanced north battering the Soviet flank formations and supporting the link-up on 'Erika'. With that link lost barely a week later the Flemings were used as a fire-brigade and rushed to wherever there was most pressure on the southern jaw of the pincer to hold back the constant Russian assaults. The German line was made up of several lines of defence, the farthest forward being light recce screens, with the main defence in the HKL (the *Haupt Kampf Linien*) – the Main Battle Line. It was this line of fortified bunkers and trenches that had to be held against the Soviet assaults, and it was here that the Flemish were constantly deployed to bear the brunt of the fighting. As the weather hotted up the landscape changed dramatically with snow being replaced by swamp and ground water. Moving around was nightmarish, even on the few corduroy roads and paths, and both men and equipment were continually coated in stinking, cloying mud. The fighting was bitter and bloody and dominated by infantry clashes, as both sides had relatively little armour and few opportunities to use it on the ground. Men tended to be left where they fell. The Flemish did their utmost to recover the bodies of their fallen comrades but for the attacking Russians this was a luxury they could often not afford. The result is difficult to imagine. The rising temperatures, the humidity, the abundant bacteria in the swamp and the awesome clouds of flies made for a putrefying mix. The stench was utterly loathsome and bodies decomposed at terrific rates.

From March 16 through to the beginning of April the Legion held the line against Russian artillery fire and the occasional attack, but on 2 April two much more determined assaults were made by the Russians led by groups of T-34 tanks. Ill-equipped with anti-tank weapons it was only the intervention of a specialist tank-busting team from the Spanish Blue Division that enabled the Flemings to stop the attack. This success did not come without a price as their newly-promoted commander, Michael Lippert, was badly wounded, hospitalised and replaced. He would never return to the Legion, a fact which the majority of his men would not be too sorry about.

The now nominally leaderless Flemings were again coming under heavy Russian tank attack until on April 11 they were pulled out of the line to Chichulino to rest and be re-grouped. By this time, despite the return of numbers of legionnaires from their hospital beds having recovered from frostbite or battle wounds, the SS-Legion Flandern was down to a rump and was merged with other remnants from its parent formation, the 2. SS-Infanterie Brigade, to form a useable *kampfgruppe* (battlegroup formation able to fight independently). In this set-up the Flemings fought on and were even reinforced by over a hundred new recruits at the end of May who had just finished their training at Graz in Austria.

Week after week at the end of April and the beginning of May the Soviets continued to try and widen their link back to their own forces and push open the jaws of the Wehrmacht pincers. Massed infantry assaults were launched against the thinning Flemish lines only to leave another tidal mark of dead Red Army men lying in knots for the flies to feast on. It was a scene worthy of Dante.

Finally, at the end of the first week of May, a reinforced 58th Infantry Division assault re-took 'Erika' from Vlasov's exhausted Siberians. Six weeks after first taking the scrubland clearing of 'Erika' the pincers of the encirclement were now firmly shut and would remain so. The end for Vlasov and his Army was now merely a matter of time. For the Soviet commander the time to hold his ground was now gone and he gave orders for an all-out assault on 'Erika' to breach the German line and lead his depleted forces back east. For the Germans and their allies this too was their moment of truth. The commanding general of Eighteenth Army, General of Cavalry Georg Lindemann, issued his Order of the Day on 20 May that simply stated: 'The Russians are pulling out of the Volkhov Pocket.'

Once again, and with renewed fury, the reduced Red Army formations charged at the Flemish strongpoints and were mown down in their hundreds. One failed infantry attack was followed by another, as desperation set in amongst the remnants of the 2nd Shock Army. Russian casualties steadily mounted. Rations for the Russian soldiers were now down to a meagre 300 grammes of bread a day. Artillery, mortar and infantry gun fire churned the marshy ground and blew the trees to stumps and matchsticks. Water filled every shell hole and every slit trench and bunker, it was Passchaendale in the Great War all over again. But as May came to a bloody end, so did organised Russian resistance in the Volkhov Pocket.

New commanders for the SS-Legion Flandern

With Lippert's wounding the search was on for a new commander for the Flandern. The man chosen was an aristocrat from a distinguished military lineage, SS-Obersturmbannfuhrer Hans-Albert von Lettow-Vorbeck, an extremely different character from the aloof and contemptuous Lippert. Hans-Albert von Lettow-Vorbeck was a nephew of the famous World War I hero, General Paul von Lettow-Vorbeck, who had led a tiny Imperial German force and defied the might of the British Empire for so long in a game of cat and mouse on the east African savannah. Having served in the SS-Wiking he was well accustomed to the needs of the foreign freiwillige and had come across Flemish volunteers before in the ranks of that elite division. There were almost 700 of them in the Wiking. In preparation for his command he was sent to Flanders to meet the likes of Staf De Clercq and Jef Van De Wiele of DeVlag to ensure their continued backing for the Legion, especially in maintaining the flow of volunteers. He was a big hit and listened attentively to the issues the VNV raised, in particular about the lack of respect accorded to Flemish nationalist aspirations and the treatment of Flemish culture by a minority of German instructors and superiors. All looked well set, but events caught up when the Commander of the Freikorps Danmark, the charismatic and popular Count Christian Frederik von Schalburg, was killed in action on the Eastern Front at Demyansk. To fill the gap von Lettow-Vorbeck was rushed to the front to lead the Danes but was himself killed in action just ten days later. The Flemings had now lost their second commander in the space of just over two months.

The Legion needed a commander and one was found in the form of the 46-year-old Austrian, SS-Obersturmbannführer Josef Fitzhum. Appointed on 20 June 1942 Fitzhum was only ever intended to be a stopgap, his intended home being the Flemings' sister unit, the SS-Legion Niederlande.

Mopping up – the end on the Volkhov

Exhausted, starving and with ammunition fast running out, the remaining Soviet troops began to throw down their weapons and surrender to the nearest Heer or Waffen-SS units. But many did not heed the signs of surrender around them and significant pockets of resistance remained to be overcome by the Germans and their allies. The SS-Legion Flandern was now greatly reduced in strength and could only muster 13 officers, 26 NCOs and 288 legionnaires, about a third of its original complement. The Flemings were assigned to Kampfgruppe 'Burk', commanded by SS-Sturmbannführer Burk, consisting of a portion of the brigade staff from the 2.SS-Infanterie Brigade, a Heer battalion from the 20th Motorised Division and the 232nd Security Battalion of second-echelon troops. Alongside the Kampfgruppe were two Spanish battalions assigned to help clear the sister villages of Bol Samosje and Mal Samosje. The Spanish spearheaded the assault but faltered and so the Flemish took over and spent the next four days fighting through the area. Some two hundred Soviet soldiers were killed and 13 bunkers were destroyed, but at the loss of 41 Flemish casualties, including 11 men dead. The roster was now down to just six officers, 23 NCOs and 257 men available for combat.

By 20 June the Legion was so below strength that as soon as Fitzhum was appointed he had it combined with a Spanish battalion from the decimated Blue Division, and a convalescent company formed of men still recovering from wounds, to make a viable kampfgruppe. Tasked with mopping up the hard core of Soviet resistance the composite unit attacked on 21 June for the next five days straight. Bunker after bunker fell but Flemish casualties mounted too, before the Legion was pulled out of the line at the beginning of July for a well earned rest.

The old SS-Legion Flandern was now almost unrecognisable, it had been worn away on the Volkhov. The Legion held a memorial service on 11 July 1942, as they did every year to commemorate the Battle of Kortrijk, where they buried the bodies they had recovered of their fallen comrades and Fitzhum decorated survivors as well as speaking of their bravery and brotherhood with the Germans in the struggle against bolshevism. This would be Fitzhum's last engagement with the Legion, as he was replaced by a permanent commander on the same day.

The Russians themselves had fought to near annihilation. But another Kiev this was not to be. The heady days for the Wehrmacht of 1941, with its mass surrenders, were gone. The Red Army of 1942 had progressed a great deal from those dark days and the bag was pretty empty for the tired Wehrmacht formations. Of the original 200,000 Red Army men in the Pocket only some 32,000 surrendered, with almost three times that number killed. The rest had managed to withdraw through 'Erika' while it was still in Russian hands or had slipped through other holes in the net, holes that the much-depleted SS and Heer units just could not plug. This was the warning sign for the *Ostheer* (the German Army in the East) that the Volkhov battles brought. In the summer of 1941 superior German tactics and weaponry had combined to shatter a Red Army still suffering from the purges, and well over three million Soviet soldiers had gone into captivity when encircled by swiftly manoeuvring Wehrmacht units. Now this was not to be repeated. The Red Army and its soldiers had learnt valuable lessons. In 1941 the Volkhov would have easily produced over a hundred thousand prisoners, but in 1942 it produced less than a third of that. The Volkhov defeat sent shock waves through the STAVKA, but in reality it should have had that effect on the German High Command. In the short term the 2nd Shock Army was nevertheless finished as a formation and wiped off the Red Army order of battle; but not for long, and the Flemish would meet it again.

Another change at the top

SS-Obersturmbannführer Josef Fitzhum had commanded the Legion during the summer battles to finish the Pocket but following the Legion's withdrawal to rest at the beginning of July he was then officially posted to become the new commander of the Flemings' sister formation, the Dutch

SS-Legion Niederlande. Before his official transfer he was called away to prepare for his new posting and during his absence he was substituted as caretaker commander by SS-Hauptsturmführer Gerhard Hallman, the Chief-of-Staff of the 2. SS-Infanterie Brigade. This was a holding appointment only, Fitzhum came back for the memorial service on 11 July but was already on his way out and was replaced the very same day by the newly-designated commander of the SS-Legion Flandern, SS-Hauptsturmführer, soon promoted to SS-Sturmbannführer, Conrad A. Schellong. Auspicously taking command on the anniversary of the famous Battle of Kortrijk, this was the beginning of Conrad Schellong's association with the Flemish. He would now serve with them until the very end of the War in Europe.

Conrad A. Schellong

Born on February 7, 1910 in the medieval east German city of Dresden in Saxony, Conrad Schellong was like so many other Germans of his post-war generation in his yearning for order and a return to glory for Germany. As a young man he finished school and trained for business, becoming an intern in a local firm. There he worked hard and was finally taken on fulltime as a salesman, his future seemed assured. That was until the Great Depression hit in 1931 and he was made redundant like millions of his fellow Germans. Just 23 years old and already thrown on the scrapheap he was unable to find work for two years and instead turned to politics. He was already a member of the rightwing *Wehrzwolf* organisation at the time but his enforced idleness made him even more politically motivated and in 1932 he joined the brownshirt Sturmabteilung, the SA, as a stormtrooper when he finally found work as a labourer on an East Prussian farm. He then transferred from the SA to Heinrich Himmler's fledgling SS on 28 December 1932, with a membership number of 135,553, shortly after joining the Nazi Party itself, on 1 December 1932, with a membership number of 1,428,412.

He left the farm to join the Hilfspolizei before becoming a member of the Totenkopf organisation under Theodor Eicke. He served in the concentration camp guard unit, the SS-Oberkommando Sachsen, before joining the SS-Totenkopf Regiment 1 Oberbayern. These years as a guard commander in the concentration camps would later come back and haunt Schellong decades later. The Oberbayern Regiment was also a guard unit in the concentration camp system but as the Waffen-SS grew it was incorporated as a lead combat formation in the newly-established field unit, the 3rd SS Division Totenkopf. As such, Schellong was one of the very first officers in a division that was to earn an astonishing reputation for bravery and brutality in almost equal measure. He served in the Totenkopf Division throughout the first three years of the War, fighting in Poland, France and

Russia and earning himself the Iron Cross 2nd Class as a company commander before being transferred to the staff of the SS-Legion Niederlande in early 1942. He went on to command the Dutch Legion for a short time during which he was awarded the Iron Cross 1st Class. On the back of that service he was considered a good choice to head up the Flemings in the SS-Legion Flandern and changed places with Josef Fitzhum, who went across to command the Niederlande. Fitzhum had shown some aptitude for commanding freiwillige and he would continue to serve with them for most of the war until he was killed in action in Albania on 1 January 1945.

After action report

The legacy of the Volkhov for the Flemish was mixed. After a predictably uncertain start they had performed particularly well in the latter stages of the battle and had been mentioned in Wehrmacht dispatches on no less than three occasions, earning themselves a well-deserved reputation for steadfastness and courage under fire. This differed greatly from their initial shortcomings, which were outlined comprehensively in an after-action report by their own 1a (Operations Officer) at the beginning of March. Those comments on recent operations included the following rebukes:

1. Poor reconnaissance of enemy field positions and strength. Attacks not conducted with air and artillery support.
2. Too few German officers and NCOs have been in the companies. As soon as the Company Commander is killed or wounded the attacks stalls. As soon as a new leader arrives, the attack resumes. The troops are good but lack leadership.
3. Insufficent liaison between regimental Headquarters and the Legion.
4. Unsatisfactory evacuation of the wounded.
5. Unsuccessful coordination with Spanish units on flank.
6. Artillery fired on registration points, rather than by direct observation from the frontlines.

On a positive note at the time the same report complimented the Legion on its excellent handling of ammunition and supplies as well as cooperation with neighbouring German units. As the Legion became more experienced these shortcomings were overcome,and the key observation had been the recognition that the Flemings themselves were of a high standard. It is axiomatic that time can work to better military processes such as bringing down accurate artillery fire, but if the quality of the troops is low to start with there is truly a mountain to climb; this was clearly not the case with the Flemish.

By the end of the battles on the Volkhov the Flemings' growing reputation had been recognised with the award of a host of medals, including the first Flemish recipient of the coveted Iron Cross 1st Class to the young Jules Geurts, and in Conrad Schellong they now had a new commander who, although not exactly adored by his legionnaires, would stay with them through thick and thin for the rest of the War. However, they had suffered horrendous privations and casualties. Frostbite and shrapnel had ripped through their ranks with equal force and German field hospitals and cemeteries were filled with Flemish legionnaires. But as with so many other Wehrmacht units in the summer of 1942, what the surviving Flemish now had in abundance was combat experience. There was now a pool of young Flemings who had survived the horrors of the Russian winter and fought some of the Red Army's crack units to a standstill. This was crucial in laying the foundations for the future. Lessons learned on the Volkhov would be invaluable in the Ukraine in 1943 and even more so at the Narva in 1944. The idealistic young men from Flanders were now true *Oostfronters* (Legion slang for Russian Front veterans).

Jules Geurts – SS-Legion Flandern poster boy

Like so many of his fellow legionnaires Jules (also called Juul) Geurts came from a family with strong Flemish nationalist sympathies. Born on 24 February 1923 in the village of Waterschei in east Flanders, where his family owned and ran the local flour mill, the young Geurts imbibed the Flemish folklore of Kortrijk and the Frontpartij and engaged in the same sort of low-level anti-Walloon vandalism as his contemporary Georg D'Haese over in Lede. At the time of the German invasion he was already active in the VNV as a fresh-faced and idealistic 17-year-old. He joined the movement's paramilitary wing, the Black Brigade, and became a devotee of the charismatic Reimond Tollenaere. Quite tall and with a relatively slight build, Geurts found he thoroughly enjoyed life in uniform and when the call went out to form the SS-Legion Flandern he stepped forward with his leader and became one of the first to enlist in the Waffen-SS on 6 August 1941.

As luck would have it he was posted, along with Tollenaere, into the Legion's 2nd Company, the famous 'Circus Breymann'. He went through his bloody initiation in northern Russia and soon established a reputation for himself as a brave and resourceful infantryman. Like his compatriot, Remy Schrijnen, Geurts took on one of the most dangerous tasks at the front and became a *Fussmelder*, a company runner, often exposing himself to enemy fire as he carried messages between positions. In fact he was Tollenaere's own runner up until the latter's death at the end of January 1942. As a result of his bravery Geurts was one of the first Flemings to be awarded the Iron Class 2nd Class, on 20 March 1942, during the height of the Volkhov fighting. He became the very first Flemish recipient of the coveted Iron Cross 1st Class just three months later, on 2 July 1942, after the Legion was pulled out of the frontline to rest and refit. The award itself was made by the commander of the Heer's Eighteenth Army, General Georg Lindemann, at his headquarters at Raglitza on 5 July.

The award caused a sensation and Geurts was feted in the German and Flemish press as a heroic role model. He became a poster boy for the SS-Legion Flandern and the whole legionary movement, literally. Soon his face was plastered all over billboards, recruitment posters and even postcards to try and encourage more young men to enlist. Like Degrelle for the Walloons and Mooyman for the Dutch, Geurts became a Flemish talisman. Whether this acted as a spur or not it is impossible to tell but Geurts continued to put himself in danger at the front and never shied away from the most difficult tasks. In many ways his attitude at the front was very much like another, later idol of the Flemings, Remy Schrijnen.

Maps and a tall man

Interestingly the greatest legacy of the Volkhov lay not in a huge haul of prisoners, masses of booty or strategic advantage, but elsewhere, in the person of just one man and three lorryloads of paper. Lieutenant-General Andrei Andreivich Vlasov did not manage to escape east from his doomed Army but instead went into hiding in the forests and swamps of the region. Hunted remorselessly by the Wehrmacht he was eventually taken prisoner by the headman of a local Russian village who handed him over to the Intelligence Officer of the German XXVIII Corps, Hauptmann von Schwerdtner, who happened to be in the area investigating reports of sightings of the elusive Vlasov. Locked in a shed with no-one but a female orderly, he cut a sorry figure, gaunt, exhausted, no longer clean shaven, his uniform caked in mud. He stumbled out into the light holding his hands high and surrendered to the astonished Wehrmacht officer. For the next three years he was to cast a huge shadow over the Russo-German conflict in the East, and it all started on the Volkhov when he was abandoned by Stalin and had to watch as his once-proud Army slowly died.

The other find of huge significance was a haul of maps. The Wehrmacht had always been desperately short of accurate maps of the Soviet Union and that weakness severely hampered operations. However it was discovered during the standard debriefing of prisoners that an entire Red Army cartographic unit had been part of the trapped 2nd Shock Army, and rather than lose its precious stock of maps when captured it had diverted a water course and buried them in the dried up river bed. They had then let the water flow again through its original course and so effectively hidden their treasure trove of geographic detail. The Germans now knew the location and once dug up, the three lorry loads of maps divulged their secrets. They covered the whole western area of the Soviet Union up to and beyond the Urals in the east, and in a very short time they were copied and supplied to the entire Ostheer. It was the greatest cartographic find of the War.

Back to the siege of Leningrad

Following its mauling in the Pocket and Schellong's appointment the Legion enjoyed almost a whole month's rest and refit out of the front line. The time was desperately needed to reinforce the unit and get it back to some sort of strength. Recruits appeared to swell the depleted ranks and many previously wounded men came back with their injuries healed and their convalescence over. Worn out and lost equipment was replaced, promotions were made and confirmed and even some leave was taken. Most importantly for their future survival back in the line, the infantry squads ('sections' in British Army parlance) and heavy weapons teams were filled out and given time and space to go through their paces. New volunteers got to know their roles as well as their comrades and soak up all the invaluable lessons they would need to stay alive at the front. For the *alte Hasen* – the old hares (Wehrmacht slang for experienced combat veterans), it was a time to be thankful they were alive after the Volkhov and 'Erika', and to mentally prepare themselves to go through it all again when the call came that would take them back to the struggle.

That call came on 24 July, coinciding with a renewed push to tighten the noose around Leningrad with the launching of Germany's Operation Northern Light. Following the seizure of the fortress of Sevastopol in the Crimea by General Erich von Manstein and his Eleventh Army it was decided to transfer both him and elements of his Army to duplicate the feat and seize Leningrad. His command group, siege artillery and four divisions came north to join seven divisions from Army Group North for the assault. But even at this fairly early stage of the War the Wehrmacht was lacking in strength and the number of troops allocated were insufficient for the task. The Wehrmacht had not even been able to completely encircle Soviet Russia's second city and every man was needed to try and hold the blockade as it stood. The chances of taking the city by assault were slim to nil.

For the still weak Flandern this meant taking its place in the concentric lines of trenches facing the city as part of its old formation the 2. SS-Infanterie Brigade (mot.). The Brigade was then part of the Heer's L Corps to the south of Leningrad near Pushkin on the Izhora River. For the first weeks of August the Flandern came under intermittent attack, along with its Latvian and Dutch SS neighbours, from probing groups of Soviet tanks and infantry; and in the middle of August the Russians spiced this up by employing psychologiocal warfare tactics. The Russians used batteries of loudspeakers blaring out propaganda in Flemish, and inviting the slightly deafened legionnaires to throw down their arms, leave their German commanders and come and join their fraternal Soviet brothers who would shower them with gifts and hospitality! Unsurprisingly, this offer was not taken up.

First offensive at Lake Ladoga

The Flandern had barely got wet in the trenches when the planned Operation Northern Light was thrown completely out of kilter by a surprise Russian offensive launched on 27 August at Lake Ladoga, the first in an eventual series of three. The Red Army broke through the Eighteenth Army front in several places and tried to link up at Mga to the south east of the city to cut off the Wehrmacht forces further north and west on the shores of the lake. The Flandern was flung into the fighting along with every man that Manstein could muster. The fighting was short and sharp and the Red Army was sent packing and their offensive cancelled by 2 October. However, it meant the suspension of Operation Northern Light which was never again resurrected. With this decision the initiative in the campaign in the north of Russia was effectively handed to the Red Army, from now onwards all the Wehrmacht could do was to react to their opponent's moves, now more than ever the German war in the north was to be one of defence, defence, defence.

The rest of the autumn and most of the winter of 1942 to 1943 was spent by the Flemings in utterly miserable conditions. As in every trench system ever devised by man in any war ever fought it was in reality an incredibly efficient water catchment collection device designed to rot men's feet and spirits! The bottom of the trenches were typically at least a foot under water and needed constant bailing out of both water and the inevitable mud and detritus of men living in cramped conditions for months. Quiet for often weeks on end, the line would periodically burst into life with the Russians probing it for weak spots with patrols, artillery fire and tank and infantry assault.

Slowly the Flemings were brought back up to some sort of strength. In October alone some 200 new volunteers arrived, along with a handful of returning injured such as SS-Untersturmführer Jack Delbaere. The Wehrmacht had also learned from its last winter in Russia and this time around they were determined not to be caught out, so supplies of real winter clothing were issued to the troops as well as special gun greases and lubricants to keep the guns firing and the vehicles moving. All the time the

Flandern looked to strengthen its positions, so whenever stocks of defence stores such as barbed wire became available they were used to beef up the positions against inevitable Russian attack. As winter wore on this tactic proved its worth: a series of Russian infantry assaults, in November in particular, slowed and were then held by multiple wire obstacles that were covered by direct fields of fire from the Flemish. This is the basic secret to the success of any obstacle, in order to be an obstacle it must either be covered by direct fire, such as machine-guns or anti-tank weapons, or by observed indirect fire, that is artillery or mortar fire controlled by an observing fire controller. This was exactly what the Flemings had in place and the result was heavy Russian casualties showing very little in return. Just before Christmas the Flemish went over to the offensive with an attack on a series of Russian bunkers covering a minefield, but the Soviets had learned their battle lessons too and the attack faltered and died away in the face of concentrated defensive fire. With Christmas coming both sides warily let each other be and prepared for the next round.

Second and third offensives at Lake Ladoga

That next round would not be long coming as, not content with their failure the previous autumn, the Red Army tried again in January 1943 to trap the Wehrmacht on Lake Ladoga by piercing the front of Eighteenth Army and taking Mga in their second Ladoga offensive, sometimes confusingly called the First Ladoga Battle by the Germans. This time they succeeded and the trapped Germans had to fight through to the west, back to their own lines and safety. This meant that although the siege of Leningrad was not officially over – it would still come under intermittent artillery and air attack – the city would never be seriously threatened again. The tide had indeed turned against the Germans and their allies in the East.

The Flandern had spent the last few weeks on a variety of tasks including training new Latvian SS units on heavy weapons and forming a new anti-tank platoon, as their own anti-tank company was detached to support the 4th SS-Polizei Division. With the support companies engaged the 1st, 2nd and 3rd rifle companies were rotated out of the Leningrad trenches on 12 February 1943 to become the brigade reserve behind the emplaced Spaniards of the Blue Division near the small town of Krasny-Bor. Little did they know that they stood directly in the planned path of a Red Army offensive designed to shatter the Wehrmacht front in the north of Russia. Emboldened by their victory at Mga and still smarting from the failed Volkhov offensive the STAVKA determined to try again to completely relieve Leningrad and trap and destroy the besieging Wehrmacht forces. The Red Army sought to build on their existing momentum by launching a third Ladoga offensive, again rather confusingly called the

Second Ladoga Battle by the Wehrmacht. The offensive began with a huge frontal assault on 10 February 1943 south of Kolpino, tasked initially with surrounding Pogostschje, with the brunt falling on the Spaniards of the Blue Division. The SS-Legion Flandern found itself called to help stem the tide as the vastly outnumbered Spaniards were butchered in the snow and gave ground.

Attrition at Krasny-Bor

The Flemish were grouped with several Latvian formations and sent to join the 254th Infantry Division on the western flank of the breakthrough at first to slow and then halt the Russians so that larger German units could counter-attack and seal off the hole in the front. Though this was only possible after more than a month of very heavy fighting.

This spell of action around the town of Krasny-Bor is often cited by surviving veterans as some of the hardest they were ever involved in. It was a desperate struggle by the severely overstretched Wehrmacht forces to hold back a Red Army that was continually increasing in numbers, equipment and tactical know-how. The battle itself received little attention at a time when the whole of Germany was still reeling from a host of disasters on both the Eastern Front and in the Mediterranean. With Friedrich von Paulus's surrender at Stalingrad Germany had lost its first full field army since Jena in Napoleon's day, and this would be swiftly followed by another at the fall of Tunis and the loss of all of North Africa. Down in southern Russia the resurgent Red Army was driving west to the city of Karkhov and on every front it seemed the Axis was in full retreat. At Karkhov at least, the Waffen-SS under Paul Hausser would turn the tide back in Nazi Germany's favour, but elsewhere there was little for Germany and her allies to cheer.

In the snow and cold of northern Russia the rest of the War seemed a long way away as the much-diminished SS-Legion Flandern fought for its life at at Krasny-Bor. Only some 450 men strong, the Flemings were placed under the direct command of the 254th Infantry Division to hold the newly-established line against any further Soviet attacks.

The first half of March passed quietly enough with merely patrol activity on both sides but then exploded in the third week when the Red Army renewed its offensive, aiming squarely at the 254th and the Blue Division. Both divisions were hit extremely hard and gave ground with the Spanish in particular suffering huge casualties and their lines cracking. To restore the situation the Flandern was sent in on a coordinated and supported counter-attack to retake the lost Spanish frontline and stabilise the front.

Flemings forward!

On March 22 1943, covered by Stuka ground attack aircraft, panzer and artillery support, the few hundred survivors of the SS-Legion Flandern climbed out of their trenches, organized themselves into attack formation and advanced with bayonets fixed and grenades primed. As the thin line of legionnaires moved forward the Stukas flew off to avoid hitting their own troops, and then the panzers stopped as they had orders not to risk themselves by going beyond the most forward German positions. The Flemings were now on their own except for a creeping artillery barrage that provided them with some blessed cover as they raced to cross no-man's land and reach the Russians in the old Spanish positions before the Russians could start fixing them with fire. Lungs bursting and legs pumping, the Flemish grenadiers made it across and got in amongst the defending Russians.

The fighting in the fortification line was vicious. Each bunker in turn was cut off from its neighbours by fire and then a squad of legionnaires would move forward, under covering fire, to shove grenades through its firing slits and then take it at the point of the bayonet. With the bunker clear another squad of Flemings would join their comrades in the newly-captured position and stand in the blood and muck of its dead Russian defenders. Covered by their comrades they would then take their turn to storm the next bunker in line, and so on. Trench and bunker fighting is slow, gritty work dominated by weight of fire and resolution. Running at an enemy bunker firing a tommy gun from the hip before using your teeth to pull the pin on a grenade is strictly for the movies and the insane. Anyone running towards a bunker is cut down pretty quickly and if you try to pull a grenade pin with your teeth you will lose a tooth! For the attackers the only way is on your belly using every scrap of cover and fold in the ground to stay as close as possible to the earth and stay alive. For the defender it is a test of nerve to stay in your position knowing a man you can't see is crawling towards you and in a few minutes will put a grenade into the bottom of your bunker that will spray you with red hot, razor-sharp shrapnel. It is little consolation to know that grenades are not designed to kill you in the blast, but more to injure and shock you so you are incapable of resistance. Once the grenade has gone off the grenadier is then straight in and shoots or bayonets any survivors; in the rush of bloodlust and adrenalin there is very little chance of surrender. As bunker after bunker fell to the relentless Flemish the Russians finally cracked and abandoned the line, leaving it to be occupied by the victorious Flemings. The struggle was not over quite yet. A Russian deserter told the Flandern it was to be hit by a counter-attack led by T-34s the next morning. The intelligence was spot on and as March 23 dawned the Red Army threw a massed tank and infantry assault at the decimated unit. The Flemings only integral anti-tank weapons were a few boxes of Teller anti-tank mines and bundled hand-grenades, but they used these effectively until support came from an 88mm battery that appeared behind the Flemings and began to pulverise the Russian assault. The Soviets did not back off and pressed forward again until they were fighting hand-to-hand in the line. The Legion's Commander, SS-Sturmbannführer Conrad Schellong, now showed his metal and gathered together every man he could find capable of firing a weapon, including the drivers, cooks, mechanics and signallers, and led them into the line to join the battle. The next few minutes of fighting were crucial and would decide the outcome of the battle. On this occasion fate favoured the Flemish as the leading Russian T-34 threw a tread and its neighbouring tank was brewed up by a well-placed magnetic mine. Owing to the lie of the land this meant the way forward was blocked for the remaining T-34s and the German anti-tank guns reacted with purposeful glee and swamped the stalled tanks with a deluge of fire. Tank after tank was blown to pieces and, shorn of their support, their supporting infantry were easy meat for the Flemish machine-guns. Russian dead began to pile up and with no way forward they retreated. The punch-drunk Flemish had won, but they got no respite for it. They were not relieved and had to stay in their newly-recaptured positions burying their dead as best they could and even fending off a half-hearted Russian attack on March 28. Finally, on March 30, the pathetic handful of survivors were pulled out of the line. The Soviets called off their latest Ladoga offensive the following day.

From an establishment of nearly 1,200 men, only some 450 had still been in action come the last battle at the Spanish line near Krasny-Bor. Eight days after that battle began only some 50 unwounded members of the Flandern were left to be relieved from the line. From an original five very strong companies there were barely two platoons of men left standing. Krasny-Bor had effectively wiped out the SS-Legion Flandern as a fighting force.

With the defeat of the Soviet offensive at Ladoga the remnants of the SS-Legion Flandern were finally withdrawn from the Russian Front altogether on 14 April 1943 and sent to refit and reform in its old stomping ground at Debica in Poland. The Flandern had endured fifteen months of more or less continuous combat at the front. From such a low ebb, where now for the Flemish?

Death of a Flemish hero

One of the many Flemish legionnaires who fell during the Lake Ladoga offensives was the SS-Legion Flandern's own pin-up boy, Jules Geurts. He was forward of the front trenches covering a team of German assault pioneers as they were trying to clear a minefield they had themselves laid earlier when he was shot by a Soviet sniper. During the ensuing chaos he was also injured by an exploding mine. As he lay dying his last words were said to be "I am thirsty ... it is over for me." Geurts, still only nineteen years old and holder of the Iron Cross 1st and 2nd Class, was killed in action in the second week of January 1943.

Back home in Flanders: politics

As the SS-Legion Flandern matured at the front into a hard bitten, experienced fighting unit, the political movement of Flemish nationalism that had to a large extent produced them, was disintegrating. The heady days of 1941 and the dominance of the VNV were long gone. With the amalgamation of almost all Flemish collaborationst parties into the VNV the bearded Staf De Clercq had promoted himself to the new post of *Algemeen Leider* (General Leader), and had renamed his party the *Eenheidsbeweging VNV* (the Unity Movement VNV), but it was all a mirage. DeVlag and the Flemish SS were both allowed their continued independence by the occupying Germans and lost no time in setting themselves up in opposition to De Clercq and his pretensions to power. The VNV instituted a cabinet of sorts, the so-called *Raad van Leiding* (the Leadership Council) which was intended to form the basis of a provisional Flemish government. This was often ignored by the Germans in favour of their own administration and the likes of Jef Van De Wiele and his DeVlag men. The reality in Flanders, as everywhere else in Nazi-occupied Europe, was that the the overarching concern of the occupiers was exploitation. What could Nazi Germany extract from Flanders in the way of economic and military benefits? This was of paramount importance to Falkenhausen and his staff, not how they could prepare Flanders and the VNV for future political power.

To this end, the Germans sponsored the creation of a host of local, Flemish paramilitary organisations of various sizes to carry the burden of occupation instead of their own forces. This policy saw the creation of, among others, an auxiliary rural police to guard harvest and agricultural production called the *Boerenwacht* that had 27,790 members by the summer of 1942, and a counterpart for factories called the *Vlaamsche Wacht* (later called the *Wacht Brigade*) of some 4,000 men. As elsewhere in occupied Europe the German Organization Todt labour service recruited in Flanders taking over 30,000 civilian workers and almost 5,000 uniformed Flemish guards into its own *Schutzkommando*. The paramilitary Nazi transport corps, the NSKK, also set about recruiting in Flanders and over 4,000 men were enlisted by the end of 1942; this included almost the entire VNV DM-MB (the Dietsche Militie – Motor Brigade), the motorised sister organisation to Tollenaere's VNV Black Brigade. The Nazis were also very keen to attract non-Todt civilian workers to Germany and the Flemish were encouraged to volunteer, with the promise of excellent treatment and good wages, and Remy Schrijnen was one such willing recruit. Initially recruitment was purely voluntary and some 300,000 Belgians, both Flemings and Walloons, went to Germany. But as the War progressed and Germany's need for labour increased, from October 1942 workers were compulsorily rounded up for transportation to the Reich.

Staf De Clercq dies

Flemish nationalism had already lost two of its charismatic standard bearers by the summer of 1942 with the execution in France of Joris Van Severen and the death in Russia of Dr Reimond Tollenaere. Now it lost its political centre when at the relatively young age of fifty-eight Staf De Clercq suffered a heart attack on the morning of 22 October 1942 and died. The news was greeted with dismay by the majority of the Legion at the front, who felt Flanders had now lost its best hope of independence under a strong leader. Incidentally the same effect was seen in the French SS Charlemagne Division when the PPF party leader Jacques Doriot was killed in an Allied air attack. De Clercq himself had appointed a successor in case of his death, the respected doctor of law and philosophy and VNV Governor of Ghent, Dr Hendrik Elias. Intelligent and learned though he was, Elias was no political giant and under his leadership the VNV became increasingly irrelevant. Membership slumped while DeVlag's star continued to rise and by August 1943 it claimed a membership of 51,000. By contrast the VNV stopped publishing its membership figures as numbers fell and the VNV's institutions, such as the Black Brigade, were more and more taken over directly by the Germans. Collaboration from the VNV began to fracture and in August 1943 the head of the VNV youth wing, Dr Edgar Lehembre, went so far as to inform the German authorities that he could no longer cooperate with the Hitler Youth as a partner organisation. The Germans were outraged and Elias quickly dismissed Lehembre to try and placate them, but the writing was on the wall. As central control weakened, the fringes of the VNV began to fray and to its everlasting shame the spectre of anti-semitism reared its head in the organisation. The Nazis were, of course, instituting their Final Solution across Europe and were herding Jews onto cattle trucks and thence to the death camps of Auschwitz, Treblinka and others in the east. The centre of Belgian Jewry was in the ancient Flemish city of Antwerp, also the centre of Flemish fascism, and here it was the local VNV Governor, Herremans, who worked with the Flemish SS and the Germans to forcibly expel the Jewish community who had lived there for centuries. With the active help of local collaborators the Jews, men, women and children, were put on trains and sent to their deaths.

Names to remember

Having finally got into the Waffen-SS, via his mountain soldier application, Remy Schrijnen began his training at Klagenfurt before moving on to Graz in Austria, and then finally attending the SS-Panzerjäger School at Hilvorsum in the Netherlands. It was here that he would begin his familiarisation with the weapon, the 75mm PAK towed anti-tank gun, that would become forever associated with him and the war he would fight on the Russian Front. As it turned out at Hilvorsum he would meet a host of figures, all staff members at the School, who would later figure prominently in both the SS-Legion Flandern and the SS-Sturmbrigade Langemarck, including his future commanders Alfons Gradmeyer and August Knorr. Schrijnen himself said of his training:

> The training in the Waffen-SS was very hard and among other things included learning the *Parademarsch* (goose step), training for combat at the front, and of course lots of sporting activity. As a recruit I thought the training was very good and covered everything one needed to know. Our instructors were all specialists with years of experience. They treated us just like they treated the German recruits.

With his training complete Schrijnen and his fellow recruits were dispatched to the Legion on the Leningrad front. As he was anti-tank trained Schrijnen was assigned to Willi Dethier's 5th Panzerjäger Company with SS-Untersturmführer Johannes Gläser as his platoon commander. There, just like Jules Geurts, he volunteered for the dangerous role of *Fussmelder*, company runner. Communication is always preferable at the front over the field telephone or radio if at all possible and secure, but with telephone lines shredded by artillery fire and open to being tapped into when out of direct line of sight, and radio often failing or being used by the enemy to locate targets for artillery strikes, it came down, and still does, to men carrying verbal or written messages between commanders and sub-units. Schrijnen said he wanted to follow in Hitler's footsteps in volunteering for what was a dangerous role: Hitler had won the Iron Cross 1st Class as a Fussmelder in World War I. It was in this job that Schrijnen established a reputation as a soldier not given to blind obedience or being particularly deferential to rank. He became self-reliant in the field, independent of thought and action, and discovered in himself a real liking for battle, a thirst for combat as it were that made a mark on him. It was in this role too that he began his long association and friendship with other Flemish stalwarts of the Legion, men who he would fight with right through to the end, such as Juul Fieremans, Paul Rubens and Alfons Van Broeck. More and more, Schrijnen was being recognised as one of the hard core in the Flandern.

Research carried out in recent years has identified the concept of what might be called the '10%ers', the men who are a small minority in a force but through their efforts impact massively on the outcome of a battle. These men are not strategic decision makers, the Rommels and Pattons, but privates, NCOs and junior officers who absolutely excel in combat. The concept holds that the vast majority of men in action fight from a sense of self-preservation and duty and will act with the prevailing mood of logic. So, for example, they will stay in their trenches firing at attacking troops as long as they feel on balance it is safer to be there than not, and that the numbers of attackers are not so vast as to make it a racing certainty that they will be overwhelmed and killed. A '10%er' on the other hand does not think like that at all. For the '10%er' the fight itself is everything and inspires actions from them, most often carried out with no real thought, that go against the prevailing sense of logic that dictates their comrades' actions. Given the same scenario of trench defence one of these men would never abandon their post but would use every weapon to hand to stop the enemy assault, and failing that may well actually attack the oncoming mass! Unsurprisingly, it is these soldiers who figure heavily in the annals of military heroism and as recipients of the highest awards for bravery their countries can offer, though many of these awards are posthumous. As Schrijnen continued to build his reputation at the front he soon became marked as one of these 'special soldiers'. Arguably, no army can win without these men, though having them does not guarantee victory either.

On the Volkhov in 1942 and Krasny-Bor in 1943 were where Georg D'Haese matured into the steely combat soldier that he was when the SS-Legion Flandern was pulled out of the line to be reformed. After first fighting partisans in the snows of northern Russia he then came face to face with the Red Army itself during its ill-fated Volkhov Offensive. As casualties mounted D'Haese and his men from the 3rd Company were grouped along with Helmut Breymann's 2nd Company 'Circus' and a heavy weapons company to combat the advancing Soviets as they tried to take and secure the tactically important villages of Koptsy and Krutik. The fighting was heavy and the Flemings' casualties reflected that, with only around 100 men left from the original 388 legionnaires of Kampfgruppe Breymann at the end of the struggle. D'Haese continued to serve with the Legion during the entire Volkhov campaign, was wounded twice, and earned a hat full of medals including the Wound Badge in Black, the Infantry Assault Badge in Bronze and the Iron Cross 2nd Class. He was also promoted straight to SS-Unterscharführer, leapfrogging the rank of Rottenführer.

After seeing the spires of Leningrad once more as the Legion took its place in the besieging lines in the summer of 1942 he was deployed with the remainder of the Legion to counter the Red Army Lake Ladoga offensives around Krasny-Bor. He served in SS-Untersturmführer Vogel's

3rd Company during the fighting, which he later said was the hardest he ever endured during the war, and was one of only six men from the original complement of 137 who survived the vicious combat more or less unscathed, although 'unscathed' is a relative term, as he was wounded twice more during the battle. That made it four wounds in just 15 months for the 20-year-old Fleming.

VII

Rebirth: The SS-Sturmbrigade Langemarck

Back at Debica in Poland the remnants of the Flandern were recuperating and waiting to hear their fate decided in far away Berlin by the SS bureaucracy. Those decisions were to be momentous indeed and would set the tone and direction for the Waffen-SS and its foreign formations in particular for the rest of the war. They would also lead directly to the creation of the SS Langemarck, firstly in brigade and then divisional form, and take the Flemish to the open steppes of the Ukraine, the Blue Mountains of Estonia and the Narva River, and finally the snow-clad plains and forests of Pomerania in eastern Germany.

Overall the Wehrmacht's experiment with the legionary movement had been a success. Thousands of men had joined up from across western Europe and had proved themselves very capable soldiers in the extreme conditions of the Russian Front. True, there had been teething problems in the treatment of the foreign volunteers by some of their German instructors and commanders, and lack of early operational capability among some of the Legions, but on the whole lessons had been learned and the result was some well-earned fighting reputations for the likes of the Legions Norwegen, Flandern, Niederlande and the Freikorps Danmark. However, the original period of enlistment for the vast majority of the European legionnaires had been for a term of two years, and that time was now up. Having exclusively served in the hell that was the Russian Front, through the bitter cold of the winter 1941-1942, the murderous battles of attrition with the Red Army and partisans in 1942-1943, and having escaped being a statistic in the seemingly endless casualty lists, it was no great surprise that many of the surviving original volunteers had had enough.

The end of the Legionary system

This 'changing of the guard' was to signal the end of the legionary move-ment in its original shape. In strictly numerical terms those original vol-unteers who wanted out and had no wish to sign on again were relatively few in number compared to the available total of freiwillige. The reasons for this were twofold, firstly all the Legions had received numerous batches of reinforcements since their inception and those men had not fulfilled their two-year obligation. Secondly, the original complements of volunteers had been vastlly reduced by casualties, and so there simply were not a great number of men left to sign on again anyway.

This was not, however, the end of the foreign volunteer concept. Indeed, the end of the national legions was to herald the beginning of the great-est chapter of expansion of the Waffen-SS, and its foreign formations in particular.

The assault brigades

Reichsführer-SS Heinrich Himmler, following consultation with Gottlob Berger, had decided that the SS Legions had proved themselves in battle and could now be used to create a significant expansion of his Waffen-SS military empire. He already had plans to form new Waffen-SS field divisions based on various volksdeutsche communities from eastern and south-eastern Europe in particular, as well as more 'exotic' ethnic groups such as the Bosnian Muslims, but his eye was firmly on his favoured Western Europeans. Berger told his boss that although he would struggle to turn the remnants of the Legions into fully fledged combat divisions he could however recruit enough manpower to form a series of SS-Sturmbrigaden, SS assault brigades. These could well be an intermediate step to full divisional status, maturing the volunteers in readiness for the added complexities of operating at divisional level.

So 1943 was the year that saw the creation of Sturmbrigaden for the Walloons (newly-designated as now 'aryan' enough for the Waffen-SS!), the Dutch (a much larger formation than the others was created from them and technically termed a panzergrenadier brigade), the French (see Hitler's Gauls), and the Flemish. The Norwegians and the Danish were initially grouped with the Dutch in a new division, the 11th SS Panzergrenadier Division Nordland, but on protest from the likes of Anton Mussert and his NSB the Dutch were withdrawn to form their own, separate formation. These new assault brigades were designed as all-arms groups rather than as normal infantry regiments. As such they would be equipped to very high standards indeed in terms of wheeled transport, anti-tank, infantry and anti-aircraft guns and even have integral tracked assault guns, which although not true panzers, were still a relatively scarce resource in the Wehrmacht. This upgrading in equipment, in particular the inclusion of an integral armoured element, represented high praise indeed and demonstrated the move up the military pecking order the Legions had won by their performace in combat. At the front they were intended to operate as 'firebrigades' providing rapid reinforcement of offensive success or, as was much more likely, last-ditch defence in the face of Soviet onslaught. They were to be compatible operationally with the regular Waffen-SS divisions and operate in conjunction with them wherever possible. This policy would lead to the SS-Sturmbrigade Wallonien fighting with the SS Wiking at Cherkassy, the Flemings serving with the SS Das Reich in the Ukraine and the SS-Sturmbrigade Frankreich serving with the SS Horst Wessel in Galicia.

Calling all leaders!

As had been acknowledged by Himmler and Berger themselves back in 1942, while the general quality of foreign recruits was good, the real problem lay in lack of strong leadership at the front. While the prevailing view of class warriors has always been that gin-and-tonic swilling toff officers are at best a hindrance to the brave men 'actually doing the fighting', the Germans were exceptionally aware that this is absolute rubbish and that the real strength of a fighting formation lies in its leadership. In the line facing the enemy that meant top quality junior leaders, both officers and NCOs, and as a formation operating and manoeuvring effectively that meant top-drawer senior and staff officers. Without these the best enlisted men will falter and not fulfil their combat potential. It is as simple as that. For the Legions, and the Flemish were no exception, there had always been a shortfall in recruiting enough quality officers in particular. Many of those who did come forward had served in their own national armed forces but their training had not been of a sufficient standard to operate at the same level as their German counterparts. It must be remembered that under the Nazis the policy was to inculcate youth from an early age in paramilitary activities in the Hitler Youth and the Reich Labour Service, and then to follow that with exhaustive and rigorous military training. By that stage the junior German officer was truly a formidable beast. This was not true for many of the graduates of less comprehensive military systems elsewhere in Europe. The solution was an insistence that all foreign officers undergo training with, and be passed by, the relevant SS authorities, that is the elite officer academies at Bad Tölz and Braunschweig. Then and only then could they take up command appointments with their units. Special intakes were organized from 1942 onwards aimed specifically at training foreign volunteers on a rigorous six-month course, although this could be shorter in some instances, as it was for the French officers of the SS-Sturmbrigade Frankreich for example. Officers graduating under this system were commissioned into regular Waffen-SS rank rather than legionary status as before, and were technically indistinguishable from their German SS peers. This policy meant that by February 1943 there were a total of 47 officers and 172 officer cadets from Flanders, the Netherlands, Norway, and Denmark undergoing training at Bad Tölz. Not only did this greatly improve the leadership capacity of the foreign units but it also helped to redress the huge imbalance in officer to volunteer ratios that previously stood at just one freiwillige officer for every 120 enlisted men. For comparison, the modern British Army maintains a ratio of around one officer for every 50 men.

The problem was never completely solved as the system could never produce enough officers to fill the ranks. A ready pool of qualified officer graduates was needed from pre-war that could then just be kept topped up, but this was a luxury that the *freiwillige* never had, and indeed even the German Waffen-SS had significant problems as casualty rates mounted and the ranks of officers thinned.

What's in a name?

Mystery surrounds the logic of the choice of 'Langemarck' as the honour title for the Flemish formation designed to succeed the SS-Legion Flandern. Almost all honour titles awarded denoted either a heroic figure in Germanic history, such as Frundsberg and Hohenstaufen, or if the units members were foreigners it usually took the form of their country title, Wallonia for example. There were exceptions of course, Charlemagne for the French, but even in the weird world of Waffen-SS honorifics the use of Langemarck was extremely odd. Langemarck, spelt *Langemark* in Flemish, was actually a geographical place, a small village in the Ypres salient of Flanders that had become a battlefield in 1914 in the early, ignorant days of World War I. It was there that high idealism met high velocity ammunition and lost. Answering the Kaiser's call to arms large numbers of university students had donned Imperial German Army uniform and marched confidently to the front grouped in all-volunteer battalions, high on enthusiasm and exceedingly low on practical experience. The result can be imagined – bloody slaughter. The charging students had rushed forward singing the German national anthem to be mown down by nothing more advanced than machine-gunners who had mastered the simple task of traversing their gun barrels. As the guns swept left and right Germany lost a generation of its brightest young men, and with them much of its pre-war innocence as well. As could be expected, the name of the Battle of Langemarck became one that was heavy with meaning in Germany and it belonged to a whole lineage of formations before it finally came to the Flemish.

New name or old?

For the Germans it has always been assumed that the use of the name was intended as a sign of German-Flemish camaraderie, while many of the Flemings themselves took it as a slight, as it meant nothing to them and their own nationalist struggle. Having investigated it I believe the use of the name Langemarck came, not from any thought-through policy of the SS authorities, but rather from happenstance. The unit chosen to act as the German cadre for the new Flemish assault brigade was already called 'Langemarck', and with its Flemish connotations it was probably deemed acceptable to leave it as it was. Nothing more sinister or underhand than that. (When considering the military, and that goes for every nation's military, it is often best to think in terms of cock-up rather than conspiracy.) The use of a battle honour name, such as Langemarck, is always intended to commemorate the sacrifice of one's own soldiers at the time and not to insult or cause offence to others. In the British Army each infantry regiment has a particular day of the year on which it celebrates a famous battle of its forbears, one day to remember so many, and for the admirable English line infantry of the 1st Battalion The Royal Anglian Regiment for instance, that day is 1 August, Minden Day. Minden was an eighteenth-century battle fought, and won, by the British in Germany against the French, but that has never stopped the battalion from celebrating it with any nearby Frenchmen. The use of the name does not indicate a slur on France but rather a sombre, though definitely not sober, invitation to soldiers to reflect on their history as well as their future. Langemarck was intended to be just such a name.

The first formation to be granted the honorific Langemarck was actually the SS-Legion Flandern's old stable mate from the 2. SS-Infanterie Brigade (mot.), and the fighting at Leningrad and the Volkhov, the Totenkopf's 4th SS Infanterie Standarte. Prior to the War in the late thirties, as Himmler and Berger conspired to increase the size of the Waffen-SS, they had instituted the Totenkopf formations on a regional basis and used them, although not exclusively, to police and man the growing concentration camp system. Admittedly this was well before the creation of the dedicated death camps for which the concentration camp system became infamous, but even so they were still academies of brutality. With the creation of the 3rd SS Division Totenkopf to serve as a field formation several of these regiments had been absorbed into its ranks, but there was not room for all of them. Those remaining Totenkopf regiments, such as the 4th SS Infanterie Standarte, were then placed into the 1. and 2. SS-Infanterie Brigades as future potential replacements for Totenkopf losses and cadres for new Waffen-SS formations. As such, the regiment was fulfilling one of its original goals when selected to be the *Stamm-Einheit* (cadre formation) to help form the new Flemish Sturmbrigade. As with the Legion, the Totenkopf men had been fighting almost continuously at the Front for many, many months and had been reduced in strength from their original 3,000 down at one point to a miniscule 180 effectives. They officially received the Langemarck title on 20 April 1942 when fighting on the Volkhov. In June 1942 the shattered remnants of the regiment were merged with the divisional motorcycle battalion of the 2nd SS Panzergrenadier Divsion Das Reich to form an unnumbered infantry regiment bearing the Langemarck name within Das Reich itself. The Langemarck regiment then served with the Das Reich throughout the autumn and winter of 1942 and through into spring 1943, fighting in the successful Kharkov battles alongside the Leibstandarte before being detached and marked as a component of the newly-proposed Sturmbrigade.

The Langemarck forms

The decision to utilise the Langemarck regiment as the cadre was taken in early 1943 by the SS-Führungshauptamt (responsible for unit establishment), with Berger's SS-Hauptamt working to fill it. The idea was to use the shattered Totenkopf/Das Reich Langemarck veterans, alongside the remaining Flemish legionnaires, as the cadre for a rebuilt and expanded Flemish volunteer unit, an assault brigade, entitled the 6th SS-Freiwilligen Sturmbrigade Langemarck. This unit, based on its German/Flemish cadre would be filled out with a new wave of volunteers from Flanders. The official date of incorporation was 31 May 1943 when the Flemings, who had been resting for the last two months in Debica in Poland, were amalgamated with the ex-Totenkopf/Das Reich men and declared to be one new unit.

Debica had been a rallying point for the Flemish after the bitter battles at Krasny-Bor. Those who had been on external courses filtered back and hundreds of wounded men returned to duty following convalescence. This meant that by the date of incorporation the new Sturmbrigade could muster some 600 veteran Flemish legionnaires. It would be these men, and their German compatriots from the Totenkopf/Das Reich, who would form the essential core of the new formation. They were the underpinning upon which the Sturmbrigade would either be built or would fall.

With the cadre in place what was needed now were the mass of recruits, the main body of troops who would be moulded by their experienced comrades and their training into a fighting formation. Berger drafted in those Flemish recruits and replacements already in the SS depots, but it was clear a new wave of recruitment was needed and the intention was to use the anniversary of the Battle of Kortrijk to spur the recruiting effort back in Flanders and elsewhere in Europe. But with the breakdown of support for the VNV in Flanders following Staf De Clercq's death in autumn 1942 and the subsequent frosting of relations between it and the Nazis, the VNV as the major source of recruitment (some 50 to 60% of the previous total) was drying up. More Flemish SS did come forward, as did supporters of DeVlag, but the numbers were not huge, the last 300 arriving in Debica from the collection centre at Ghent on 27 July. Luckily for Berger and his extravagant promises to Himmler, an answer had presented itself in late April 1943, foreign workers in the Reich.

There had previously been a ban on recruiting from this pool of labour as it had been brought to Germany, and was needed for war production. Individuals were allowed to volunteer if they wished, indeed Remy Schrijnen had been one, but no formal recruiting drives were allowed. However, post-Stalingrad even Albert Speer's Labour Ministry realized that manpower at the front was the priority and the direct recruitment ban was lifted. This proved to be a boon for Berger and his energetic teams of recruiters. By July 1943 Berger reported his success to Himmler in signing up no less than 2,500 Western European volunteers from the foreign labour pool alone, and forecast another 6,500 enlistments by mid-September. Beating even his own predictions Berger actually obtained 8,105 recruits by mid-August, but only 3,154 proved to be of the requisite standard for entry. For the Flemish it meant a total of 1,069 new recruits, or 'New Marchers' as Waffen-SS veterans termed them, of which 529 were finally accepted into the Sturmbrigade. Recruits were enticed to join by propaganda films which they were invited to attend free of charge, as well as the plastering of their workplaces with recruitment posters glamorising the battles in the East and the Waffen-SS in general.

The most effective technique however proved to be to use actual veterans from the Legions who spoke at rallies of their fellow-countrymen and extolled the virtues of their experience and the threat from the East of bolshevism. It was a powerful combination and one that relied on fostering an atmosphere that encouraged volunteering and did not rely on coercion, of which there was scant evidence. Those that did join up really did want to. Interestingly there was only very limited use of anti-Semitic propaganda, this not being seen as a powerful motivator for potential volunteers.

Milovice and the reorganisation

By the end of July 1943 the newly-established 6th SS-Freiwilligen Sturmbrigade Langemarck (hereafter called simply the SS-Sturmbrigade Langemarck) was transferred en masse to the SS training grounds near the village of Milovice (also spelt Milovitz) in Bohemia, some 30 miles north-east of Prague, for work-up and field exercises, which would last for most of the latter half of 1943 and would put the unit in good stead when its name was called to head back to the Eastern Front.

The establishment of the Sturmbrigade was originally set at a strength of 1,700 men, to be organised into two grenadier battalions with a staff and supporting sub-units. The first battalion of four companies was to be infantry, the first three being motorised infantry and the fourth being a support company equipped with heavy mortars and machine-guns. The second battalion, of a further five companies, was to provide the real punching power of the Sturmbrigade with an armoured company equipped with Sturmgeschütz tracked self-propelled guns – basically a cheap, turretless tank – a panzerjäger company equipped with towed 75mm PAK anti-tank guns, a heavy infantry gun company equipped with infantry cannons and heavy machine-guns to act as the Sturmbrigade's integral artillery arm, and lastly, two anti-aircraft flak companies, the first equipped with light towed 20mm FLAK guns, and the second equipped with the superfluous towed 88mm FLAK gun that was also renowned as a tank-killer par excellence. There would also be a tenth reserve company, the Marsch Kompanie, that would act as a pool of trained reinforcements to keep the combat companies up to strength, and the usual supporting elements of course: signals, medics, cooks and logistics personnel. All of these elements were to be fully motorised to provide the formation with real manoeuvrability and significantly increase their operational utility. This was a huge break with the past, when the Legions had simply been infantry heavy formations with little in the way of advanced technical capability or heavy weapons establishment. With German war production struggling to supply and equip the Wehrmacht the fact that the Flemish SS-Sturmbrigade Langemarck was going to include significant numbers of armoured vehicles and heavy weapons was a clear sign of the unit's perceived combat worth, and a nod to its fighting reputation built on the Volkhov and at Krasny-Bor.

Order of battle and command roster

The official order of battle for the 6th SS-Freiwilligen Sturmbrigade Langemarck was as follows:

- Stab der Brigade (Brigade Headquarters)
  Brigade Commander   SS-Sturmbannführer Conrad
                                Schellong (German)
  Adjutant   SS-Untersturmführer Wilhelm
                                Teichert (German)

- Stab Kompanie (headquarters company)
  Commander   SS-Untersturmführer Rudolf Six
                                (German – killed in action May 1945)
  Motorcycle dispatch rider platoon SS-Oberscharführer Fritz
                                Taktasch (German)
  Assault pioneer platoon   SS-Untersturmführer Karl Prade
                                (German – killed in action in the
                                Ukraine February 1944)
  Signals platoon   SS- Untersturmführer Hendrik van

War reporters platoon	den Abeele (Flemish) SS-Oberscharführer Raf van Hulse (Flemish – former Commander of the Flemish SS) See below
Feldpost Number 44853	

News at the front

As an aside to this interesting addition of an entire platoon of war report-ers, it had always been a major tool of the Nazis in general and the Waffen-SS in particular to use the media to get its message across to a wider audience. Uniformed war reporters were always with frontline units from January 1940, when the very first SS-Kriegsberichter-Kompanie (Waffen-SS war reporters company) was formed to send stories and pictures back home to keep up morale and encourage recruitment and support. The SS after all had its own magazine, *Das Schwarze Korps* (The Black Corps), and newspapers were produced for the foreign volunteer contingents in their own languages as well as in German. In December 1943 the Waffen-SS went so far as to form an entire regiment of reporters, the SS-Kriegsberichter-Standarte 'Kurt Eggers', named after the former editor of Das Schwarze Korps who was killed in action at Kharkov on 13 August 1943, and com-manded by the SS propagandist Gunter d'Alquen. All Waffen-SS reporters were amalgamated into this formation but were always distributed among their parent combat formations. Influential Flemish members of the regi-ment included Hugo Lindekens and Jan Buyse, an ex-SS-Legion Flandern man who was promoted to SS-Untersturmfuhrer in 1944 and went on to command the war reporters' platoon attached to the Langemarck. He was also a holder of the Iron Class 2nd Class.

- 1st Battalion (1/6. Bde)
Feldpost Number 34695A-D

• 1. Kompanie	(1st Company – infantry)
Company Commander	SS-Obersturmführer Kurt Mahrenholz (German, ex-Legion 1st Company platoon commander)
1st Platoon Commander	SS-Untersturmführer Karl-August Jenssen (German – killed in action on January 3 1944 in the Ukraine)
2nd Platoon Commander	SS-Untersturmführer de Backer (Flemish – killed in action on January 1 1944 in the Ukraine along with his entire platoon!)
3rd Platoon Commander	SS-Hauptsturmführer Andreas Cambie

| | (Flemish – killed in action on March 8 1944) |
| 4th Platoon Commander | SS-Oberscharführer Peters (German) |

• 2. Kompanie	(2nd Company – infantry)
Company Commander	SS-Untersturmführer Sven Martenson (German, ex-Legion 2nd Company platoon commander – killed in action)
1st Platoon Commander	SS-Hauptscharführer Steiniger (German)
2nd Platoon Commander	SS-Untersturmführer Johann Güldentope (Flemish)
3rd Platoon Commander	SS-Obersturmführer Delft (Flemish)
4th Platoon Commander	SS-Untersturmführer Andreas Stevens (Flemish)

• 3. Kompanie	(3rd Company – infantry)
Company Commander	SS-Untersturmführer Vogel (German, ex-Legion 3rd Company platoon commander)
1st Platoon Commander	SS-Untersturmführer Herbert Karhl (German, ex-Legion 3rd Company platoon commander – killed in action on February 24 1944 in the Ukraine)
2nd Platoon Commander	SS-Untersturmführer Georg Bruyninckx (Flemish)
3rd Platoon Commander	SS-Untersturmführer Demeester (Flemish)
4th Platoon Commander	SS-Hauptscharführer Laublicher (German)

• 4. (schwer) Kompanie (4th Company – heavy infantry)	
Company Commander	SS-Untersturmführer Leo van der Ween (Flemish – killed in action on February 15 1944 in the Ukraine)
1st Platoon Commander	SS-Hauptscharführer Ollendorp (German)
2nd Platoon Commander	SS-Oberscharführer Blum (German)
3rd Platoon Commander	SS-Oberscharführer Huber (German)
4th Platoon Commander	SS-Oberscharführer Goemans (Flemish)

• 2nd Battalion (2/6. Bde)
Feldpost Number 17662A-D

| • 5. (infanterie) | (5th Company – infantry-guns) -granatwerfer) Kompanie |
| Company Commander | SS-Untersturmführer Willi Köhn (German, ex-Legion 3rd Company |

platoon commander)

1st Battery Commander	SS-Untersturmführer Remi Bogaert (Flemish – killed in action on March 4 1944 in the Ukraine)
2nd Battery Commander	SS-Hauptscharführer Wagner (German)
3rd Heavy Battery Commander	SS-Hauptscharführer Blohm (German)

Feldpost Number 37892

• 6. Panzerjäger Kompanie	(6th Company – towed anti-tank guns)
Company Commander	SS-Hauptsturmführer August Knorr (German - missing in action on March 5 1944 in the Ukraine)
1st Platoon Commander	SS-Untersturmführer Anton Kotlowski (Austrian)
2nd Platoon Commander	SS-Untersturmführer Hugo Mortier (Flemish)

(Mortier replaced the original German Commander SS-Untersturmführer Alois Herzog)

3rd Platoon Commander	SS-Oberscharführer Alfons Gradmeyer (German – killed in action on January 6 1944 in the Ukraine)

Feldpost Number 21836

• 7. Sturmgeschütz Kompanie	(7th Company tracked self- propelled guns)
Company Commander	SS-Hauptsturmführer Karl Weingärtner (Austrian, ex-Legion 5th Panzerjäger Company Commander – killed in action on January 3 1944 in the Ukraine)
1st Battery Commander	SS-Untersturmführer Friedrich Ritzau (German, ex-Legion 2nd Company platoon commander)
2nd Battery Commander	SS-Untersturmführer Johannes Gläser (German, ex-Legion 5th Panzerjäger Company platoon commander)
3rd Battery Commander	SS-Untersturmführer August Heyerick (Flemish)

Feldpost Number 40035

• 8. Licht FLAK Kompanie	(8th light anti-aircraft guns)
Company Commander	SS-Untersturmführer Otto Uytersprot

(Flemish)

1st Battery Commander	SS-Untersturmführer Issel (German)
2nd Battery Commander	SS-Oberscharführer Tinke (German)
3rd Battery Commander	SS-Oberscharführer Johannes Weber (German)

Feldpost Number 45840

This Company struggled to fill its complement due to lack of equipment so that at the front it could only field one battery.

• 9. schwer FLAK Kompanie	(9th heavy anti-aircraft guns)
Company Commander	SS-Hauptsturmführer Willi Dethier (German, ex-Legion 5th Company Commander)
1st Battery Commander	SS-Obersturmführer Karl-Heinz Gustavson (German)
2nd Battery Commander	SS-Untersturmführer Cesar Geerts (Flemish)
3rd Battery Commander	SS-Untersturmführer Meelman (German)

Feldpost Number 45214

As with its sister light anti-aircraft company, this sub-unit struggled to form owing to lack of equipment and could only ever field a single battery of deadly 88mms; this significantly reduced the Sturmbrigade's anti-tank capability.

• 10. Marsch Kompanie	(10th replacement company)
Company Commander	SS-Untersturmführer Wilhelm Schaumann (German)

Feldpost Number 56414

HIWIS and Finns

Even with a good number of the old legion 'hares' signing back on, the ex-Totenkpof/Das Reich men and the new recruits from Flanders and the German war industries, there was still a shortfall in the strength of the Sturmbrigade. As with every Wehrmacht unit serving in the Russian theatre of operations, one of the ways the formation increased its strength was by incorporating Russian volunteers, the so-called *hilfswillige* – HIWIS, onto its roll. These men had often deserted from the Red Army or were captured by a Wehrmacht unit who then employed them as a useful source of labour to carry out tasks such as dig latrines, mend vehicles, cook meals and carry ammunition. In such circumstances it was not a massive step for a man to go from carrying ammunition to an anti-tank gun to actually loading it. Taken onto the ration roll for the SS-Sturmbrigade Langemarck were 137 such HIWIS.

This took the Sturmbrigade's strength up to 2,205 men, comprising 42 officers (20 under strength), 162 NCOs (more than 200 under strength), and 1,864 enlisted men (this doesn't include the HIWIS). Further small contingents of new Fleimish recruits came in over the summer and autumn and were incorporated into the Sturmbrigade, but even though this took the total to around 2,500 it could not hide the huge shortfalls. Yet, almost unbelievably, at the same time not all Flemings joining the Waffen-SS were concentrated in the Langemarck. Some volunteers were sent direct to the SS Wiking as replacements for the grenadier companies, and yet more were sent as technical replacements to other Waffen-SS field divisions such as Das Reich. It was, however, recognised by the SS-Hauptamt that the infantry complement in the Sturmbrigade was low for the likely battles of attrition it would face and so it was decided to beef up the grenadier numbers by importing an entire formed Finnish SS volunteer battalion. A flick of a pen in Berger's office and the SS-Sturmbrigade Langemarck was now a truly international unit with at least five nationalities represented, if you count the *volksdeutsche* men among the Das Reich transferees as a nationality.

It was not only in numbers of infantrymen but crucially in leaders and equipment that the Sturmbrigade fell short. The more heavy weapons a unit had, the more effective it was at the front was the general rule of thumb, especially against an equipment-rich enemy like the Red Army, and those men and their weapons needed leading, and leaders always suffered high casualty rates. It was clear, even before the formation was sent back to the Eastern Front, that while not a one-shot weapon in terms of operational effectiveness, it could not hope to last indefinitely as a viable fighting force without significant reinforcement of both men and material.

Uniforms and insignia

Members of the Sturmbrigade wore standard Waffen-SS uniform but were authorised to wear the trifos, the sun-wheel swastika, rather than the normal sig runes on their right collar patch. This only heightened confusion with some volunteers refusing to wear the trifos as they considered it to denote inferiority in the pecking order of the Waffen-SS, and others seeing it as a mark of national distinction. Some of the men did wear it, including Schellong who was keen to set an example, but in reality most just wore the sig runes, mainly for convenience. As you would expect, Remy Schrijnen took a contrary view and though at first he felt insulted by being told to wear the trifos he then decided to continue to wear it when his comrades switched to the sig runes so he could cock a snook at the SS authorities. To denote their Flemish status a new yellow and black lion arm shield was produced and worn by members below the SS eagle on the left upper arm, higher than in the old Legion. They also wore a new cuff title, *Langemarck* , on their lower left arm. There were at least three variations of this cuff title produced in black and silver aluminium flatwire, both machine-woven and machine-embroidered.

Getting to know you

It was a strange and unsettling time for the new Sturmbrigade members. For the Flemings it meant getting used to serving in a much more mixed nationality unit, and for the ex-Totenkopf/Das Reich troopers it was equally difficult to get used to being in a unit that was not predominantly German. The Finns must just have been bewildered! There were the obvious language issues, but much more besides. 'Racially' close (a dangerous word to use in a history such as this) the Germans and Flemings may have been, but they were still two distinct cultures with two sets of traditions and histories. For all but the most educated Germans the Battle of the Golden Spurs and names such as Pieter De Connick and Staf De Clercq meant nothing. In their talk of the Flemish flatlands and resentment of Gallic-Walloon repression and chauvinism, the Germans found their new comrades-in-arms to be quite alien. By this time too of course, Degrelle was a household name in Germany and the Germans found the Flemings' emnity for the Walloons difficult to understand. The Flemings were also suffering from some doubts about the future for their homeland. Many had joined expecting to see the VNV work with the Germans to establish an independent Flanders, perhaps even a 'Greater Netherlands' incorporating Holland as well, but with De Clercq's death and the disintegration of the VNV that goal seemed to be receding. They now saw that their unit had been upgraded but was no longer wholly Flemish in character and even the name it bore was not their own!

Despite all these differences, what bound the members of the new unit together was shared experience, in particular the realisation that the Eastern Front was the bedrock of all their combat records and that at the end of a hard day's training at Milovice when the men relaxed in the canteens and bars with a well-deserved beer, they could all talk about the horrors of a Russian winter and what it was like to stand in a trench looking over a gun sight at hordes of Red Army men screaming their blood-curdling 'urrahs!'. This made the politics of home seem far away and the men started to settle down to some seriously hard training and preparation.

As summer became autumn and then winter the SS-Sturmbrigade was still very much in transition to becoming fully combat-ready, but as was increasingly the case in a manpower-strapped Third Reich, events overtook the Langemarck. It was soon going to be time to go back to the War.

VIII

Dogged defence in the Ukraine

With the disaster at Stalingrad still fresh in the national conciousness, Nazi Germany had one last opportunity to regain the initiative in the East. Without it, a Wehrmacht that was fighting a war on two fronts would suffer fatally from the shortage of men and material that was already seriously beginning to bite. If the Soviets could dictate the pace and focus of the campaign on the Eastern Front then there would be next to no chance of avoiding eventual defeat. The SS victory at Kharkov had checked the Red Army and given the Germans a breathing space, thus the summer of 1943 would be decisive. The result was that Adolf Hitler gambled all on Operation Citadel, the crushing of the Kursk salient in south central Russia by coordinated assaults from both Army Group Centre and Army Group South. This offensive was designed to wrestle the initiative on the Russian Front back to Nazi Germany. But the offensive lacked surprise, overwhelming force or most crucially, any strategic or tactical subtlety. Where a thrust towards Moscow or a daring push back towards Stalingrad and the Caucasus utilising double envelopments of Soviet armies, or even a sudden swing north to roll up the Soviet frontline would have been classic Wehrmacht operations, the crude sledgehammering of the assault at Kursk was playing the Soviets at their own game. It was blunt weight of steel against weight of steel, and in any such contest there was only ever going to be one winner. Kursk was the most dull-witted German offensive of the war bar none and consigned them to ultimate defeat in the East.

Immediately following the abject failure and cancellation of the offensive, when it became clear after the brutal tank bloodbath at Prokhorovka that the Wehrmacht was spent and the Western Allies had launched Operation Husky and landed on Sicily, the Red Army did what it did so well: it counter-punched with overwhelming force. Using its colossal reserves of men and equipment the Red Army had not finished burying its 250,000-plus battle dead from Kursk (and had shrugged off the loss there of over a thousand tanks) when it launched a steamroller of a counter-offensive at the exhausted Heer and Waffen-SS formations. Already bled white on the endless Soviet anti-tank gun lines, mine belts and oceans of tanks, the shredded flower of the Wehrmacht was now hit full-on by a wave of fresh Soviet divisions hungry for victory. The result was desperate defence and retreat by an ever-shrinking Ostheer. The already depleted Wehrmacht formations had been dramatically further reduced in the space of a few weeks and were now being hungrily torn at by a confident, well-equipped and well-led Red Army.

As the SS-Sturmbrigade Langemarck was continuing to put its new recruits through their paces in Bohemia and getting hold of as much equipment as possible, back in the East the Red Army was pushing ever westwards through the autumn and early winter of 1943, crossing back into the Ukraine in the south, taking Belgorod and then Kharkov and finally liberating the ancient Ukrainian capital of Kiev on 5 November, as the Russians tore hole after hole in the German lines and poured through into western Ukraine. To sustain an offensive on this scale and intensity for so long is truly awe inspiring and testimony to how far the Soviets had come since the cataclysms of 1941. The front eventually stabilised just before Christmas 1943 but this was a false dawn for the Wehrmacht and they knew it. Intelligence from Reinhard Gehlen's specialist Abwehr section, *Fremde Heere Ost* – Enemy Armies East – and overwhelming local evidence from the frontlines, clearly indicated the Soviets were just drawing breath and were preparing to strike again. However, it was thought the lull would last until the new year of 1944, giving the exhausted Ostheer the fragile peace of a quiet Christmas, fingers crossed.

Meanwhile, back in Bohemia, Conrad Schellong led the Sturmbrigade on a parade through the streets of Prague to celebrate the successful formation and training of the unit. He then reported to the SS-Führungshauptamt that the Sturmbrigade was ready for action.

Back at the front all was indeed quiet, though not for long. Following Kursk it was the Soviets who held the initiative and they were not about to give the invaders a moment's peace. At 0600hrs on Christmas Eve 1943 the Soviets renewed their earlier offensive with a terrific hour-long artillery bombardment that deluged the German lines with high explosive and was then followed up by massed infantry and armour assaults across all of Manstein's Army Group South. Four whole Soviet Fronts, the 1st to 4th Ukrainian from north to south respectively, went on the offensive. The German line was held in some places, significantly by the SS Das Reich kampfgruppe, former home of many of the Langemarck's German cadre, but elsewhere the under-strength Wehrmacht units were simply annihilated. The Red Army poured westwards and the whole southern front was in danger of collapse. Troops were desperately needed to bolster the front, and ready or not, every formation that could move up to the line was called for.

The Flemish arrive in the Ukraine

The Ukraine is a land of open steppes and endless plains, agriculturally rich and criss-crossed north to south by a series of large rivers, including the mighty Dnieper. In many ways the area could have been designed for modern mobile warfare, key points being the major road and rail junctions as well as the ever-important river bridges that would serve as choke points for any defender or attacker. Domination of those pieces of key ground would enable a force to manoeuvre successfully and defeat an enemy. In the summer of 1941 the Wehrmacht had used its tactical and technological superiority to control the Ukrainian battlefield and win major battles, culminating in the largest ever encirclement victory in the history of warfare at Kiev that bagged over 665,000 Red Army prisoners. In the winter of 1943 everything had changed for the Wehrmacht; but the fundamentals for a successful campaign in the Ukraine were still the same and it was going to be mobile forces, able to move quickly and have the punching power to act decisively, that would be needed if the Wehrmacht was to stave off looming defeat. The SS-Sturmbrigade Langemarck with its motorised infantry and anti-tank weapons and, crucially, its armoured Sturmgeschütz tracked self-propelled guns, would be an asset in such a theatre, and this is where, assigned to Army Group South, they would go.

The Sturmbrigade received its movement orders and immediately went, by rail, to Chudniv in the Ukraine on Boxing Day, 26 December 1943, arriving on New Year's Eve. The die was cast and the Flemings of the 6th SS-Sturmbrigade Langemarck were back off to war.

Fighting with the elite SS Kampfgruppe Lammerding (Das Reich)

Prior to the renewed Soviet offensive the decision had been made to withdraw the shattered 2nd SS-Panzergrenadier Division Das Reich from the Eastern Front and send it to southern France to reform and retrain as a fully fledged panzer division. Having not stopped fighting since the disastrous Kursk offensive in the summer, the division was already a shadow of its former powerful self; but even now the situation was still so grave that Army Group South could not afford to let the division go in its entirety. So a compromise was struck, whereby the majority of the division and its infrastructure were withdrawn just before Christmas, but on 17 December a 5,000-man all-arms kampfgruppe of infantry, armour and artillery under the Das Reich commander, SS-Oberführer Heinz Lammerding, was formed to be left behind to continue fighting. The kampfgruppe had fared pretty well against the initial Boxing Day offensive, although casualties had been heavy, but was soon swamped by the Red Army advance and left struggling westwards to extricate itself from potential disaster.

This then was the Langemarck's first task. As they disembarked from their trains and were given an operational deployment area, key sub-units of the Sturmbrigade were moved forward to try and hold off the advancing Russian forward troops to allow the surrounded Das Reich to break-out west from its *kessel*, cauldron or pocket, near Zhitomir. As could be expected in a defensive phase of combat it was August Knorr's 6th Panzerjäger, or PAK, Company that went into action first, with SS-Oberscharführer Alfons Gradmeyer's 3rd Platoon leading the way in a series of rapid fire engagements against T34s and Soviet infantry. In fact, it was Remy Schrijnen and his crew who took first blood by knocking out three T34s trying to cut off a supply road. The move was successful and, along with other units, the Langemarck helped the Das Reich kampf-gruppe and the Leibstandarte escape and head west.

Other engagements followed around the villages of Tschudinov and Olszanka, with more and more of the Langemarck committed and acquitting itself fairly well; but there were problems. The PAK Company in particular hit trouble. First it committed a blue on blue and destroyed two withdrawing Das Reich panzers, mistaking them for Russians, then it lost several guns and two of its platoon commanders to enemy fire as Gradmeyer was killed along with almost an entire gun crew and Mortier was injured in the face. Finally, one of the remaining gun crews lost their nerve and ran from the action, leaving their cannon and tow truck behind intact. The German commander of the crew, SS-Unterscharführer Kleinmann, an ex-policeman from Hamburg, was arrested for cowardice following the incident and sentenced to seven years' continuous service at the front as a result. It was an inauspicious start and the Flemings felt unsettled in their new role, in a new sector of the Eastern Front, and in the chaos resulting from the huge Russian offensive.

Retreat to Yampil

Now, as part of the Fourth Panzer Army, the Das Reich kampfgruppe was grouped with its old running mate the Leibstandarte to act as a firebrigade for the front. The SS-Sturmbrigade Langemarck was added to this force on an ad hoc basis to fulfil its previously designated role of providing additional firepower and strength to the Waffen-SS field divisions. The remainder of German-held Ukraine was being overrun by the Red Army at a terrific rate. All of eastern Ukraine had gone before 1943 was out and now most of western Ukraine was gone too. The Wehrmacht was being unceremoniously bundled towards the Ukrainian–Moldovan border and the Carpathians. The fight was on to try and stem the Red tide, extricate as much of the Wehrmacht intact from southern Russia and the Ukraine as possible and try and create a defensible frontline. In the maelstrom of early 1944 that was a tall order. The resultant fighting was to test the Langemarck to the limit in its very first campaign, as frontlines disintegrated and all semblance of order disappeared, to be replaced by a swirl of combat where units of both sides moved over the battlefield and were as likely to pop up in the rear of an enemy formation or position as in front of it. The fighting was going to echo the savagery of Krasny-Bor of the previous year as the Flemish and their German, volksdeutsche and Finnish comrades struggled to survive the first few months of 1944. The Langemarck was not the only Belgian Waffen-SS formation fighting for its life on the southern front in the new year, as Degrelle and the Walloon Sturmbrigade were surrounded, along with the SS Wiking, at Cherkassy, not far from the Langemarck and Das Reich. It was a recurring feature of the campaign that winter and spring, as the retreating Wehrmacht forces were constantly being encircled by fast-moving Red Army units and having to fight their way out.

The Flemish, along with their SS compatriots in the Das Reich and Leibstandarte, were heading due west in an effort to get ahead of the advancing Red Army and try to set up a solid line. This phase of operations is known in military parlance as 'withdrawal in contact', and is just about the hardest stage of combat to carry out successfully. It requires resolution and firepower in rearguard defence, mobility in manoeuvre, aggression in counter-attack and above all, luck! Against a numerically and materially superior enemy such as the Red Army it was this last ingredient that the Flemings would need most of all. The Sturmbrigade began to leapfrog backwards towards the west with the heavy sub-units, most often the anti-tank panzerjäger teams, providing rear cover for the mass of the formation, with the grenadiers giving localised infantry support. When ready, and during a break in the fighting, the panzerjägers would then up sticks and bug out west following their comrades. So a pattern soon established itself, the SS men holding during the day and fighting off the advancing Russians, then slipping away as night fell and retreating to another position by daybreak. Back west went the Flemings, giving up first Burkovzy, then Sseverinovka, and all the time getting closer to the key border town of Yampil. Yampil itself (also spelt Jambol, Jampol, and Yampol), sits on a crossing of the Nistru River and forms the border between the Ukraine and present-day Moldova, then called Bessarabia, and its ethnic Rouman population.

The situation worsened for the Flemish on 17 February, when a report on so-called partisans at the village of Tschepetovka in the brigade's rear actually turned out to refer to advance penetrations of the Red Army seeking to cut off a major part of the Wehrmacht forces in the south. The discovery set off another rush westwards to avoid encirclement and the

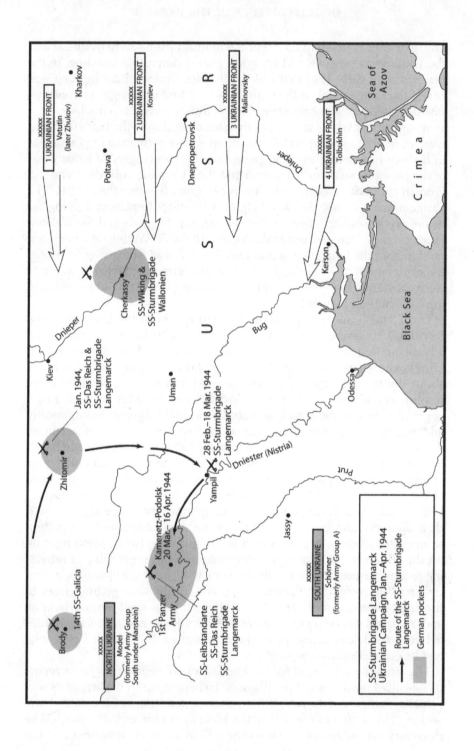

Flemish went into their fighting retreat mode again, as they leapfrogged from Zaslav to Klembovka, to Bjelgorodka, to Sinjutki. At last, on February 28, the first of the Flemings arrived in Yampil on the old border between the Ukraine and Bessarabia. Short of three years after crossing into the Ukraine, the Wehrmacht had as good as been thrown out.

Defence of Yampil

The Sturmbrigade's role at Yampil was meant to be as an anchor for the left flank of LIX Corps of the Fourth Panzer Army. The triumphant Soviets had torn a yawning 40-mile hole in the line to the west of the Army and had dangerously exposed the entire Wehrmacht formation to becoming surrounded. From the start it was clear that disaster threatened and the Sturmbrigade would be lucky to survive the conflagration. Even before the whole unit was in Yampil, Russian troops were clearly seen to the west behind the town and as sub-units arrived they were thrown into the fighting against battalion-sized Soviet attacks. The fighting was intense and without quarter. The assault on 29 February alone cost the Flemish 13 men killed and 45 wounded. During the following days, alongside their Das Reich comrades, the Flemings manoeuvred around the Yampil sector as they desperately tried to concentrate their dwindling forces against the more or less constant Soviet assaults. The fighting was now reaching a crescendo as the Red Army threw what was intended to be an overwhelming attack at the Flemings on 2 March, to unhinge the defence in the sector so that they could then turn south, to cut off Tarnopol, and north to encircle Hube's entire First Panzer Army. The assault came at the Flemish from two directions at once and resulted in hand-to-hand combat in the trenches. Casualties swiftly mounted but the Sturmbrigade would not be beaten and even launched savage local counter-attacks to fling the Russians back onto the steppe. The battle raged all day and night but by the morning of 3 March it was obvious the Sturmbrigade could not hold much longer and Schellong won agreement from higher command to withdraw his men before they were annihilated.

Retreat and massacre

Getting out of Yampil was easier said than done and, in the inevitable confusion arising from the situation, the effort would lead to disaster for the Langemarck. To help cover the withdrawal Lammerding sent the highly decorated SS-Obersturmführer Hermann Bolte, and his mixed Company of less than 10 panzers and Sturmgeschütze, to Yampil to assist the Flemish. The Das Reich armour was grouped with Knorr's PAK

Company to provide the rearguard for the retreat and stay in Yampil until everyone else was clear of the town. Under this cover the mass of the Sturmbrigade, including most of its heavy equipment, managed to retreat in some semblance of order, but Russian pressure on the town continued to mount. On March 5 a Soviet artillery shell landed just yards away from a staff car carrying the PAK Company Commander, SS-Hauptsturmführer August Knorr, and his Flemish driver SS-Mann Edmond van Winckel. The blast threw both men out of the vehicle and though eyewitnesses state they were both seen alive and moving they were obviously stunned and injured. Before they could be reached, and right in front of the eyes of their Flemish comrades, a Russian tank drove over the two men at full tilt. They were never seen again, and although both were officially posted as Missing in Action rather than Killed there was no doubt that they had been pulverised by tank tracks. The Sturmbrigade then received another blow when its Commander, Conrad Schellong, was wounded and had to be evacuated on March 8. He had lost the little finger on his right hand and was replaced as overall commander from the ranks of the PAK Company by SS-Hauptsturmführer Willi Dethier. The fighting continued unabated and the mixed Das Reich/Langemarck force was still in Yampil on March 18. By now the town's few defenders had been fighting continuously for a fortnight and were utterly exhausted. Resupply was non-existent, the men had not eaten a hot meal for days and the bitter cold was wearing away spirits. Even more crucially, the ammunition was almost all gone, and without it the men were defenceless. A last Soviet assault went in and wiped out the remaining Das Reich armour, after which organised defence collapsed. The few survivors were rounded up by the victorious Russians and then herded to a field on the outskirts of the town, where they were ordered to strip naked. The SS men did as they were told and stood there in the snow shivering in front of a row of Soviet tanks. Without warning, one of the tanks opened up on the prisoners with its machine-gun, to be followed immediately by the others. Every prisoner was butchered.

The Russians had paid a heavy price for their victory. Nineteen Soviet tanks were left burning on the steppe, along with 24 anti-tank guns, 18 mortars and 11 artillery pieces destroyed, and surrounding the town lay over 2,000 Russian dead. The Flemings' defence of Yampil also saved Tarnopol to the south from being encircled and earned Schellong the German Cross in Gold, one level below the Knight's Cross, from a grateful Lammerding.

The rest of the Sturmbrigade was now a 'mini wandering pocket' as it worked its way out of the encirclement of Yampil and headed to the relative safety of the German lines at Staro-Konstantinov, eventually reached on 19 March. There, despite the terrible state of the unit and its horrific casualties, there was no time for rest as it was deployed immediately in the area of Proskurov to try and help seal another huge new gap torn in the lines by the Red Army between the Fourth Panzer Army in the south and the First Panzer Army to its north. The exhausted attempt to hold Zhukov's 1st and Koniev's 2nd Ukrainian Fronts was unsuccessful and in days the First Panzer Army, including the Leibstandarte, Lammerding's Das Reich kampfgruppe and the SS-Sturmbrigade Langemarck, were surrounded in the Kamenets-Podolsk Pocket (also known as the Hube Pocket after First Panzer Army's Commander).

The Kamenets-Podolsk Pocket

Cherkassy was the pocket battle that caught everyone's attention at the time, with the horrendous weather conditions, the stubborn heroism of SS-Obergruppenführer Herbert Otto Gille's SS Wiking and the SS Wallonien among others, and the terrible casualties of the break-out that saw only 32,000 of the encircled 56,000 men come out alive. By contrast, Kamenets-Podolsk was almost low key, despite the fact that more Wehrmacht troops, some 200,000, were surrounded than was the case at Cherkassy. Lessons from Cherkassy had been learned by the OKW and the decision was made to airlift huge supplies of fuel and ammunition into the Pocket, not only to support the break-out but to ensure the heavy equipment did not have to be left behind. The Red Army had now been advancing for over two months straight and was at the end of long supply lines, it was running out of steam. This enabled the encircled troops to establish an aggressive defence of the Pocket and gave time for OKW to rush reinforcements to the front to lead a counter-offensive to reach the stranded men. These were not just any old reinforcements, they were the newly constituted II SS Panzer Corps comprising Willi Bittrich's 9th SS Panzer Division Hohenstaufen and Karl von Treuenfeld's 10th SS Panzer Division Frundsberg. (As an interesting footnote, the Hohenstaufen had spent the majority of its work-up time at the Maria ter Heide training grounds next to the Field of the Golden Spurs at Kortrijk in Flanders.)

Both formations were brand new, having just completed their training, fully manned with mainly volksdeutsche recruits grouped around experienced cadres from the Leibstandarte and the Das Reich, and superbly equipped. Using an average of 144 trains per day the Corps was sent from France to the Ukraine to try and stave off calamitous defeat.

The break-out

On 27 March the two newly-arrived SS panzer divisions spearheaded a relief offensive for Fourth Panzer Army aimed at the Pocket. At the same time during a dreadful blizzard, that gave great cover, the surrounded

First Panzer Army began its break-out attempt spearheaded on its side by the panzers and grenadiers of the Leibstandarte. The Langemarck played its part by defending its assigned sector in the Pocket but was too weak to lend the Leibstandarte much of a hand as they attacked west. Indeed by this time the space between individual Flemish slit trenches was now routinely 400 metres and sometimes even greater. With the range of personal weapons being most effective at 300 metres or less, it was obvious that the Flemings would have trouble just supporting each other in their holes.

The fighting to relieve the Pocket was particularly fierce as the Russians strove to stop the surrounded troops from escaping. STAVKA scented another Stalingrad and threw in massed tank attacks against the advancing II SS Panzer Corps as they were loath to see the Germans and their allies live to fight another day. In the middle of this struggle, on 2 April, Hitler lost confidence in Manstein and replaced him with Field Marshal Walther Model, at the same time as renaming Army Group South as Army Group North Ukraine. This had no immediate effect on the situation but for once the Germans were too strong and Soviet tank casualties went into the hundreds as the superlative gunnery of the SS panzer crews chewed them up.

Late in the afternoon of 7 April the Frundsberg's 6th SS Panzer Company, under the command of a wounded SS-Hauptsturmführer Franke, met the lead elements of the First Panzer Army's 6th Panzer Division at Buszacz, and the Kamenets-Podolsk Pocket had been relieved. Over the next nine days Hube successfully withdrew the First Panzer Army, including the decimated Langemarck, back across into German-held territory west of the Seret River without losing either significant numbers of men or heavy weapons, the equipment and manpower that the Wehrmacht could ill-afford to lose.

Counting the cost

The SS-Sturmbrigade Langemarck was finally in relative safety and was ordered firstly to Jaslo in Polish Galicia and then, by train, back once more to Debica to be reformed yet again just a short three and a half months after first being committed to the fighting in the Ukraine. As a fighting unit the Sturmbrigade was shattered. It had lost nearly all its heavy equipment, particularly its armour component, along with an astonishing 75%-plus of its combat strength as casualties. In total, barely 400 unwounded survivors of the Sturmbrigade had made it out of the Ukraine, with the fighting around Yampil in particular taking a terrible toll of the young Flemish grenadiers. As a percentage, casualties were highest among the command elements of the unit, with the brigade commander, every company commander and nearly all of the platoon commanders being wounded or killed.

1. Postcard of a Flemish Waffen-SS freiwillige. Volunteers back home in Flanders on leave often had these type of shots taken for family and friends; for them their service was something to be proud of. (Courtesy of Rene Chavez)

2. A pre-war photo of Joris Van Severen, the ex-Belgian Army officer and head of Dinaso who was executed by the French police in Abbeville as a 'precaution'.

3. Joris Van Severen, the charismatic head of the Dinaso movement, had the potential to become the Flemish 'Quisling' leader but was shot by French gendarmes before even committing a crime.

4. Volunteers in the Vlaamsche SS and the NSJV Youth wing, the majority of the Vlaamsche SS and many NSJV members would go on to serve in the Waffen-SS during the War. (Courtesy of Luc De Bast)

5. Banleider (Major) Maurice Dekeyser of the VNV's paramilitary Black Brigade. The Black Brigade was a major source of recruits for the Flemish Waffen-SS throughout the War. (Courtesy of Luc De Bast)

6. The five-man Raad van Leiding 'cabinet' of the VNV established in October 1940 to try and govern occupied Flanders. From left to right: Staf De Clercq, Hendrik J. Elias, Reimond Tollenaere, Gerard Romsée and Ernest Van Den Berghe. De Clerq and Tollenaere would not survive the War.

7. The Kortrijk Memorial in 1941 on commemoration day of the Flemish victory at the Battle of the Golden Spurs in 1302.

8. Gustave 'Staf' De Clercq, charismatic leader of the Flemish nationalist Vlaamsch Nationaal Verbond.

9. Staf De Clercq (in the middle with the arm raised), addresses a rally of VNV supporters in Brussels' central Market Square.

10. Reimond Tollenaere, the pre-War leader of the VNV's Black Brigade paramilitary wing, before he became one of the first volunteers in the SS-Legion Flandern.

11. SS-Untersturmführer Reimond Tollenaere on the Russian Front in the winter of 1941. His position as leader of the Dietsche Militie Zwarte Brigade (the Black Brigade) was taken by Joris van Steenlandt.

12. The VNV newspaper, *Volk en Staat*, carries the front page story of the death of the ex-head of the VNV's Black Brigade, Reimond Tollenaere, on the Russian Front in January 1942.

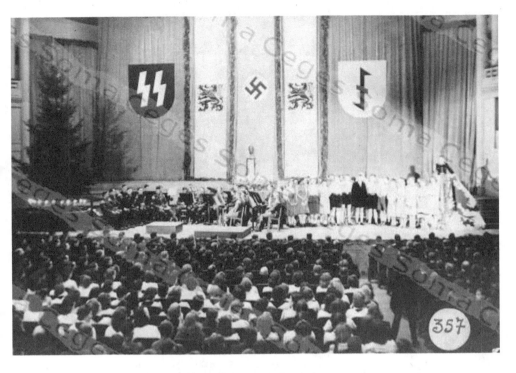

Above: **13.** A VNV rally during the occupation of Flanders.

Below: **14.** Staf De Clercq in a postcard posing with SS-Legion Flandern veterans, the commemorative picture of Reimond Tollenaere on the wall probably means this photo was taken after his death to Spanish artillery fire at Koptsy on 21 January 1942; and of course before Staf De Clercq's death from a heart attack on 22 October 1942. (Courtesy of Rene Chavez)

Left: **15.** Following his death on 22 October 1942, Staf De Clercq is buried with full honours.

Below: **16.** An honour guard of Flemish Waffen-SS and VNV members stand watch over Staf De Clercq's tomb.

17. Dr Hendrik J. Elias, member of the VNV 'shadow' government for Flanders, the Raad Van Leiding. He assumed leadership of the VNV after Staf De Clercq's death.

18. Dr Hendrik J. Elias at a VNV rally. Before assuming the movement's leadership he was the VNV Governor of Ghent.

19. Dr Edgar Lehembre, leader of the VNV's youth wing, the Nationaal-Socialistische Jeugd Verbond, and Jetje Claessens, leader of the Dietsche Meisjes Scharen (literally the Netherlandic maidens platoons), the female section of the VNV's youth wing, at a rally on 14 June 1942.

20. A trainload of SS-Legion Flandern volunteers rolls out of Flanders on 10 November 1941 bound for the Eastern Front.

21. Waffen-SS Oberscharführer Ward Buntinx was a Fleming who spent his wartime career serving in the elite SS panzer divisions rather than any of the wholly Flemish units. He ended up fighting alongside both the Flemings and Walloons in 1945 in the bitter battles around Stargard in Pomerania. (Courtesy of Luc De Bast)

22. Born on 2 September 1920 Frans Verdonck was another Fleming who did not serve with either the SS-Langemarck or its predecessors. Instead he fought in the SS-Das Reich's 2nd SS Panzer Regiment until his death in action on 28 August 1943 in the fighting at Kharkov. (Courtesy of Luc De Bast)

Above: **23.** The Flemish lion arm shield of the 27th SS-Langemarck Division. (Courtesy of Luc De Bast)

Above: **25.** An Algemeene-SS (also called Vlaamsche SS or SS-Vlaanderen) Scharleider (German rank equivalent SS-Unterscharführer) from Gent. (Courtesy of Luc De Bast)

Opposite below: **24.** The trifos swastika worn by some Flemish Waffen-SS volunteers in the SS-Sturmbrigade Langemarck and SS-Division Langemarck in place of the normal SS collar tab runes, but by necessity most Flemish Waffen-SS men wore the standard sig runes instead. (Courtesy of Luc De Bast)

Above: **26.** Max von Tilborg was a member of the 1 SS-Standarte Flandern (German spelling), the paramilitary wing of the Flemish Germanic SS. The photo shows the elongated swastika worn on the cap and the sig runes badge worn on the upper left arm. (Courtesy of Luc De Bast)

Left: **27.** An SS-Legion Flandern volunteer showing the Flemish lion collar badge as well as his cuff title and arm shield on his left arm. (Courtesy of Luc De Bast)

28. It was not only Flemish men who served at the front during the War, this postcard is of a Flemish volunteer nurse in the German Red Cross, she is wearing the Flemish lion arm shield on her upper right arm. (Courtesy of Luc De Bast)

29. Flemish Waffen-SS war reporters back home in Flanders with a portrait of the VNV Black Brigade leader, Reimond Tollenaere, in the background. (Courtesy of Luc De Bast)

30. SS-Oberscharführer Raf Van Hulse (on left with glasses), ex-head of the Vlaamsche SS, after he became a war reporter in the Waffen-SS. Van Hulse went on to lead the war reporters platoon in the SS-Sturmbrigade Langemarck. (Courtesy of Luc De Bast)

31. On the right of this picture is a publicity shot of the Flemish Knight's Cross winner Remy Schrijnen sporting both his medal and the trifos collar tab, while the background picture is of a platoon of Flemish Waffen-SS volunteers on the Eastern Front. (Courtesy of Luc De Bast)

Above: **32.** Extremely rare photo of the wedding of the Flemish SS-Sturmmann Peter De Wit. He is wearing the VNV Black Brigade Reimond Tollenaere Honour Medal and the Infantry Assault Badge. As his cuff title denotes, De Wit was one of the many Flemings serving in the SS-Das Reich but what is interesting to note is that he is also wearing a Flemish lion arm shield. (Courtesy of Luc De Bast)

Right: **33.** Karel De Maeyer wearing his Iron Cross 2nd Class ribbon, Wound Badge in Gold, Infantry Assault Badge and the Reimond Tollenaere Honour Medal showing he was a member of the VNV's Black Brigade before volunteering for the Waffen-SS. He wears the Langemarck cuff title but not the new BEVO arm eagle designed for the Flemish Langemarck volunteers. (Courtesy of Luc De Bast)

Above: **34.** Flemish volunteers in the SS-Nordwest Regiment relax with an evening of music and drink. (Courtesy of Luc De Bast)

Left: **35.** Original arm badge of the Flemish NSKK Transport Brigade. More than 4,000 Flemings enlisted in the Brigade in 1941 and 1942 alone. (Courtesy of Luc De Bast)

Above left: **36.** SS-Unterscharfuhrer Etienne Anneesens wearing his Iron Cross 2nd Class and the commemorative Joris Van Severen badge, showing he was a pre-War member of the Dinaso movement. (Courtesy of Luc De Bast)

Above right: **37.** SS-Legion Flandern volunteer, SS-Unterscharführer Bert Mathys, sporting his Iron Cross 2nd Class won in combat on the Eastern Front. (Courtesy of Luc De Bast)

38. A march of the VNV's youth wing, the NSJV, through Brussels in 1943. The flag shows the stylized stormy petrel that was their emblem. In Flemish this bird was called the *blauwvoet* and figured prominently in Flemish nationalist organisations such as Dinaso's youth wing, the Verbond van Jongdinaso Vendels. (Courtesy of Luc De Bast)

39. SS-Unterscharführer Frans Werrebroek; according to Georg D'Haese, Werrebroek was 'one of the most loyal, brave and dependable soldiers during the heavy fighting in the Volkhov Pocket and before Leningrad, where he fought as an SS-Sturmmann.' Werrebroek went on to serve as a platoon leader in KG Schellong during the fighting in Pomerania in 1945. (Courtesy of Luc De Bast)

40. SS-Oberscharführer Cardoen, commander of 3 Platoon from the 3rd Company of I.SS/Freiwilligen-Grenadier Regiment 67. Cardoen fought in Rehmann's battalion in Kampfgruppe Schellong in Pomerania in 1945. This picture of Cardoen was taken when he was an SS-Sturmmann serving in the SS-Deutschland Regiment in the elite SS-Division Das Reich prior to his service with the SS-Division Langemarck. (Courtesy of Luc De Bast)

Above: **41.** Postcard of the Flemish Iron Cross winner Jules Geurts and a Flemish volunteer nurse in the German Red Cross. (Courtesy of Rene Chavez)

Left: **42.** Recruiting poster for the SS-Westland Regiment made up of volunteers from Flanders and the Netherlands.

43. Recruiting poster for the SS-Legion Flandern, imploring would-be volunteers to go to the Brussels recruitment office.

44. An anti-semitic recruiting poster for the 27th SS-Division Langemarck.

45. Recruiting poster for the SS-Sturmbrigade Langemarck.

46. SS-Sturmmann Jules 'Juul' Geurts, the first Flemish recipient of the Iron Cross 1st Class on 2 July 1942. He was killed in action during the fighting near Lake Ladoga in the second week of January 1943. (Courtesy of Sébastian J. Bianchi)

47. Anti-tank gunner Remy Schrijnen (on left) with his company commander the Austrian SS-Untersturmführer Anton Kotlowski. (Courtesy of Kris Simoens)

48. Remy Schrijnen seen here sporting the Iron Cross 2nd Class ribbon, the Infantry Assault Badge and the Iron Cross 1st Class. (Courtesy of Kris Simoens)

49. Schrijnen proudly shows off his Knight's Cross won for outstanding bravery at the 'Battle of the European SS' at Narva in Estonia. (Courtesy of Kris Simoens)

50. Schrijnen seen wearing the sunwheel swastika, the trifos, which was a source of resentment for some Flemish volunteers but was one of pride for the ever-independent Schrijnen. (Courtesy of Kris Simoens)

51. Following the award of the Knight's Cross, SS-Sturmmann Remy Schrijnen is paraded in front of his Flemish comrades as an example to emulate. The parade was at the Knovitz training grounds. On Schrijnen's right is the Flemings' long-time commander Conrad Schellong and to the left is Schellong's Adjutant, SS-Untersturmführer Wilhelm Teichert. (Courtesy of Kris Simoens)

The Flemings were not alone in being greatly diminished. At the end of the campaign the Leibstandarte had only 1,229 men left as combat effectives, equipped with three panzers and four assault guns from a previous divisional armour total of 160. As for Heinz Lammerding's Das Reich kampfgruppe, when it was finally relieved from the front and boarded a train on 20 April to take the survivors back to their parent division in far-away Toulouse, there were only 800 survivors out of the original complement of 5,000 men. Manstein who, before his replacement by Field Marshal Walther Model, commanded Army Group South said of the Ukraine fighting:

> Our forces had finally reached the point of exhaustion. The German divisions ... were literally burned out ... The fighting had eaten away at the very core of the fighting units. How could we wage effective counter-attacks, for example, when an entire Panzerkorps had only 24 panzers ready for battle? (From Michael Reynolds, *The Devil's Adjutant*, Spellmount Publishing, 1995)

Non-Langemarck Flemings at the front

The Langemarck men were not the only Flemings serving in the Waffen-SS who distinguished themselves in the Ukraine battles of 1943-1944. There were still a considerable number of Flemish volunteers serving in the 5th SS Panzergrenadier Division Wiking and they fought valiantly at Cherkassy, and of even more interest there were even a small number in the Kampfgruppe Lammerding fighting alongside their Flemish brethren in the SS-Sturmbrigade Langemarck. One of the Flemish Das Reich men, SS-Oberscharführer Georges Colemonts, was listed in the Wehrmacht Bulletin and the Roll of Honour on 27 August 1943 for his courage as a panzer driver during the fighting around Kharkov.

Home in Flanders: resistance

For the Flemings on the Eastern Front home seemed a very long way away, but just as their nationalist aspirations began to recede the peace of their homeland also began to suffer from the slow but perceptible growth of resistance.

Active Belgian resistance among both the Flemish and Walloon populations was never strong and always divided. That is not to say that the majority of the citizenry were pro-German, rather that they chose a passive path of resistance and not an active one. That was the case across most of western Europe. The numbers of active resistors and collaborators, the two extremes if you like, were relatively low, with the majority of people sitting in the middle. In Belgium the division, as you would anticipate, was firstly along racial lines – between the Flemings and Walloons – but was also a political one, as with everywhere else in occupied Europe, between the communists and non-communists. In line with the Nazi-Soviet Non-aggression Pact of 1939, the Belgian communists, who were Walloon-dominated, adhered strictly to the policy line from Moscow and did not contest the initial German occupation in 1940. This 'politics before country', *Internationale* approach was mirrored across Europe by all the homegrown communist parties and was the cause of widespread resentment, particularly with early resistors, as on occasions they were actively hindered and informed on by their own communist countrymen, as directed by Stalin.

The main non-communist national resistance organisation in Belgium was the *Mouvement National Belge* headed by a World War I veteran, Camille Joset, and its attention was firmly on intelligence gathering for the Allies in London and industrial espionage and not armed action. It was mildly successful but was hit hard when Joset and his chief lieutenants were arrested en masse in 1942 and the movement fell into disarray. As the Gallic name of the Mouvement suggests it was a Walloon-orientated organisation. In Flanders the Antwerp-based *Witte Brigade* was the main non-communist resistance set-up and enjoyed some limited success, again, like their Walloon neighbours, excelling at industrial espionage rather than armed conflict.

Following the launch of Operation Barbarossa however, the cry of course went out from Moscow for all foreign communists to perform a volte face and attack the Germans at every opportunity. Already used to strict discipline, acting clandestinely and organised in secretive cell structures, the various European communist parties, Belgium's included, were tailor-made for this new role and were often by far the most effective resistance groups at hitting the Germans and their allies. In Belgium the local communists formed the catchily titled, *Armée Belge des Partisans du Front de l'Indépendence et de la Libération* (FIL for short). The assassination of local collaborators was a favoured tool of the FIL and between 1942 and 1944 the communists killed about 1,000 pro-German Belgians across the country. Degrelle's own brother was a victim, being gunned down in his hometown of Charleroi, and in Flanders the FIL claimed their highest profile victim on 4 December 1942 when they assassinated SS-Onderstormleider (SS-Untersturmführer) August Schollen of the Flemish SS in Brussels. Schollen was only 27 years old but was already a senior figure in the 1. Standarten der Germaansche SS Vlaanderen. His death was a serious blow to the organisation. He was buried by his comrades with full honours in a military funeral on 8 December, less than two months after Staf De Clercq was also put in the ground.

The Germans themselves were targets as well of course and from 1941 to liberation in 1944 some 500 Germans were killed in the Brussels region alone by the resistance. Although this must be seen in the context of a war where 1,000 Germans were being killed every single day in the Normandy fighting post-D-Day.

A Spanish proposal

In one of the many bizarre twists that accompanied the freiwillige movement, while the Sturmbrigade Langemarck was fighting for its life in Yampil back in March, in Germany the camp authorities at the Leibstandarte barracks in Berlin-Lichterfelde (which, incidentally, was also the recruiting centre for the Langemarck) had been approached by Alphonse Van Horembeke, a francophone Fleming who had fought for Franco in the Spanish Foreign Legion in the Civil War and had then worked for the Falangist Youth in Vizcaya. Van Horembeke had secretly crossed the Spanish-French border and travelled to Germany with an extraordinary proposal. Franco had long since ordered the Blue Division home to provide reassurance to the Allies on his country's neutrality but there was still a number of Spaniards who were determined to fight with the Wehrmacht in the war against the Bolsheviks. Small numbers of Spaniards ended up in a whole range of weird and wonderful German and German-sponsored military formations, but Van Horembeke was sent to make contact specifically with the SS-Sturmbrigade Langemarck, by his friends in the Falangist Youth, to offer 400 or more young Spanish volunteers to serve alongside the Flemish in their assault brigade. The Flemish had been chosen because of the amicable relationship they had struck up with the Blue Division during the fighting outside Leningrad and on the Volkhov in the old SS-Legion Flandern days. (The fact that Reimond Tollenaere was killed by a Spanish artillery shell was probably not mentioned during the meeting.) Nothing came of the proposal however as back in Spain the Ministry of Foreign Affairs had gotten wind of it and moved quickly to stamp on the idea. The last thing Franco's regime needed when it was absolutely clear the Allies would win the war was to be associated with the losing side. Though Spaniards did serve with Degrelle's Walloons as Van Horembeke was directed to the Walloon training camp at the Debica complex. Here he found an old friend from his Spanish Civil War days and together they set out to recruit Spaniards into the Walloon Sturmbrigade, with Degrelle's blessing of course.

Names to remember

On the establishment of the Sturmbrigade Remy Schrijnen had transferred from his position as a foot messenger to that of a Richtschütze, a No.1

gunner, on a towed 75mm PAK anti-tank gun. Having learnt his trade as a simple grenadier he had now found his 'home' in a military sense. For the rest of the War he would be found sitting behind the gunner's sight staring coolly at the next tank or gun he was going to destroy. More than any other weapon it was the 75mm (and the men like Dries Anseeuw and Toon Pauli who manned them) that would provide the Flemish with the majority of their fire support for the next two years; and in Remy Schrijnen they had found a man who knew exactly how to use it.

From the start of the deployment in the Ukraine he began to amass an awesome tally of kills and a justified reputation for bravery, coolness under fire and an unorthodox streak that would forever be his hallmark. Alongside one of his crew who spoke Russian, Anton Dersmenscheck who was born in the Ukraine, he would lead 'unofficial' night-time recce patrols out into no-man's land to gather intelligence and feed it back. During the days he was perfecting his soon to be famous *Kopfstellung* gun position as the best way to use his weapon, and all the while tank after tank and gun after gun fell victim to his courage and accuracy.

Alongside his collection of kills he was also collecting wounds. He had been wounded three times already in the fighting around Leningrad and Ladoga, but down in the Ukraine he chalked up another four separate wounds and was first awarded the Wound Badge in Black and then Silver while still recovering in hospital in mid-March 1944. This was followed in May by the award of the Iron Cross 2nd Class, the first member of his company to receive the award. One incident best describes Schrijnen's behaviour at the front and gives a clue to his later heroism at Narva. On this occasion his gun was coming under increasing fire from a large number of Russian anti-tank guns. With the situation getting worse Schrijnen sent the rest of the crew back to the relative safety of company headquarters while he stayed and fought the gun alone. His company commander, August Knorr, saw this and without a moment's hesitation ran through the enemy fire until he reached Schrijnen and took over as his loader. The two of them then destroyed all the opposing Russian guns one-by-one.

Georg D'Haese missed the Ukrainain campaign as he had been selected for officer training following his showing in the SS-Legion Flandern and during the fighting at Krasny-Bor in particular. He attended that mecca for freiwillige officer cadets, the elite SS Officer Academy at Bad Tölz. His course began on 6 September 1943 and he passed out on March 11, 1944 after eight gruelling months of intense instruction, which saw him promoted to SS-Standartenoberjunker. He went directly from Bad Tölz to Knovitz to marry up with the remnants of the Sturmbrigade following its battles in the Ukraine, and it was there on June 21 1944 that he received news of his commission as a fully-fledged SS-Untersturmführer, and was subsequently given his first company command.

IX

The Legend of Narva:
The Battle of the European SS

The new year of 1944, as the Langemarck could attest to in the Ukraine, had brought nothing but pain for the Ostheer. The initiative in the East was now irreversibly with the Soviets and they could use their huge superiority in men and material wherever they saw fit to drive back the exhausted Germans and their allies. In fact so powerful had the Red Army become that their offensive against Army Group South was not the only game in town. Over a thousand miles to the north at the other end of the Russian Front the decision had been taken to finally remove the Nazi threat from Leningrad and push the Wehrmacht back out of the Soviet Union, through the Baltic States and Poland to the very eastern borders of the Reich itself.

Leningrad finally freed

A short two weeks after the Langemarck was firing its first shots down in the Ukraine, the troops of General Govorov's Leningrad Front, including a reconstituted 2nd Shock Army, launched a full-scale offensive on the night of 13–14 January from their Oranienbaum Pocket enclave to the west of Leningrad that smashed into the outnumbered and ill-prepared Wehrmacht units facing them. The offensive swept aside the inexperienced 9th and 10th Luftwaffe field divisions holding the line, although this was unsurprising as these formations were created by drafting in unemployed ground crew and logistics staff and attempting to make infantrymen of them. As such, these units were no match for the Russian bulldozer that hit them at full tilt. The Germans hurried to react but the result was that the trench lines surrounding Leningrad, which had been so resolutely held for so long by the likes of the Flemish, were breached and a general withdrawal was necessary to avoid the threat of encirclement. As the Germans disappeared south and west, a calm settled over Leningrad as, finally, following so much agony, the epic siege of Soviet Russia's second city was officially, irrevocably lifted on 19 January 1944, after more than 900 days of struggle.

Steiner's III (germanisches) SS Panzer Corps

It was during this battle in the north that the Red Army first came up against SS-Gruppenführer Felix Steiner's newly-constituted III (germanisches) SS Panzer Corps. Comprising the Scandinavians of the 11th SS-Freiwilligen Panzergrenadier Division Nordland and the Dutchmen of the 4th SS-Freiwilligen Panzergrenadier Brigade Nederland as its basic units, it was this Corps that would quickly become the home of some of those acknowledged to be amongst the finest foreign volunteer formations to fight with the Wehrmacht during the war and worthy successors to the first such grouping of freiwillige in the 2. SS-Infanterie Brigade. In early January 1944 the Corps was still in its embryonic form and had been rushed forward to stiffen the Luftwaffe defence lines west of Leningrad. As the ex-ground crew were butchered in the snow or fled west it was the Norwegians, Danes and Swedes of the Nordland who formed the mainstay of the resistance. At Gubianzy, for example, over 60 Soviet T-34s attacked the town and were met by the armour of the Nordland's Reconnaisance Battalion. The outnumbered SS panzer crews set about the mass of Soviet tanks with a will. In no time at all, 50 of the Red Army tanks lay burning in and around the town and the remainder fled. Not a single Nordland panzer was lost. But even Steiner's men were unable to do anything more than slow the pace of the Red Army advance. In just one week the whole Wehrmacht front was ruptured beyond repair and by 26 January a full scale withdrawal back to the Luga River, some 60 miles (100 kilometres) to the west, was underway.

In a re-run of 1942, the Soviet Volkhov Front also advanced, but this time there was no stopping them. Novgord was liberated in late January. All along the northern sector of the Russian Front the Wehrmacht was under huge pressure and was forced to conduct a desperate, fighting withdrawal through the rest of winter and spring. The Germans and their allies continued to have local successes against their materially superior enemy but this merely slowed down the rate of withdrawal.

First battle of Narva

The Europeans of Steiner's Corps were soon joined by a further tranche of volunteers in the form of the Waffen-SS's Baltic divisions; the Latvians of the 15th Waffen-Grenadier Division der SS (lettische Nr.1) and the 19th

Waffen-Grenadier Division der SS (lettische Nr.2), and the Estonians of the 20th Waffen-Grenadier Division der SS (estnische Nr.1). For these men this was about defending their homes and families and they fought grimly as they went backwards step by step. This, effectively, was the first battle of Narva. Narva was not a battle like Kursk that was fought out in a few days, it was more like Volkhov or Stalingrad in being a series of battles around a single zone fought over a few months.

For the initial phase of combat around Narva, when it first began to be referred to as the 'Battle of the European SS', the Flemish were actually at the other end of the Russian Front fighting down south in the Ukraine. But for the Flemish their time would come. By the end of June 1944, after more than four and a half months of continuous fighting, the Red Army had freed almost all of northern Russia from the invader and stood at the very gates of Estonia on the Narva River.

Yet another reorganisation in Debica

Meanwhile, back at the old home of the Polish Army cavalry in Debica, the trains from Jaslo pulled in and a few hundred Flemings, Germans and a handful of Hiwis disembarked and marched to one of the local barracks on what was one of the Waffen-SS's largest training complexes in the whole of Europe. The men were tired and travel-stained, their uniforms and kit tattered and their equipment battered. Many of the survivors were ex-Legion Flandern men who had used every ounce of experience and guile they had learned at Leningrad, Krasny-Bor and on the Volkhov to get themselves out of the Ukraine alive; but for a sizable number the retreat through the south had been their first time in battle, and it had left its mark. True, they had taken part in a remarkable escape. They, the First Panzer Army, and indeed all of Army Group South, had somehow managed to keep four Red Army Fronts at bay and break out from not one, not two, but three pockets (Korsun, Cherkassy and Kamenets-Podolsk) during the campaign. Casualties had been high in both men and equipment, but the Soviets had paid for their victories in full and hundreds of thousands of Russians lay dead or wounded on the vast Ukrainian steppe.For the men of the Langemarck the only thing they had known as a new SS-Sturmbrigade was the bitter taste of retreat and defeat. But they had proved themselves, they had been able to make the leap from motorised infantry to an all-arms grouping, to manoeuvre and coordinate with some of the best formations the Germans had to offer, and to stand their ground against overwhelming Russian force. It had been Himmler and Berger's decision to upgrade the Flemings to Sturmbrigade status and they liked what they saw and heard. The order went out, the SS-Sturmbrigade Langemarck would rise again from the ashes of the Ukraine, it was time to rebuild.

SS-Sturmbrigade Langemarck 'Mark II'

Having rested a short while in Debica the Flemings were sent on to Knovitz in Czechoslovakia where the new brigade was to take shape and carry out its work-up training. The new unit was to be larger than its earlier incarnation, totalling 14 companies rather than the original nine, with close to three thousand men. There was to be a formal two battalion and supporting companies set-up, with both battalions comprising four infantry and one panzerjäger anti-tank company each. There would also be no less than four other heavy companies, one each for light and heavy anti-aircraft, one of Sturmgeschütz self-propelled guns and a new addition of an artillery company. The total effect would be to double the number of grenadiers while also increasing the unit's overall punching power with integral armour and artillery. Significantly there would also be a much larger anti-tank element to the Sturmbrigade. The order of battle was set as follows:

- Stab der Brigade (Brigade Headquarters)

Brigade Commander   SS-Obersturmbannführer Conrad Schellong
                      (German – recovering from wounds and
                      newly-promoted)

Adjutant   SS-Obersturmführer Wilhelm Teichert
                      (German – newly-promoted)

- 1st Battalion (I. Bataillon)

Battalion Commander   SS-Hauptsturmführer Wilhelm Rehmann
                      (German, ex-Sturmbrigade platoon com
                      mander and temporary 3rd Company
                      Commander)

Adjutant   SS-Untersturmführer Walther Van
                      Leemputten (Flemish – born in Putney,
                      London)

- 1. Kompanie   91st Company -infantry)
Company Commander SS-Untersturmführer Frans Swinnen (Flemish)

- 2. Kompanie   (2nd Company - infantry)
Company Commander   SS-Untersturmführer Henri Van Mol
                      (Flemish)

- 3. Kompanie   (3rd Company – infantry)
Company Commander   SS-Untersturmführer Georg D'Haese
                      (Flemish, ex-Legion grenadier)

- 4. Kompanie   (4th Company - infantry)
Company Commander   SS-Untersturmführer Van Ossel (Flemish)

- 5. Panzerjäger   (5th Company – PAK towed anti-tank guns)
Kompanie
Company Commander   SS-Untersturmführer Marcel Laperre
(Flemish)

- 2nd Battalion (II. Bataillon)
Battalion Commander   SS-Hauptsturmführer Johannes Oehms
(German)
Adjutant   SS-Obersturmführer Ludwig Plabst
(German)

- 6. Kompanie   (6th Company – infantry)
Company Commander   SS-Untersturmführer Wilhelm Schaumann
(German, ex-Sturmbrigade10th Marsch
replacement Company Commander)

- 7. Kompanie   (7th Company – infantry)
Company Commander   SS-Untersturmführer Tops (Flemish)

- 8. Kompanie   (8th Company - infantry)
Company Commander   SS-Untersturmführer Demeester (Flemish,
ex-platoon commander Sturmbrigade 3rd
Company)

- 9. Kompanie   (9th Company - infantry)
Company Commander   SS-Untersturmführer Jack Delbaere
(Flemish, ex-platoon commander 4th heavy
weapons Company Legion Flandern)

- 10. Panzerjäger   (10th Company – PAK towed anti-tank
Kompanie   guns)
Company Commander   SS-Untersturmführer Anton Kotlowski
(Austrian, ex-platoon commander
Sturmbrigade 6th Company – wounded in
the Ukraine)

There were also the Sturmbrigade's heavy companies:
- 11. Artillerie   (11th Company – towed artillery)
Kompanie
Company Commander   SS-Obersturmführer Horst Hinrichs
(German)

- 12. Sturmgeschutz Kompanie   (12th Company – towed artillery)

Company Commander   SS-Hauptsturmführer Willi Sprenger (German)

- 13. Licht FLAK Kompanie   (13th Company - light anti-aircraft guns)

Company Commander   SS-Untersturmführer Otto Uytersprot (Flemish, ex-Sturmbrigade light FLAK Company Commander)

- 14. schwer FLAK Kompanie   (14th Company - heavy anti-aircraft guns)

Company Commander   SS-Obersturmführer Karl-Heinz Gustavson (German, ex-battery commander Sturmbrigade heavy FLAK Company)

The reality gap

Wonderful though this new structure looked on paper it was never likely to become reality on the ground. The original Sturmbrigade had struggled to fill its establishment, particularly as regards heavy weapons such as anti-aircraft guns, and in the spring of 1944 it was unlikely that bomb-ravaged German war production would be able to furnish the Flemish with their new equipment needs. As for the manpower to fill the ranks, this too was almost impossible to find. The old Sturmbrigade had trawled the ranks of the Flemish SS and DeVlag, as well as incorporating Reichs and volksdeutsche, but those particular wells were running dry. The VNV, which had always been the backbone of the Flemish contribution to the war in the East, was in freefall. Those members who saw the future of Flanders inextricably aligned with Nazi Germany headed off to DeVlag, while the mass of nationalists became increasingly disilliusioned with the illusory fruits of collaboration. Elias tried to hold the movement together but to little avail. The German administration was openly dismissive of the cause of an independent Flanders and yet was strident in its demands for more volunteers to join the war effort.

As in other occupied countries in Western Europe the SS recruiting authorities began to cast their eyes over other potential sources of manpower to replace the haemorrhaging of the ranks caused by the slaughter on the Russian Front. But in the meantime the recruiting offices in Flanders – there were 23 in total across Belgium – went into overdrive and drummed up support for the reconstitution of the Langemarck. The likes of Jef Van De Wiele from DeVlag toured the region holding rallies and exhorting young Flemings to step forward and play their part in the anti-bolshevik crusade in the East. Mountains of propaganda were aimed at those who had shown any previous interest in putting on a collabora-tionist uniform of any type and the SS 'marketing machine' did what it did best and romanticised the brutal attrition of the Russian Front, magically transforming it into a noble and just cause.

Even now, with the writing on the wall for Nazi Germany for all to see, there was still a supply of volunteers willing to come forward. It was by no means a flood though and it was obvious it would take quite some time to get the new Sturmbrigade up to any sort of strength. Luckily for the future of the Langemarck, a new crop of commissioned Flemish offi-cers were just passing out of Bad Tölz. This included the likes of Walther Van Leemputten, Marcel Laperre, Luc Bottu, Jef Van Bockel, Hutten and Roger Groenvinck. These were the men who would lead the Langemarck through the last climactic year of the war and to the bitter end. But before that, they would face their own Thermopylae.

Bigger than Overlord

On 22 June 1944, three years to the day since Hitler launched Operation Barbarossa and less than three weeks after D-Day, the Soviets opened their Operation Bagration offensive with an artillery barrage that seemed to shake the very foundations of the earth. The aim of Bagration was simple, liberate Belorussia and completely annihilate Army Group Centre. The attack was gigantic in every aspect. Launched over a frontage of more than 450 miles the Red Army had massed four entire Fronts, each the size of a full-strength Wehrmacht Army, comprising 166 divisions equipped with 5,200 tanks and self-propelled guns, supported by 31,000 guns and mortars and 6,000 planes, and supplied by a fleet of 12,000 lorries. Behind the German lines, over 143,000 communist partisans went into action blowing up every single railway line in Belorussia and paralysing German attempts at resupply and reinforcement. The Red Army had even pre-pared 294,000 hospital beds for its anticipated wounded.

The Russians crashed into Field Marshal Busch's depleted forces and broke the front line in six different places in the first five days alone. The Soviets proceeded to pour through the gaps, bypassing surviv-ing Wehrmacht units and racing ever westwards to encircle even more stranded troops. The Red Army advanced at a rate of 10 to 15 miles a day while the beleaguered Germans were prevented from building a new frontline by one of Hitler's criminally stupid 'stand and fight' orders. The inevitable result was military catastrophe on a scale greater even than Stalingrad. Losses amounted to 350,000 men as 25 divisions were simply wiped off the Wehrmacht order of battle. Coincidentally it was during this offensive that the hitherto undistinguished French volunteers of the LVF would make their name on the Bobr River, while 1,000 of their fellow

French brothers-in-arms from the SS-Sturmbrigade Frankreich would do the same in Galicia. For both it would begin the journey to their last stand together in the ruins of Berlin less than a year later (see *Hitler's Gauls*).

In the north

The Red Army had already tried just about everything to wipe out the bridgehead on the east bank of the Narva River that had been so stubbornly held by Steiner's men for the entire spring and early summer. They had even resorted to an amphibious landing along the coast to try and outflank the position, but in the end it was sheer weight of numbers and exhaustion on the part of the SS men that won the day for the Soviets. The bridgehead on the east bank could no longer be held by the forces available and so the decision was made to withdraw back across the river, give up the city of Narva itself, and retreat to the pre-prepared Tannenberg Line defences 15 miles to the west.

The Red Army had also precipitated a further German withdrawal by its actions further south. In the wake of Bagration the STAVKA decided to maximise its advantage by trying to destroy the Wehrmacht's Army Group North as well as Army Group Centre. Their thinking was clear; if they could replicate their success against Küchler's forces, then up to half of the Wehrmacht on the Eastern Front could be wiped out by the end of summer and the war might be over by Christmas. The first phase of the plan was an attack on the junction of Army Groups Centre and North that tore a 15-mile-wide hole in the line and sent more than 29 Red Army divisions rushing along the Duna River valley towards the borders of Latvia and Lithuania.

The second phase was a concerted assault on the Narva. There would be no subtlety this time, no cunning attacks by sea, airborne subterfuge or diversionary feints. This would be a battle of weight. Weight of high explosive, weight of steel and weight of sheer flesh, and the Red Army was determined not to be denied. The 3rd Baltic Front, later redesignated the Narva Operational Group with the addition of extra forces, deployed 20 full-strength Red Army infantry divisions with six armoured brigades, an entire Front's-worth of artillery regiments, plus massed air support, all concentrated to take on the III (germanisches) SS Panzer Corps. Nominally at a strength of three infantry divisions, a panzergrenadier division and the Dutch panzergrenadier brigade, the SS Panzer Corps was a shadow of its former self by July 1944. Months of hard combat with few replacements meant the likelihood of the Corps standing up to the planned assault was slim. They needed help. That help would come from their fellow Europeans from the little country of Belgium. Having survived the cauldron of Cherkassy, 452 Walloons would come from their reorganisation point at Debica, and from Knovitz would come the Flemings.

The Flemish head for Narva

Berger and his recruiters had been as busy as ever in Flanders and among the ranks of Flanders paramilitary organisations and had managed to sign up a thousand volunteers or more. Along with the Ukrainian campaign survivors and injured men returning from convalescence, the SS-Sturmbrigade Langemarck 'mark II' had a strength of 1,731 by the beginning of July 1944 at its training camp in Knovitz. However it was still far from being combat ready and even its Commander, Conrad Schellong, was still recovering from his injuries and unfit for duty. But time was a luxury the manpower-starved Wehrmacht could no longer afford and orders came down to form a kampfgruppe of available men and send them to Narva as quickly as possible. This was standard Wehrmacht practice, the needs of the front were paramount and if that meant taking what they could get from the training grounds and depots to confront a short-term crisis then so be it. Das Reich had done it in the Ukraine in 1943-1944, as had innumerable units as the situation in the East worsened. This time it would be Langemarck's turn.

Kampfgruppe Rehmann

With Schellong still out of the picture it was decided to give the Langemarck command to SS-Hauptsturmführer Wilhelm Rehmann, and therefore form Kampfgruppe Rehmann, as Oehm's 2nd Battalion was only just being formed. The unit was to be based on Rehmann's 1st Battalion and its five companies, four infantry and one PAK. However while the infantry companies were nearing their establishment strength, Laperre's anti-tank company was still embryonic and only one platoon was ready to go. All in all, Kampfgruppe Rehmann boasted less than 500 men and three solitary 75mm anti-tank guns. It had a handful of trucks to move the troops, but no armour or integral artillery. The order of battle was as follows:

KG Commander	SS-Hauptsturmführer Wilhelm Rehmann (German, ex-Sturmbrigade platoon comander and temporary 3rd Company Commander)
Adjutant	SS-Untersturmführer Walther Van Leemputten (Flemish)
Doctor	Leutnant Dr Hertgens (German – Luftwaffe, served with the Sturmbrigade)
• 1. Kompanie	(1st Company -infantry)
Company Commander	SS-Untersturmführer Frans Swinnen (Flemish)

- 2. Kompanie   (2nd Company - infantry)
- Company Commander   SS-Untersturmführer Henri Van Mol (Flemish)

- 3. Kompanie   (3rd Company - infantry)
- Company Commander   SS-Untersturmführer Georg D'Haese (Flemish, ex-Legion grenadier)

- 4. Kompanie   (4th Company – infantry)
- Company Commander   SS-Untersturmführer Van Ossel (Flemish)

As it transpired upon arrival on the Narva front SS-Untersturmführer Van Ossel was given command of an Estonian company from the 20th SS Division that had lost all of its officers in the recent combat; as a result the 4th Company was disbanded and its platoons distributed among the other three to increase their strength.

- Panzerjäger Zug   (Anti-tank platoon – 3 x PAK towed anti-tank guns)
- Platoon Commander   SS-Untersturmführer Marcel Laperre (Flemish)
- 1. Geschütz (gun team)   SS-Unterscharführer Bert D'Hollander (Flemish, ex-Legion Flandern)
- 2. Geschütz   SS-Unterscharführer Eduard Reeb (German, ex-Legion Flandern)
- 3. Geschütz   SS-Unterscharführer Jef Grootaers (Flemish, ex-Sturmbrigade) Each gun team typically consisted of about 7 men.

Kampfgruppe (KG) Rehmann paraded on 19 July and boarded a train at Beneschau, near Knovitz, to travel non-stop to Steiner's Headquarters in Estonia at Toila, from where they would be deployed as necessary.

What difference could such a small force make? True, as an all-arms Sturmbrigade in the Ukraine the Flemings had made an impact, but that was with four times the manpower and a supply of heavy weapons. As it turned out, sending these few Flemish to Narva with hardly any equipment only added to the mystique of their contribution. Most of them would not be coming back, they would end up buried in Estonia's Blue Mountains, but for those that did return reputations would be made, and also destroyed. The men who went were among the cream of the Flemish contribution to the German effort in the East during the War. Narva was to become their battle, their legend, and it was there that a relative handful of Flemings would earn their place among the pantheon of the European SS. Remy Schrijnen, Georg D'Haese, Marcel Laperre, Dries Anseeuw, Jan De Wilde and Leo Tollanaere, these were the men who were the hard wood of the Langemarck, the names from Narva, the names who would define the Flemish for the rest of the war.

The Dutch Seyffardt Regiment wiped out

Named after the famous First World War battle that saw the German Army under Hindenburg trounce an advancing Tsarist Russian Army, the *Tannenbergstellung* (Tannenberg Line) was not an impressive set of fortifications with a continuous series of prepared trenches and bunkers covered by belts of mines and barbed wire. Rather it was a line on a map that sought to use a series of natural features, such as the high ground of the Swedish Wall in the north (an earth fortification built back in 1704), as well as intermittent pre-prepared positions, to stop the Russian advance.

The pullback from Narva to the Tannenberg Line itself did not go as planned. Crossing the river north and south of the city the Soviets attempted to encircle the III (germansiches) SS Panzer Corps before it could reach the relative safety of the Tannenberg defences. In the south stubborn resistance by the Heer's 11th Infantry Division held the Soviet pincer, but in the north the Estonians of the 20th SS could not repeat that feat and were pushed back, allowing the Russians to swing down south and surround the retreating SS-Legion Niederlande veterans of the Dutch SS-Freiwilligen Panzergrenadier Regiment 48 General Seyffardt. A relief attempt failed and the regiment, in British Army terms an entire brigade, was crushed. Only 20% of the volunteers from the General Seyffardt managed to escape, including the old Legion Flandern veteran, Helmut Breymann, who had commanded the famous 2nd Company 'Circus Breymann' in the first battles at Leningrad. He had been the commander of the Dutch regiment's 2nd Battalion but had now seen his unit shredded. Although he survived the slaughter of his regiment in front of the Tannenberg Line he would be killed in action a few days later on the Narva.

The three hills

From the city of Narva, and Russian-held Hungerburg to the north, a series of roads ran southwest before doglegging up northwest and then straight through to the Estonian capital of Tallinn, then called Reval, on the coast. Parallel to these roads, but further south, was the railway line that again connected the capital to the river city. While the rail line would be very important for logistics and resupply when Tallinn was captured, what was needed by an advancing army was then, and still is now, a major road network. The majority of an army's transport is wheeled and does not adapt well to cross-country movement. Tracked vehicles like tanks are designed to go offroad but the reality is that this is the exception rather than the rule and such movement is hugely wearing on the vehicles and men, and it drinks fuel at a prodigous rate. Even marching infantry and horsedrawn wagons, still very prevalent in the Second World War, move far quicker on road than off it and although some offensives, such as Manstein's Sedan attack in 1940 in France, utilised areas regarded as impassable for vehicles, the vast majority of assaults have the freeing of the transport network as a primary objective.

Most of the roads in the area came to clear junctions in front of three prominent hills, through which the main Narva-Tallinn road weaved on its way to Sillamae to the west. These roads were critical, and it was clear then that whoever controlled them controlled the battlefield. The hills themselves run directly east to west and provide a panoramic view across the plain back to the city of Narva. The furthest east, and therefore the first hill the Red Army would come up against, was called *Kinderheim-Höhe*, Orphanage Hill, after a deserted orphanage built on its summit. Next in line to the west was *Grenadier-Höhe*, Grenadier Hill, and then finally came *69.9-Höhe*, 69.9 Hill, so-called after its spot height on the map. This last hill was called *Liebes-Höhe*, Love's Hill, by the Flemish themselves. To avoid confusion, and because it was not the Flemish but the Estonians and Nordland men who defended it, it will be referred to as 69.9 Hill.

Control of these three hills would enable the defenders to bring direct fire weapons, such as anti-tank guns, panzer guns and so on, to bear along a lot of the road network and the surrounding area that was in range, while also bringing down observed indirect fire, from artillery and mortars, right up to the western edge of Narva city itself. The hills then were the lynchpin of the entire defence line. If they fell then the Tannenberg Line would be breached and the whole SS Corps threatened with disaster. All three needed to be defended to the last, and key to them all was the very first, the most easterly, the hill the Soviets would attack first, Orphanage Hill. This hill was the final destination for Kampfgruppe Rehmann.

Steiner's dispositions

To meet the Red Army onslaught Steiner deployed his limited formations in the following manner: on the coast to the north were the Estonians of the 20th SS Division, with the two battalions of the Dutch SS-Freiwilligen Panzergrenadier Regiment 49 De Ruiter (this was instead of a regiment's usual three) to their south along with their Pioneer Battalion, number 54, from the 4th SS-Freiwilligen Panzergrenadier Brigade. These three battalions were tasked with covering all the way south to the main Tallinn road. From there south to the railway line were the Scandinavians of the

2nd and 3rd Battalions of the Nordland's SS-Panzergrenadier Regiment 24 Danmark and the 3rd Battalion of SS-Panzergrenadier Regiment 23 Norge. Both regiments were down to two grenadier battalions instead of the usual three through casualties, and even the surviving companies were rarely more than a hundred men strong. Nordland's SS-Panzer Artillerie Regiment 11 was also down there to provide support along the whole frontage. Grenadier and 69.9 Hills were defended by the Estonians and two companies from the Nordland's Pionier-Bataillon 11. Orphanage Hill itself was to be screened by the Dutch but not directly defended by them; with their having taken so many casualties in the recent fighting it was decided to reinforce them with the small Flemish Langemarck contingent. It was hoped that KG Rehmann would beef up the Dutch defence and enable it to hold the front of the three hills. With orders given the Flemings moved up onto Orphanage Hill on the night of 25 July and dug in to be ready for the inevitable Soviet juggernaut. As indicated earlier, the Flemish were going to face the Red Army's 2nd Shock Army, this formation having been reconstituted after its annihilation in the Volkhov Pocket by, among others, the SS-Legion Flandern.

25 July: eve of battle

In mid-summer that far north the nights are very short, lasting only a few hours, but for the Flemings it was crucial to get to Orphanage Hill and get into position before daybreak allowed the Soviets to either attack or bring down artillery fire on them before they were ready and secure deep in the comforting earth.

Defensive positions are all about the ground. The first thing any commander worth their salt does when assigned an area to defend is to get onto the ground and, if at all possible, to view it from the enemy's direction. That way you can see the lay of the land through your enemy's eyes and you can use that information to place your own troops and equipment assets accordingly. You then re-check after you have dug in to ensure camouflage is working and to double-check the decisions you have made. 'Can I see any gunpits, are any of my men skylined, are there any piles of thrown-up earth that give positions away?' These are the questions you look to answer but this is not always possible in the face of a swiftly advancing enemy. There is then a mass of other data to take into consideration; the range and characteristics of your own weapon systems, ability to achieve interlocking fields of fire, counter-attack and withdrawal routes and the practical application of all of these aspects. There is no point, for instance, in placing one of your anti-tank weapons to cover a road junction if that junction is out of range of the weapon itself. This may seem obvious but in the tension before battle even simple things can become incredibly difficult. In fact, an adage experienced soldiers often use to measure a unit's value in combat is their 'ability to do the simple things well under the most difficult of conditions'.

Then of course there is the availability or scarcity of defence stores such as barbed wire and mines, and key issues such as the siting of pre-selected and recorded artillery shoots, so-called DF's (Defensive Fire). These are critical, as weight of high explosive is a boon in any battle. Any approach routes that cannot be covered by direct fire, or main axes of advance for the enemy, can be selected by commanders and passed to the artillery for them to fire a few rounds on to, the fall of shot is then observed and corrections sent to the gunners who adjust as necessary. When they are dead on the target is recorded, that is the exact position of the guns in terms of elevation, direction, explosive charge and so on is written down, and the target is given a code number. During battle all a commander then has to do is contact the guns and ask for that target to be hit by giving its code number, in a few seconds a torrent of shells lands on the enemy causing mayhem, and the enemy have no warning they are about to be hit as the guns have not had to range themselves in. This is a huge advantage as the vast majority of casualties caused by artillery occur within the first 30 seconds of a barrage.

Given its mission, equipment and the ground, SS-Hauptsturmführer Rehmann positioned his small command with the grenadier companies forward and facing east in the direction of the expected Red Army assault. They were spread out in a rough arrowhead formation on the flat land at the base of Orphanage Hill, to the right of the road running from the forest to the east that then weaved between Grenadier Hill and 69.9 Hill to their rear. Henri Van Mol's 2nd Company was up forward in the centre, Georg D'Haese's 3rd Company was on his left and slightly back and Frans Swinnen's 1st Company was on the right and again slightly behind. From the base of Orphanage Hill to the forest in the east was about 600 metres, so whilst it would be a stretch for some of their personal weapons to cover all the ground up to the wood this would not be a problem for their section machine-guns, which contribute most of a unit's firepower. It also meant the Flemish had good, open fields of fire. Rehmann's '1 company up, 2 back' formation is slightly unusual in that it tends to cut down the frontage a unit can cover and can act to isolate the lead company. A more normal '2-up, 1 in reserve' formation doubles the frontage a unit can bring direct fire onto, while enabling all companies to mutually support each other, the third company can then act as reserve and counter-attack force as necessary.

To direct the fighting Rehmann positioned his Command Post behind the grenadier companies and slightly elevated on the forward, eastern slope of Orphanage Hill below the orphanage on the summit itself. The Langemarck's medical post, manned by Dr Hertgens and his medics, was just to the rear of Hill 69.9. To the south of the hills were swamps that made the ground unsuitable for tanks, and so secured the Flemish right flank; but of course as the main Soviet threat was through massed armour it was the placing of his three 75mm PAK guns that was absolutely crucial. Harsh but true: the grenadier companies were not there as the mainstay of the defence but first and foremost to protect those three guns from enemy infantry. Large foot soldier assaults would be hit by artillery to cause maximum casualties and break up the momentum and rythmn of any attack and then it was down to the grenadiers in their holes to cut down anybody that tried to carry on towards the guns, likewise any infantry supporting advancing tanks. But the line would not be breached by infantry. Tanks were the threat, and they had to be stopped.

The tale of the three PAKs

Conventional wisdom in the German anti-tank gun world was that the best way to deploy towed guns was in linear 'fronts' covering a broad area. The guns should be dug in on low, flat, featureless terrain that would mean they did not stand out and so were less likely to be the target for air or artillery strikes. Laperre, as the platoon commander, was in charge of siting the PAKs as long as this conformed to his Commander's intentions for the battle, but Rehmann intervened directly in this key decision. He adhered to convention with regards to Reeb's and Grootaer's guns asking Laperre to site them on the open ground to the north and just back from Orphanage Hill, so they could use their range to hit enemy armour coming out of the forest and along the road but stay out of the ground fight. But, inexplicably, he decided to put D'Hollander's PAK on the eastern, forward slope of Orphanage Hill close to his Command Post. Experienced anti-tankers like Remy Schrijnen were horrified and protested loudly. D'Hollander himself was very unhappy with Rehmann's siting decision; he was an ex-Legion Flandern veteran who had worked his way up through the ranks and had just returned from the successful completion of an SS NCO's course at Lauenberg, and he thought the gun position was too exposed and too far forward, and would quickly be right in the middle of the battlefield and overrun. Rehmann ignored all the warnings. It is a foolish officer indeed who ignores his senior soldiers and NCOs; if you do then you better be right...

As for Laperre he sited Reeb's and Grootaer's guns only to find later on that night that Schrijnen, as the No.1 gunner (the Richtschütze) and not the gun commander it must be added, had disagreed with his view and moved Grootaer's gun to a position of his own choosing, a siting Schrijnen had come up with on his own and called the *Kopfstellung*. Laperre angrily questioned why his orders had not been obeyed but was given short shrift by the diminutive Schrijnen who rounded on him and in no uncertain terms told him that he and he alone made the decision about where the gun was sited and that even though Laperre was the platoon commander he could like it or lump it! Taken aback by the effrontery of a man who was not even a senior NCO, Laperre nevertheless remembered what his fellow Flemish officers had told him of Schrijnen and how it was best to trust his judgement and he let the gun stay where it was. This was the second fateful decision made that first night.

Remy Schrijnen and his *Kopfstellung*

As already noted, the standard wisdom in positioning an anti-tank gun was to dig it in on a low, flat, featureless piece of ground so that it in no way stood out from its surroundings and drew fire. While fighting in the Ukraine as a PAK crewman Schrijnen had found that this siting philosophy had some major drawbacks, of which the worst was that this position meant a gun would more often than not be firing upwards at an angle to hit a Soviet tank and this greatly increased the deflective effectiveness of the Soviets' use of sloping armour. PAK shells would 'bounce off' Russian tanks. Schrijnen believed that it was far better to find a slightly elevated position for the gun with no background. Firstly, this would obviate the problem of deflection as the gun would firing down onto the Soviet tanks and so be able to hit their far weaker top armour; and secondly, it would give enemy tank gunners a very difficult shot in trying to judge the exact position of the gun, as it would have no backdrop behind it to act as an aid to judging distance. Schrijnen also insisted in laying out large amounts of canvas sheeting, the *Zelt bähne*, to the front and sides of the gun. Normally used to provide tent-like shelter for the crew it had the effect, as long as it was kept relatively damp, of hugely reducing the telltale dustcloud that a PAK threw up when it fired. The likes of August Knorr and Willi Dethier thought the *Kopfstellung* position was dangerous and were very much against it during the fighting in the Ukraine, but Schrijnen persevered and by the time he was at Narva no-one was prepared to gainsay the intense SS-Sturmmann with such a fearsome reputation. His gun would stay where it was.

Wednesday 26 July 1944: Day 1

It had been light since before 4 o'clock that morning but it wasn't until gone midday that the Red Army began its attack on Orphanage Hill. First in were dive bombers, the dreaded Russian Stormoviks, laying a carpet of high explosive and shrapnel on probable defensive positions. Then came the full weight of the Soviet artillery arm; truck-borne Katyusha multiple rocket launchers, heavy and medium artillery pieces and mortars. The Russian artillery observers did not know where the Flemings' positions were, so the tactic they employed was to simply work the fire forwards and backwards over the terrain, levelling everything and concentrating on likely points of cover. The effect was like scouring the earth. Every tree in the area, including the small woods on the three hills, was reduced to matchsticks and a stump. The lush greenness of the Estonian countryside in high summer was ploughed up into furrowed mud and dirt. For the Flemings lying in their pairs in slit trenches there was nothing they could do but sit tight and take it. The noise was deafening and made communication between positions impossible, men couldn't hear themselves speak, let alone talk to others. When a shell landed close they were showered by dirt, stones and debris, the dust was choking and covered everything. Shell bursts shattered eardrums and caused nose bleeds, and if an explosion was particularly near it would send shock waves through the ground that would collapse trench walls burying the men inside. Putting your head up out of the trench meant running the risk of being hit in the head by a razor sharp fragment of red hot shrapnel. Your helmet might stop it but it might not, and a jagged piece of metal travelling as fast as a bullet would take half your head off. But the men had to keep on peering out to see what was happening, they had to know when the Russians were coming. Three German panzers, almost certainly from the Nordland, did appear at one point in the late afternoon next to Reeb's gun and began to lay down fire on the Russian positions in the woodline to the east but were soon forced to withdraw under heavy fire, with one of them brewing up after a direct hit. A couple of the crew survived the hit but were machine-gunned down as they tried to reach cover. Apart from that the battle up to that point was pretty much one-sided, with the Flemish having to soak up the punishment that was being meted out.

First blood to the Russians

Under such a terrific bombardment it was inevitable that casualties would be heavy. Grenadiers from all three infantry companies were pulverised. 1st Company on the right flank lost its commander, SS-Untersturmführer Frans Swinnen, while 2nd Company out front lost not only its commander, SS-Untersturmführer Henri Van Mol, but also one of its platoon commanders, SS-Untersturmführer Jef Van Bockel. On the slopes of Orphanage Hill itself the Kampfgruppe headquarters took a direct hit that killed or wounded most of the runners and forward medics and wounded SS-Hauptsturmführer Rehmann himself.

The events that followed this shell blast have been the cause of much controversy ever since. What is indisputable is that Rehmann was wounded on the throat by shrapnel and took himself to a field hospital behind the three hills. After treatment he returned to his command and then ordered one of the surviving motorcycle messengers, Schrijnen's old friend from the Legion days Alfons 'Fons' Van Broeck, to accompany him to Felix Steiner's Corps Headquarters to the west. Once there, Rehmann reported to Steiner and updated him on the situation regarding his Kampfgruppe. What exactly was said between the Flemings' Commanding Officer and the tough, charismatic Steiner no-one knows, but the exchange was short and brutal and resulted in Rehmann being ordered to the rear and replaced by the 21-year-old Flemish commander of 3rd Company, Georg D'Haese.

D'Haese had been wounded as well, though not badly, in the opening bombardment but in contrast to Rehmann had not sought medical attention in the rear and was still with his command. In recognition of the change in leadership the Flemish were now rechristened Kampfgruppe D'Haese. This was a significant expression of appreciation. In the winter of 1941-1942 the SS-Legion Flandern was considered by the Wehrmacht to be a unit with limited combat value best suited for rear area security duties or quiet sectors of the front, and to sustain even that, a German leadership cadre was a necessity. Now, by the summer of 1944, the Flemings had transformed that view to one where they were seen as first-rate combat troops suited for some of the toughest assignments at the front and with a hard core of leaders who were overwhelmingly Flemish freiwillige and who were now for the very first time commanded by one of their own.

The Kampfgruppe that D'Haese took over was bleeding. The three infantry companies and the headquarters staff had taken dozens of casualties, and even worse, he had lost one of his precious 75mm anti-tank guns. The voices of experience among the PAK crews were proved right when it became obvious to Bert D'Hollander that his gun was exposed and in danger of being overrun and captured by the enemy. He sent his crew to the rear and blew up his own gun to deny it to the Soviets, but something went wrong and he did not get clear in time. Possibly setting an incorrect fuse on the explosives – they were colour coded to show the length of delay before exploding – he was blown to pieces. Now the Flemings were down to Reeb's and Grootaer's guns.

Panzer Alarm!

After D'Haese took command the Russians tried their first real foray out of the woods to the east. Five T-34s rumbled out of a fire break and fanned out, parallel with the road, heading towards the Flemish trenches. It did not take long for the tanks to cover the open ground and some of the less experienced grenadiers and commanders became very nervous about why their two remaining PAKs were not engaging them. Then a bare couple of hundred metres short of the first Flemish positions the T-34s slowed, turned round and headed back to the woods. The whole exercise had been a ruse to try and draw the Flemings' fire and the five Soviet tanks were live bait. The Russian commander had hoped the tanks would be fired on and then his artillery could identify the positions of the anti-tank guns and obliterate them. But experience told and the Russians were left guessing.

Their response was typical, a massed tank assault. Yet another artillery barrage was put down on the hills and the land around them but this time the bombardment was short and was swiftly followed by the roar of engines as a mailed fist of Soviet armour charged out of the woods and towards Orphanage Hill. This was no ruse and the Flemish knew it. Almost immediately the PAKs began firing and within minutes four T-34s were burning furiously. Under the concentrated and accurate fire of the two anti-tank guns the remaining Russians retreated to the relative safety of the woods.

There were no more attacks that day, and with nightfall the PAK crews manually dragged their guns back to the safety of Hill 69.9 to avoid them being attacked by probing Russian night patrols. Night-time at the front was an infantryman's battle alone, with the Flemish grenadiers listening intently to any sounds that might give away the presence of infiltrating Russians. Shots punctuated the night with tracer zig-zagging across the sky and the open land between the woods to the east and Orphanage Hill. But the summer night was short and after a couple of hours rest the crews manhandled their guns back to their firing positions.

Thursday 27 July 1944: Day 2

With the dawn came the Russians. There was no more subtlety now, the Red Army was determined to break through the Tannenberg Line and it would do it by sheer weight of numbers. Attacks on the Flemish trenches were interspersed by artillery bombardments so as to give the defenders no respite. The grenadiers also noticed that there were frequent firefights out to the east and soon they realised that it was groups of stragglers, many of them survivors from the Dutch General Seyffardt regiment, who were trying vainly to break through to the safety of their own lines. Very few made it, the majority were wiped out as they struggled to find a path through the massed Soviet assault troops. Then disaster struck as a shell landed close to Reeb's gun and badly damaged it. Miraculously, the crew were unscathed but the PAK itself was a mess and was sent to the work-shop in the rear to be repaired. In the meantime the crew were split up between the infantry companies, and as it turned out the gun would not make it back to the battle in time. The only heavy weapon the Flemings now possessed was SS-Unterscharführer Jef Grootaer's 75mm anti-tank gun.

Scenting a breakthrough the Soviets threw everything at the thin line of freiwillige in front of them. Waves of infantry stormed out of the woods to the east and rushed across the open ground towards the slopes of Orphanage Hill screaming their battle cries of 'Urrah!', their breath hot with a double ration of vodka gulped down as they waited on their start lines. But the Flemish stood their ground and poured fire into the ranks of Red Army soldiers, mowing them down in their hundreds. The churned up ground was soon littered with corpses and the wounded as each fresh attack was thrown back. As each assault failed the Soviets responded by plastering the area with ever more high explosive in an attempt to literally blow the stubborn defenders away, and although it did indeed grind the Flemings down, its greatest impact was on the poor Russian injured left on the field, who had no chance of survival but had to lie there and wait to be killed by their own guns.

To the east the city of Narva was still burning. The ancient Hermannsburg Fortress of the Teutonic Knights on the western bank of the river was in ruins, as was its Tsarist counter-part Ivangorod on the eastern shore, but even through the flames the Red Army was able to continue pouring men and material over hastily erected combat bridges to fling at the dwindling numbers of men facing them in the Tannenberg Line. At this time of the summer, just as the nights were short the days were long and there was no let up for the Flemings that endless Thursday afternoon, as the sun beat down on the square kilometre of land that had become their world.

Grootaer's PAK was the lynchpin of the defence. Using *Sprenggranaten* (anti-personnel high explosive shells packed with shrapnel) against the Red Army infantry and anti-tank guns in the woods the lone Flemish cannon wreaked havoc in the enemy ranks, and whenever Soviet T-34s massed for an assault the PAK switched to *Panzergranaten* (armour piercing rounds) and flung shell after shell into their turrets, smashing them to scrap metal. But the odds began to tell as the afternoon became early evening. The Russians were able to call on a constant stream of reinforcements whereas the Flemings had no reserves and received only intermittent support from the rest of the hard-pressed Corps. Steiner himself rang D'Haese:

> You have all done more than your duty with this defence. I know of the hellish barrage of fire and the bombing your unit has endured, and it isn't over yet, the Flemings must continue to hold. (From Allen Brandt, *The Last Knight of Flanders*, Schiffer Publishing, 1998)

And hold they did, although at a growing cost in lives, especially among the Kampfgruppe's leaders. As the afternoon wore on officer after officer

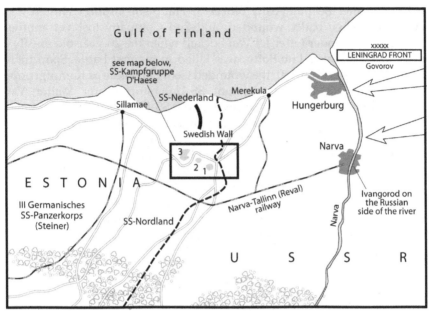

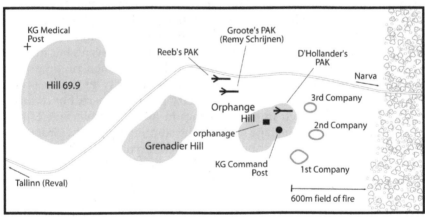

SS-Kampfgruppe D'Haese, 25–29 July 1944:
Battle of the European SS at Narva, Estonia

- - - German frontline, 25 July 1944

forest

fell. The former Belgian Army officer SS-Hauptsturmführer Hutten was evacuated when badly wounded, and 2nd Company lost yet another platoon commander (after Jef Van Bockel) when the 20-year-old ex-VNV man, SS-Oberjunker Luc Bottu, was killed in his first battle. Soon there were only four officers left; the wounded Georg D'Haese as Kampfgruppe Commander, his Flemish adjutant SS-Untersturmführer Walter Van Leemputten, Shrijnen's platoon commander SS-Untersturmführer Marcel Laperre and the young SS-Oberjunker Roger Groenvinck who had started as a platoon commander in 1st Company and was now the Company Commander after Frans Swinnen's death. Now, for the very first time in more than two-and-a-half years of Flemish involvement on the Eastern Front, their combat formation fighting in the line was not only manned overwhelmingly by Flemings, but they were being led by an officer cadre that was totally Flemish and with a Flemish officer in overall command. Germans were now a tiny minority in Kampfgruppe D'Haese.

The front fractures

With Flemish casualties rising the Red Army tried again to break the line and sent in an overwhelming mass of tanks and infantry in yet another attack. This time the hugely outnumbered Flemings could not hold and the Soviet tide swept over Orphanage Hill killing as it went, but miraculously the clash did not end in a rout, with the SS men running west towards safety. D'Haese managed to pull the majority of the survivors back onto Grenadier Hill to their secondary positions there, but as many as 60 Flemings were left in their trenches in front of Orphanage Hill or in the bombed-out orphanage itself on the summit. Critically, Grootaer's PAK stayed put just to the north. There were no officers left with these men, just a scattering of NCOs. The bulk of the Kampfgruppe now situated on Grenadier Hill acted as a blocking force preventing the Soviets from breaking out to the west, while the cut-off Flemings continued to fight and actively disrupt the Russians from trying to build up for an attack on Grenadier Hill. Surrounded by Russian infantry those few dozen Flemish SS men spat defiance and carried on killing everything that came into the range of their guns. This was the true test of a veteran unit and the men in it, the ability of the soldier to fight independently and defy the odds, to not give up but to keep on hitting and hitting hard; without them the Wehrmacht would be finished. As Paul Carrell wrote in his celebrated work on the war on the Eastern Front:

...these were the men who tackled the situations which were frequently critical for entire combat groups or divisions ... it produced that tough, patiently suffering, self-reliant, and enterprising individual fighter without whom the German armies in the East could not have survived. (From Paul Carrell, *Hitler's War on Russia*, Corgi, 1966)

Having organised the defence on Grenadier Hill, D'Haese gathered about thirty volunteers together and led them back towards Orphanage Hill to bring back their cut-off comrades. Several Sturmgeschütze from the Nordland supported the move but the Russians were determined to stop it and laid down a wall of fire in between D'Haese's relief force and the orphanage. Soon the only way forward was crawling on their bellies but even that became impossible. Just a few hundred yards short of their friends they realised there was no way on and D'Haese reluctantly called off the attempt. One further effort was made that night, with Steiner's express permission, and this time the Flemings were reinforced by some Estonians from the 20th SS Division who were also helping them defend Grenadier Hill. D'Haese led them forward again but after two hours of fighting they were no nearer their goal and, dispirited, the troops headed back and the breakthrough was cancelled. The Flemings in the orphanage now knew they were alone and they would not be rescued. They fought on, their numbers dwindling as high explosive, shrapnel and bullets took their toll and killed man after man. The rest of the Kampfgruppe listened as the firing from the orphanage gradually faded through the night, until all went silent near dawn. None of them made it back to Grenadier Hill; they were wiped out to the last man.

Friday 28 July 1944: Day 3

The Red Army had so far failed to achieve a decisive breakthrough but the commander of the 3rd Baltic Front, General Govorov, knew that if he could retain and reinforce Orphanage Hill, and then push over Grenadier and finally 69.9 Hill then he would be through the Tannenberg Line and could finish off Steiner's III (germanisches) SS Panzer Corps. He could then turn south and threaten the rest of Army Group North with destruction. For both sides, the stakes were tremendously high. Through the ruins of Narva city and Hungerburg to the north Govorov concentrated 11 of his infantry divisions and all six of his tank brigades against the weakened formations of Steiner's Corps. Even at the beginning of the fighting less than a week before the Corps's four divisions and one brigade were nowhere near full strength, but now after days of violent slaughter on both sides the Waffen-SS units were lucky to be at even half strength.

The day began as the last two had, with constant Red airforce attacks and no sign of the Luftwaffe. Everything that moved was strafed and bombs rained down on anything that looked like a target to the Russian pilots. As ever, the Soviet artillery was busy, walking curtains of high explosive backwards and forwards over the by-now desolate landscape. To add to the maelstrom, Soviet naval vessels off the coast began to bring down their own guns' fire onto the defenders, and ships' guns are very large and pack a mighty punch. There was no sign of the Kriegsmarine.

The defenders were now in a pitiful state. Exhausted after more than 48 hours of combat with only a few minutes sleep snatched here and there, their senses numbed by the constant bombardment and deafening noise, and with no hot food brought up since the first night, the men of Kampfgruppe D'Haese were nearing the end of their endurance. But it wasn't over yet.

The 10am attack

At 1000 hours the Flemings were alerted by the sound of tank engines warming up in the woods to the east. Although they could not be seen, the freiwillige knew that also in there in cover the Soviet infantry were moving from their assembly areas to their start lines. Sure enough, the barrage lifted and a tremendous wave of Russian tanks and infantry charged out of the east towards the miserably few Flemish and Estonian defenders. Steiner had concentrated all of his artillery together so it could focus its fire on specific points at decisive times; now was one of those times and the German artillery was called down and wreaked havoc amongst the brown-smocked Russian infantry. Russian tanks were hit too, and, of course, Grootaer's PAK kept on firing. At the lone gun Schrijnen was wounded in the shoulder by shrapnel and Grootaer decided to go and get help for his gunner. Leapfrogging from shellhole to shellhole, Grootaer worked his way back to the Kampfgruppe headquarters bunker to collect a medic, and then headed off back to the PAK position. Metres short of the gun, a Russian naval shell burst close by and he was killed instantly, along with the medic and several other volunteers. Schrijnen was also wounded in the blast and took some shrapnel in the face. Of the three original anti-tank gun commanders, Bert D'Hollander and Jef Grootaer were now dead and Eduard Reeb was fighting for his life in an infantry company. Their platoon commander, the young SS-Untersturmführer Marcel Laperre, was one of only four officers left in the whole Kampfgruppe and was fighting with D'Haese to try and hold the line. The lone 75mm PAK was the cornerstone of the Flemish defence and it was now all down to the young SS-Sturmmann Remy Schrijnen as its gunner.

Despite its overwhelming force the Russian attack was thrown back in disarray and a further four T-34s were left burning in front of Schrijnen's PAK. More assaults came in as the day wore on and again and again it was the high explosive *Sprenggranaten* from Schrijnen's gun that made the difference, as shell after shell burst amidst the assaulting infantry, cutting down men in their hundreds. After one such attack Schrijnen decided for no apparent reason to abandon the *Kopfstellung* position he had held for the last two-and-a-half days and move the gun some 500 metres to the left. No sooner had the move been made than a Russian naval shell landed exactly on the old site. If they had not moved the gun, the crew would have been blown to pieces and the defence would have been effectively over. As it was, Schrijnen's old comrades from the Legion, Leo Tollenaere, Fons Van Broeck and Juul Fieremans, kept on going back and forth to the rear to bring up ammunition for the gun and keep it firing. But for how much longer?

Where Knights Crosses grow

The battle was now coming to its climax. Almost three-quarters of the original Flemish Kampfgruppe of less than 500 men were out of action, either dead or badly injured. A lot of those left in the line, like D'Haese and Schrijnen, were wounded and Soviet pressure was unrelenting. With the Flemish perimeter shrinking minute by minute, D'Haese ordered another withdrawal to the west and Laperre ran to the PAK to relay the news to the crew. All of the gun team grabbed their kit with relief, ready to follow Laperre; all that is except Remy Schrijnen. 'I am staying here until I'm finished', those were his words to a shocked Laperre, who repeated his order and threatened Schrijnen with a court-martial if he did not obey. The diminutive gunner just shrugged his shoulders and stayed put. Shells were exploding all around the position and small-arms fire rattled on the protective shield of the gun as Soviet infantry pressed ever closer. There was no time to argue. Laperre gathered the rest of the crew and led them away from the gun. All of them were thinking the same thing as they headed west: 'That's the last time that any of us will see SS-Sturmmann Remy Schrijnen alive'.

The Russians were determined to prove the gun crew right and assembled one last attack that they hoped would at last sweep the stubborn Flemish defenders away. A massive force of 30 T-34s, mounted with the latest 85mm guns, plus the accompanying infantry, were gathered for the final effort of the day. To make sure of success, four of the new super-heavy Joseph Stalin tanks were added to the assault force. This tank was the Soviet response to the German Tiger tank and boasted a huge 122mm main gun and immensely thick sloped armour. The Russians were convinced that this time they would succeed and break through, victory was in sight at last.

As the tanks rolled towards his position, Schrijnen calmly sat and followed the lead T-34 through the gun's optic. He fired, the PAK's breech block leapt back with the recoil, and he raced to reload with a second anti-tank *Panzergranate* shell as quickly as possible. The first round slammed into the lead T-34, which burst into flames and ground to a halt. The rest of the advancing tanks swung their turrets towards the danger that they thought had been eliminated and as one they began to converge on the lone gun, intent on knocking it out.

In addition to imminent death, Schrijnen now met with another potential catastrophe. Having fired hundreds of rounds over the last few days the PAK's barrel and firing mechanism were caked with shell residue, gun grease and grime, and this made the spent shell case stick in the breech block. It had to be removed so that the PAK could be reloaded and reloaded fast, if not the Soviet tanks would roll over Schrijnen and his gun and that would be that. Taking the barrel poker, Schrijnen ran out from behind the gun's protective shield to the muzzle, turned his back on the mass of tanks bearing down on him and rammed the poker down the barrel to push out the shell case. He then ran back to the breech and loaded a *Panzergranate* round. Taking quick aim he fired, loaded, fired, loaded and carried on firing and loading as fast as he could in a desperate attempt to keep the tanks at bay. At that close range, even the mighty Joseph Stalin tanks had no protection against the high velocity rounds streaking towards them and were ripped apart. As the tanks charged forward they fired their main guns and machine-guns at the PAK in a World War II parody of giants duelling; but without the benefit of stabilised guns that allow modern tanks to fire accurately and move at the same time, they were unable to silence the lone Fleming. Amidst the smoke and belching fire, tank after tank was blown to pieces until at the last one of the behemoths came within yards of Schrijnen's gun and both it and the PAK fired at each other simultaneously. The Soviet machine was ripped open like a tin can, while the anti-tank gun took a direct hit and was wrecked. Remy Schrijnen himself was caught in the blast, badly wounded and knocked unconcious, and was thrown some 20 metres from the gun pit by the force of the explosion.

His battle was over but his stand had had an extraordinary impact. No less than seven Russian tanks lay smashed in front of his gun barrel, including three of the immensely powerful Joseph Stalin heavy tanks. The rest of the assault wave swept over the position towards Grenadier Hill but it had lost its momentum and punching power and the attack ran out of steam and faltered. The point of the bayonet of the entire third Baltic Front had been blunted by one man and one gun.

Late night counter-attack

With the PAK gun destroyed and the Soviet tank attack stalled, both sides seemed to take a step back and draw breath. But the pause did not last long, as the Wehrmacht's preferred method of defence was attack, attack, attack. Under the command of SS-Sturmbannführer Siegfried Scheibe from the Nederland, a counter-attack was launched by a mixed force of Norwegians, Danes and Flemings to try to retake Orphanage Hill. D'Haese and his Adjutant, Walter Van Leemputten, led the Flemish contingent and the attack itself was preceded by a short artillery barrage to soften up the Soviets, who were still not firmly emplaced on the scarred slopes of Orphanage Hill. But the assault was not strong enough and the Russians deluged the advancing Waffen-SS grenadiers with fire. The counter-attack was ground into mince-meat and the grenadiers tumbled back to their positions on Grenadier Hill. Casualties were heavy, with Scheibe wounded and Van Leemputten hit in the stomach by an exploding bullet. He was dragged back to safety by his men and evacuated but the wound was mortal and the young 29-year-old SS-Untersturmführer, actually born in Putney in London, died in a field hospital a fortnight later, on 15 August. D'Haese was wounded for the second time in the counter-attack but was able to carry on and along with Groevinck and Laperre, he was now one of only three Flemish officers left fighting. The counter-attack had failed to take back Orphanage Hill but had succeeded in throwing the Soviets off balance and winning the few defenders a vital breathing space. There would be no more attacks that night and the dog-tired Flemish were able to grab a couple of hours sleep before dawn broke and brought with it the inevitable Red Army response.

Saturday 29 July 1944: Day 4

Having come so close to victory on the preceding day, Govorov was sure that one final push would see his forces break through the thinning defence and into the rear of Army Group North. Fresh units were pushed over the river and through Narva city into assembly areas short of the three hills. The Red airforce was called into action and multiple sorties were launched against the Waffen-SS positions. Yak fighters strafed everything that moved, whilst squadrons of Stormovik ground-attack aircraft pulverised every discernible feature with rockets and bombs. The ever-superb Red Army artillery then came into play and concentrated the fire of its guns, mortars and 'Stalin's Organ' Katyusha multiple rocket-launchers onto the small sector of front around Grenadier Hill and 69.9 Hill. Grenadier Hill in particular took an extraordinary pounding as the Soviets saw it as the fulcrum of the SS defence and their immediate objective when they began their ground assault. Take Grenadier Hill swiftly, they reasoned, and the attack would gain momentum and sweep over 69.9 Hill. Once that last hill was captured then the defence would be over, with the surviving Waffen-SS men having no chance to halt the Russians on the open ground to the west of the three hills. As fire rained down on the SS grenadiers, endless streams of Soviet infantry filed onto their start lines ready for the order to attack, and more than a hundred tanks from Govorov's independent armoured brigades manoeuvred into position. After more than an hour of intense bombardment, the Red Army officers blew their whistles and the Soviet assault began.

Facing the Russians on this, the fourth consecutive day of the battle, the defensive lines were now held by a motley collection of Danes and Norwegians from the Nordland, Estonians from the 20th SS Division, some hastily scraped together German naval Marines and, of course, D'Haese and his Flemings. The units were hopelessly mixed-up, there was little in the way of coherent command and control, and since the loss of Schrijnen and his PAK, there were no more heavy weapons. There were so few men left now. Those that were still alive hadn't eaten a hot meal in days, they were filthy, unshaven and had only had a few hours sleep. Many of them were wounded but still they refused to give in, still they refused to give way. These survivors were among the cream of Western Europe's contribution to the Waffen-SS during the Second World War and they were not for retreating.

Attack and counter-attack

As the Soviet advance came forward, the wisdom of Steiner's decision to concentrate all of his Corps artillery into one force became evident. With no heavy weapons left in the line, every gun that had a shell was called upon to fire at the mass of armour bearing down on Grenadier Hill. The fire slashed through the ranks of charging infantry and smashed into tanks but still they came on. All the freiwillige had now to stop the tanks were one-shot panzer-fäusts with a range of less than a hundred metres, anti-tank Teller mines and stick grenades bundled together. Fighting soon became hand-to-hand, with soldiers using knives, pistols, grenades and entrenching tools.

Somehow, it was the Germans who found the reserves to swing the battle in their favour. From nowhere SS-Obersturmbannführer Paul-Albert Kausch appeared with the remnants of the Nordland's SS-Panzer Battalion 11 Hermann von Salza. Named after a famous Grand Master of the crusading Teutonic Knights, whose most important fortress was lying in ruins in Narva, the Nordland panzers and Sturmgeschütze tore into the stalled Russian attack. With the weight of their assault broken up by the German artillery, the Soviet machines lacked the cohesion to beat off the aggression of the Nordland counter-attack and excellent SS gunnery soon began to tell, as T-34 after T-34 brewed up. Within minutes, the tide had been turned and the Soviets were in full retreat back to the woods to the east. Kausch did not let them go easily and drove his men after them, shooting up everything they could see.

The aftermath

As the Soviets ran east, chased by the Nordland armour, the battlefield they left behind was strangely quiet and utterly desolate. Realising the fight was lost, the Soviet troops on Orphanage Hill abandoned their hard-won positions and headed after their comrades, but not before shooting any prisoners they had who were were wounded and unable to move.

Kausch's panzer drove by the wreck of Schrijnen's PAK, noting the many destroyed Soviet tanks that lay in front of its muzzle. The crew noticed a movement from a body, stopped the panzer and went outside to investigate. Unbelievably, lying wounded but definitely breathing, was the seemingly indestructible Remy Schrijnen. He was hauled onto the panzer's rear deck and taken back for medical treatment. The twice wounded Georg D'Haese was found, dazed but alive, searching 69.9 Hill for wounded comrades. As for the rest of Kampfgruppe D'Haese, only 37 of the almost 500 original members were left standing, though many of these were lightly wounded. That represents a staggering casualty rate of more than 90% in just four days. The ferocity of the fighting was such that less than 50 Flemings were captured by the Soviets during the entire battle. Of those men, only four would ever make it home, finally being released from Siberian labour camps in May 1962, after 18 years of captivity.

For the Red Army, the battle had been bloody in the extreme. Russian losses totalled 113 tanks lost, plus dozens of anti-tank guns, and thousands of dead. And even more importantly, they had been held and the Ostheer had been given a breathing space. The so-called 'Battle of the European SS' at Narva had lasted several months and the Flemish had only been involved for the last four days, but it was those days that had witnessed the crescendo of the fight and the men from the Langemarck had played their full part. With the Soviet failure to take Grenadier Hill, their entire offensive effort in the north failed. While Operation Bagration continued to rip Army Group Centre to pieces and Army Group North Ukraine (the old Army Group South) was pushed out of Soviet Russia and into Eastern Europe and the Balkans, in the north the front, temporarily, stabilised.

The Commander of the Wehrmacht's Eighteenth Army and an old friend of the Flemish from the SS-Legion Flandern days outside Leningrad, General Georg Lindemann, described the battle of Narva – and Steiner's leadership in particular – as:

> ...a defensive success for the whole Eastern Front ... holding off eleven divisions and six tank units of the Soviet 2nd Shock and 8th Armies with his weakened two divisions and single brigade.

It was General Georg Lindemann who had made the first ever award of the Iron Cross 1st Class to a Fleming, to Jules Geurts, back in Raglitza.

Names to remember

For Georg D'Haese the battle at Narva was a hard-won triumph. He had risen through the ranks from his days as a young volunteer in the SS-Legion Flandern, being wounded regularly and heaped with awards for bravery. Commanding the Flemish Kampfgruppe after Rehmann's dismissal was the pinnacle of his career during the War. Following the battle, command of the Flemish would revert to Germans for the rest of the conflict, making D'Haese the first and last Flemish field commander. Still recovering from his wounds he led the pathetic remnants of his men to the Corps Headquarters at Toila to rest and act as coastal guards. There, Steiner himself pinned his own German Cross in Gold on the young Flemish officer and handed out medals by the sack load to the survivors. In the end Steiner did not follow through with the award and unaccountably D'Haese was only awarded the Iron Cross 1st Class for his contribution at Narva. There have always been rumours that he was only denied the coveted Knights Cross because of his well-known membership of the VNV and his championing of the cause of Flemish nationalism. I have found no written evidence to substantiate these claims, and suspect that it was more likely to be down to the chaos of the time, but no matter the reason, it was from the German point of view an ignominious omission.

Strangely enough, D'Haese himself said after the war that in his opinion the battles in the Ukraine in the winter of 1943-1944 were the toughest he ever fought in and actually harder than Narva. Whatever the relative rigours of the two, the Flemish were now rightly seen as first-rate troops capable of holding their own in the hardest battles in the East. As the front settled down, there were several further Soviet attacks but they were half-hearted and gained no ground. The few Flemings were rotated back into the line over the next couple of weeks and then back out again and in that time Rehmann arrived to take up his former post. How he was viewed by the Narva survivors can only be surmised. Officers have to fight to earn respect in any army, and the Waffen-SS was no different. A man who is viewed as using a dubious wound to leave his men in the lurch is marked forever, there is no going back. Yet Rehmann would continue to serve with the Flemings for the rest of the war as a battalion commander, until being wounded again in the fighting in Pomerania in early 1945.

For Remy Schrijnen, Narva brought glory. On 1 August 1944 he was awarded the Iron Cross 1st Class and the Wound Badge in Gold, trumped when the Corps Commander, Felix Steiner himself, recommended he be admitted to the prestigious Honour Roll of the Wehrmacht. On submission of his citation, higher SS authorities decided that a Knights Cross was more appropriate, and on confirmation Schrijnen became the only Flemish recipient of Germany's highest award for courage to serve in the Langemarck. Further accolades followed as he was promoted directly from

SS-Sturmmann to SS-Unterscharführer, skipping over the SS-Rottenführer rank entirely. He was sent on a tour of Flanders and Flemish gatherings in Germany to drum up support and volunteers to serve at the front. He was even recommended for officer training at the elite Bad Tölz Academy but this he turned down, with Himmler himself unable to change his mind, despite a personal interview in Berlin. In fact, Schrijnen proved a bit of a disappointment for his German 'handlers' following his award, stubbornly refusing to do anything that he disapproved of and speaking his mind. He would not exhort youngsters in Flanders, or Flemings anywhere for that matter, to join up, insisting it was a personal matter, and even going so far as reminding the head of DeVlag, Jef Van De Wiele, that he was a VNV supporter! But heroes can get away with a lot and Schrijnen was now up there among the freiwillige stars along with the Dutchman Gerardus Mooyman, the Estonian Haralt Nugiseks, and the Dane Egon Christophersen.

During his tour an old shrapnel injury to his back flared up and had to be treated. Christmas 1944 was spent recuperating and finally Schrijnen rejoined his comrades in the newly-reformed Langemarck in February 1945. His war was not yet over.

X

Last Throw of the Dice: The Formation of the SS-Langemarck Division

The collapse and near extinction of Army Group Centre during the Red Army's Operation Bagration offensive necessitated the stripping of forces by OKW from other sectors in an attempt to shore up the frontline. For Army Group North this meant the loss of some of their best formations to their neighbouring Army Group, and a complete rethink of their strategy in containing the Red Army in the north. Govorov had failed at Narva but had succeeded in forcing Finland out of the war, and the Soviets were rapidly getting over being checked by Steiner's Corps and had regrouped, changing their point of attack. They were now aiming at Riga further south and trying to outflank all the German and allied forces to the north. In the light of this offensive the decision was made to abandon Estonia and withdraw westwards into the Courland (Kurland) Peninsula in Latvia. Estonia would then become the first country to be 'liberated' by the Red Army, although the term 'liberated' is laughably inappropriate, given the barbarity and oppression of Soviet rule. The Estonians were merely exchanging one appalling dictatorship for another.

D'Haese and his Flemings retreated westwards with the rest of the III (germanisches) SS Panzer Corp, which was slated to be the centre of the new defensive line on the Peninsula established by mid-September. The retreat was relatively uneventful, with the Soviets' offensive focus in the south. On arrival the Flemish were quickly withdrawn by the steamship *Gottland* from the port of Reval (modern-day Tallinn) across the Gulf of Riga to Swinemüde in Pomerania. Many wounded men had recovered and rejoined Kampfgruppe D'Haese in the two months since Narva, and the Flemish were back up to a strength of some 130 men as they disembarked on German soil. In their absence at the front much had been happening and the formation they came back to was a very different beast from the one they had left. No more an SS-Sturmbrigade, the Flemish were going to be nothing less than a fully-fledged Waffen-SS division!

Belgium liberated!

Between D-Day on 6 June 1944 and the beginning of November the Wehrmacht in the West lost over half a million men, and over a million in the East. Their shattered forces retreated punch-drunk. First France was liberated, and then on 3 September 1944 the British 2nd Army entered Brussels. Most of the country was left undefended by the retreating Germans and was freed within a week. Antwerp, the heartland of Flemish nationalism, fell the day after Brussels but its use to the Allies as a port would have to wait until the Germans had been cleared from the Scheldt estuary, at a cost to the Allies of over 6,000 mainly Canadian lives and several months of effort. The Higher SS and Police Leader in Belgium, SS Gruppenführer Richard Jungclaus, amalgamated the remnants of Jef François's Flemish SS and the more militant members of Jef Van De Wiele's DeVlag into a 2,500 strong Sicherheitskorps (Security Corps), one battalion of which fought with the German defenders of the Scheldt Estuary against the Canadians. This was the only recorded time that Flemish collaborators fought the Western Allies.

Post-Falaise, most of the Flemings who were working with the Germans in some capacity knew it was only a matter of time before the Allies threw the Germans out of Belgium. The change of adminstration by the Nazis – they announced that Belgium would no longer be ruled by a Military Governorship but would become a more privilieged Reichscommisariat (under the leadership of the Cologne-Aachen Gauleiter Josef Grohe) like Norway and Denmark – fooled no-one; particularly when von Falkenhausen himself was arrested by the Gestapo and implicated in the July 20 Bomb Plot on Hitler's life.

In Walloonia to the south all those who were deemed collaborators by their fellow-countrymen began to pack up and leave. To the north in the Netherlands the Nazis raised another Dutch SS division, the 34th SS-Freiwilligen Division Landstorm Nederland, from local paramilitaries in a desperate attempt to stave off their inevitable defeat. Indeed the SS-Legion Flandern's first German commander, the haughty Michael Lippert, would re-appear as the commanding officer of SS-Freiwilligen Grenadier Regiment 83 of the Landstorm Nederland and would end his war after desolutory resistance from the new formation, one of the only Waffen-SS foreign formations to ever fight against the Western Allies. In Flanders, after nearly four and a half years of occupation, local collaborators reacted as did their erstwhile comrades in France and Walloonia. They fled with their families to avoid the inevitably bloody retribution of their fellow citizens.

Collection point at Soltau

The VNV collapsed during the exodus but did not move to Nazi Germany to re-establish itself. Those organisations that did flee included most of the Sicherheitskorps, composed of Jef François's Flemish SS and Jef Van De Wiele's DeVlag, and the paramilitaries of the Vlaamsche Wacht and the Landesdienst. Although many of these latter were lukewarm converts to the Nazi cause at best and were given little option by the departing Germans but to accompany them. The number of Flemish refugees totalled tens of thousands. They arrived within the borders of Germany bedraggled, tired and confused. The Nazis, efficient as ever, designated a series of collection points for the different nationalities, be it French, Walloon, Flemish or Dutch, mostly located in Würrtemburg in the south and Westphalia in the north. The Flemish were billeted in and around the northwestern German town of Soltau, halfway between Hannover and Hamburg, and near the *Lüneburger Heide* (the Lüneburg Heath) military training area. (This whole area will be well known to any post-war British Army soldier as it is the heartland sector of the British Army on the Rhine.) Among the tide of refugees there were large numbers of able-bodied men with varying levels of military experience and commitment. In the weeks after the exodus from Flanders around 2,000 men had come forward to the authorities expressing a desire to volunteer for the Waffen-SS. Even though conditions for the Flemings and their families were cramped and food was pretty scarce, it was clear that they had nothing to go back to in Flanders. Back in Belgium one of the very first acts of the new administration post-liberation was to deprive all those who had fled to Germany, or who wore German uniform, of their Belgian citizenship. Tens of thousands of Flemish and Walloon men, women and children were now all officially 'stateless', including those still fighting on the Eastern Front.

The 27th SS-Freiwilligen Grenadier Division Langemarck (flämische Nr.1)

In this last phase of the war, as the Third Reich began to crumble to dust, there was an explosion in the number of Waffen-SS formations established. The Wehrmacht had always held Himmler's ambitions for the growth of the Waffen-SS in check and hugely restricted the expansion of his armed cohorts, and Hitler had usually sided with the Heer to avoid upsetting the generals as being the only ones capable of unseating him from power. Now with senior officers by the cartload implicated in the 20 July Bomb Plot, the shackles were off and Hitler, utilising Freisler and his special courts, went all-out to break the power of the officer class and bend it completely to his will. In reality this was a paranoiac effort: the Wehrmacht had sold its soul to the Nazis many years before and there was little appetite among the services to replace Hitler and seek a negotiated peace.

In this atmosphere, and with the Eastern Front in desperate need of manpower from whatever source, Himmler and Berger now had no curbs in their drive to expand the Waffen-SS. Out of the window went the last vestiges of the 'Aryan purity' requirements that had dictated recruitment for so long, and even the 'volunteer' concept itself, as conscription and compulsory transfer were introduced wholesale. New divisions sprung up almost overnight. Some would fight well and create names for themselves but most would end up as rumps, with divisional stature solely on paper, and would quickly disappear in the bloody slaughter against the Red Army. It was reasoned that those formations that had fought well as SS-Sturmbrigades could act as the cadres, the *Stamm-Einheiten*, for the creation of a new wave of European volunteer divisions. The influx of large numbers of refugees, following the liberation of their homelands, created pools of potential recruits that Himmler and Berger could ruthlessly exploit as even now they sought to extend their own power and influence. This new initiative saw the creation of a French Waffen-SS grenadier division, the 33rd Charlemagne, a Walloon panzergrenadier division, the 28th Wallonien, and also a new Flemish formation based on the old 6th SS-Sturmbrigade Langemarck. This formation would keep its Langemarck honorific and was given the divisional number 27. Following the battles in the Ukraine in late 1943 and spring 1944 the Sturmbrigade was being reformed in Knovitz in Czechoslovakia as a three-thousand-strong unit of some fourteen companies. Only a small number of these men went with D'Haese to fight at Narva, the rest continued to train at Knovitz until they were ordered to Soltau in the autumn to begin the formation of the new division. The upgrading of the Langemarck from a Sturmbrigade to a Division was now SS policy, so that by direct order from Himmler and the SS-Führungshauptamt the 27th SS-Freiwilligen Grenadier Division Langemarck (flämische Nr.1) was officially created on 18 October 1944.

Thomas 'Cigars' Müller

Although he was now fully recovered from losing his finger in the Ukraine and was reunited with his men, Schellong, as an SS-Obersturmbannführer, was still too junior to command a division. He would lead one of its regiments, in British Army terms a brigade, but divisional command would rest with a new appointee, SS-Standartenführer Thomas Müller. Müller was a very experienced commander, having served on both the eastern and western fronts. He had first come to prominence as the commander of the 20th SS-Panzergrenadier Regiment in the elite 9th SS Panzer Division Hohenstaufen during the division's coming of age in the Ukraine, where he encountered the Flemings during the fighting to relieve the Kamenets-Podolsk Pocket in early 1944. He then went with the Hohenstaufen to Normandy to combat the Allied invasion and actually took over command of the formation from Willi Bittrich when he was shunted up to lead both the Hohenstaufen and Frundsberg in the II SS Panzer Corps. This was an interim measure and his period of tenure only lasted from June 29 to July 10 1944. The Hohenstaufen took over 1,200 casualties during this period, defending Caen against the British and Canadians. Following such dramatic losses the Hohenstaufen was withdrawn to rest and refit in the Arnhem area of the Netherlands, where it would be a major player in the failure of Montgomery's Operation Market Garden. Müller himself was given yet another stopgap post in September as commander of the 17th SS Panzergrenadier Division Götz von Berlichingen, the only Waffen-SS division ever to fight exclusively on the Western Front, when its previous commanding officer Eduard Deisenhofer was wounded in action and sent back to Berlin to recover. Müller was quickly replaced by Gustav Mertsch and he was then assigned to Soltau to oversee the raising and deployment of the new Flemish Waffen-SS division. Nicknamed 'Cigars' because he loved them, he was a well respected officer who held both the Iron Cross 1st and 2nd Class as well as the coveted Infantry Assault Badge. He would command the Langemarck Division until the end of the war.

Uniform and insignia

Surprisingly, given the SS obsession with the minutiae of uniforms, there were no huge changes to the already established Sturmbrigade Langemarck uniform and insignia envisaged for the new division. The old debate about the use of the trifos sunwheel emblem or the standard sig runes on the right collar patch was resurrected but caused little excitement and divisional members generally wore what they already had anyway. The cuff title also remained the same.

The recruits

As a newly-recovered Conrad Schellong led his 2,000-plus Langemarck men west from Knovitz to Soltau, Georg D'Haese took his 130 Narva veterans west as well, from Pomerania to the heathland of Westphalia. Given the established strength of a grenadier infantry division was in the region of 15,000 men, it was clear that there was a dire need for a very large number of new recruits if the new division was ever going to be worthy of the name. So where were the recruits to come from?

As stated earlier, some 2,000 men from among the Flemish exiles, with a variety of backgrounds, had already come forward voluntarily since the liberation of Belgium. A further 3,000 men would come from the paramilitary Vlaamsche Wacht. This organisation was a guard unit originally established and run by the VNV to assist the police in keeping order. They also physically guarded German installations as well as the railways and the SD Headquarters in Brussels. At its peak, it consisted of four battalions based in Ghent, Antwerp, Oudenarde and Brussels, with a strength of around 4,000 men in total. Poorly armed and trained, the Vlaamsche Wacht was told following D-Day that it would fight alongside the Wehrmacht in resisting the Allies, but in reality the majority of its members fled to Soltau, where most of them ended up in the Langemarck.

The Kriegsmarine had been officially recruiting Flemings since July 1943 and as many as 500 volunteered, mainly to serve in U-boats or E-boats, but with no more ships to serve on they were transferred to the new division en masse. Numerically, the civilian worker Todt Organisation, including the 4–5,000 Flemish members of its armed protection corps, the OT Schutzkommando, was a potentially huge source and they were actively trawled for volunteers, as was the 300 or so strong teenage uniformed agricultural Landdienst. A general recruiting drive among the 300,000 Flemish workers in Germany was also carried out and yielded some results. The Langemarck's replacement depot and units were combed for men and the NSKK's contingent of over 4,000 Flemings was also targeted as a recruitment pool. However, among this flurry of activity the most controversial and ultimately tragic source of recruits was the Flemish Hitler Youth.

Before the war Hitler Youth groups had been organised in Flanders for the sons of expatriate German parents, while Flemish youngsters could join a plethora of local paramilitary youth groups including Dinaso's *Jong-Dinaso*, the rightwing *Algemeen Vlaamsch Nationaal Jeugverbond* (General Union of Flemish Nationalist Youth) or the VNV's own *Nationaal-Socialistische Jeugd Verbond* (National Socialist Youth Union). With the forced amalgamation of all political parties into the VNV in 1941, all youth movements were likewise brought together, all that is except DeVlag's, which remained independent. Van De Wiele then voluntarily merged his organisation's youth wing with the German Hitler Youth in November 1943, a path the VNV pointedly refused to follow. They did, however, allow youngsters to join the *Kadettenkorps*, also called the *Jongerenkorps*, to assist the Luftwaffe as FLAK helpers but instead of then encouraging these teenagers to join the Waffen-SS, the VNV's leader, Dr Elias, urged them to enlist in the Luftwaffe and so avoid service in the Langemarck. Never one to give up easily, Berger then began a programme encouraging these 16- and 17-year-olds to go to the so-called Hitler Youth *Wehrertüchtigungslagern*, literally 'toughening-up camps', where, away from their parents watchful gaze, they were pressured to enlist. Many did and an entire battalion was formed for the Langemarck from these boys, many with their heads stuffed full of dreams of glory. Kept together, they formed the I. SS-Grenadier Regiment

68 of the new division, their battalion commander being the decorated Danish volunteer, SS-Sturmbannführer Oluf von Krabbe. Little did they know the horrors that awaited them on the Eastern Front.

There was even talk of transferring those Flemings already serving in other Waffen-SS formations, such as the Wiking, Das Reich and Leibstandarte Adolf Hitler, over to the new unit but at this stage of the War there was never any real chance of those divisions giving up any of their members when they desperately needed every man they had. By the end of the war there would be, besides Remy Schrijnen, two Flemings (or rather more accurately two men who had been born in Flanders) who would also win the Knights Cross for bravery, one with the Leibstandarte Adolf Hitler and one with a Latvian Waffen-SS division, and both these units naturally wanted to keep soldiers of such calibre (see Chapter XII).

The end result was that on paper the new division stood at an impressive strength of some 18,000 men. In reality many of these 'willing volunteers' were nothing of the sort and had little appetite for the desperate fights to come. While there were indeed some among this new influx who sincerely wished to join the new Langemarck division and fight the advancing communist threat, the majority of these men were pretty much press-ganged into joining, and with little or no prior military training or experience they would be of limited value at the front.

To turn such a motley collection of men into a capable unit was a task that required two things above all: time to train and experienced leadership at all levels. As with so many of Himmler's formations created in the closing stages of the war, the Langemarck Division would have neither. With the Red Army and the Western Allies approaching ever nearer, it was clear that training time was fast running out, every man was needed at the front, ready or not. As for leaders they were and are essential for any fighting unit. Given enough of them even poorly trained and inexperienced troops can accomplish amazing things, but in the autumn of 1944 combat leaders were in ever dwindling supply in Nazi Germany. For instance, the average number of officers to fulfil a divisional establishment in either the Heer or Waffen-SS at the time was between 342 and 387 (the Leibstandarte SS Adolf Hitler was a notable exception, having an astonishing 678 officers in 1943!). Even with Himmler and Berger's reforms to the Waffen-SS recruitment and training regime and the institution of specific freiwillige officer courses at Bad Tölz in particular, there was never any hope of finding this many qualified leaders. When the SS-Sturmbrigade Langemarck had gone into action in the Ukraine in 1943 it had had only 42 officers, 20 under strength even then, and with casualty rates being so high the new Flemish Langemarck Division would be lucky to have a quarter of the number of well-trained officers needed to make the formation truly combat-effective. (The Flemish actually lost a Sturmbrigade veteran officer when SS-Untersturmführer Tony Combert went over to the newly-created

Wallonien as an aide to Degrelle himself. Combert was a Flemish Rexist like Paul Suys and decided to switch units to follow his old allegiances.)

The equipment

The new division was established as a grenadier formation with a divisional headquarters, three grenadier infantry regiments of two and not the more usual three or four battalions each, a panzerjäger anti-tank battalion, an artillery regiment, a combat engineer battalion and supporting elements including a supply regiment and a signals battalion. The headquarters would also comprise up to two elite grenadier battalions, an infantry gun company, a FLAK company, its own panzerjäger anti-tank company and crucially, a company of Sturmgeschütz self-propelled assault guns as an integral armour component. While being equipped at this level would not raise the division to the exalted heights of the Waffen-SS elite formations such as the Das Reich and Wiking, it would at least mean the formation would be of significant use at the front. However, in the Germany of autumn 1944 there was very little hope of equipment being provided even to this limited extent. Heavy equipment was at a premium and shortfalls, particularly in anti-tank capability, were met by the ready supply of the ubiquitous panzerfäust.

Along with the questionable quality of much of the manpower for the new formation this meant that from the very start it was clear that the Waffen-SS Langemarck Division was not going to create a step change in the Flemish contribution to the German war effort. This said, with the veterans of Leningrad, the Volkhov, Krasny-Bor and the Narva being brought together for their swansong, neither would they go down easy. The Flemings' war was not over.

Divisional Order of Battle

The proposed order of battle for the Langemarck was as follows:

• Divisionsstab (Divisional Staff and Headquarters)

Division Commander	SS-Standartenführer Thomas Müller (German)
Adjutant	SS-Obersturmführer Friedrich Seidel (German)
Chief of Staff	SS-Sturmbannführer Heinz Hufenbach (German, in post from November 1944)
Quartermaster	SS-Sturmbannführer Kurt Willamowski (German)

Feldpost Number 44853

• SS-Grenadier Regiment 66; comprising
I./SS-Grenadier Regiment 66 (each battalion had four companies)
II./SS-Grenadier Regiment 66

Regimental Commander	SS-Obersturmbannführer Conrad Schellong

Feldpost Numbers: Staff 04206, 1st Battalion 64485A-D, 2nd Battalion 17662A-D

• SS-Grenadier Regiment 67; comprising
I./SS-Grenadier Regiment 67
II./SS-Grenadier Regiment 67

Regimental Commander	SS-Sturmbannführer Otton Hansmann (German)

Feldpost Numbers: Staff 05294, 1st Battalion 34695A-D, 2nd Battalion 07073A-D

• SS-Grenadier Regiment 68; comprising
I./SS-Grenadier Regiment 68 (this battalion was mainly made up of the youths from the Flemish Hitler Youth and the 'toughening-up' camps)
II./SS-Grenadier Regiment 68

Regimental Commander	SS-Hauptsturmführer Hans Stange (German)

Feldpost Numbers: Staff 64712, 1st Battalion 04336A-D, 2nd Battalion 65078A-D

SS-Artillerie-Regiment 27	(equipped with 8 mortars and 4 infantry guns)
Regimental Commander	SS-Obersturmbannführer Holger Arentoft (German)

Feldpost Number: Staff 05814

SS-Panzerjäger Abteilung 27	(anti-tank battalion equipped with a handful of PAK guns supplemented by an establishment of 72 panzerfäusts)
Battalion Commander	SS-Hauptsturmführer Ekkehard Wangemann (German)

SS-Nachrichten Abteilung 27	(Signals Battalion)
Battalion Commander	SS-Hauptsturmführer Karl Kauss (German)

Feldpost Number: 44853

SS-Pionier-Bataillon 27   (Combat engineer battalion)
Battalion Commander   SS-Hauptsturmführer Heinrich Bauch
                                                 (German)
Feldpost Number: 66467

SS-Versorgungs-Regiment 27 (supply regiment)
Regimental Commander   SS-Sturmbannführer Heinrich
                                                 Scheingräber (German)
Feldpost Number: 66752

It was also intended that there be a field replacement battalion, SS-Feldersatz-Bataillon 27, a medical battalion, SS-Sanitäts-Abteilung 27, and a propaganda company, as divisional units. As can be deduced from the rather junior ranks of the commanders of both the 67 and 68 grenadier regiments it was considered unlikely, even at the unit's inception, that these sub-units would ever come up to full strength. The other point of note was the dearth of Flemish commanders. This was the opposite from the direction of travel over the preceding two years, when Flemings had been increasingly promoted to fill command appointments, but now, at the very culmination of the Flemish Waffen-SS experience in the war, German command reasserted itself.

The Flemish and the Battle of the Bulge

As the Germans launched their last throw of the dice in the Ardennes Offensive during Christmas 1944, the decision was taken to utilise the fledgling Langemarck Division in the West for the very first time. After the canvassing of senior Flemish leaders in the exile community however, it was decided by the OKW that theirs was not to be a combat role, but one designed purely for propaganda purposes alongside their Walloon SS comrades in the 28th SS-Freiwilligen Panzergrenadier Division Wallonien (wallonien Nr.1). The Walloons and Flemings were not to end up fighting Americans. The idea was that the two new formations would be attached to Sepp Dietrich's Sixth SS Panzer Army and follow up behind the advancing Germans to re-enter their own homelands presumably to wide acclaim and fanfare. They would then re-establish pro-German administrations and actively recruit further local volunteers for their ranks.

So it was that on Christmas Eve 1944 the SS Langemarck Division left Soltau for the border Eifel region. Attached to them was a so-called 'Ministerial Company' of Flemish civilians intended to become the new civilian adminstrators of newly-recaptured Flanders. The optimism is amazing! After a few days of the new offensive it became apparent that the Ardennes attack was faltering and that Hitler's last gamble had failed.

With no hope of moving back into Flanders the crestfallen Langemarck was sent back to its base in Soltau to continue work-up training. It was decided that a kampfgruppe should be left in the Eifel just in case the offensive did create a breakthrough and the original mission could be accomplished. Given the parlous state of training of most of the division, only the most battleworthy elements of the still-forming unit would constitute the kampfgruppe, and this meant mainly Schellong's Sturmbrigade Langemarck men from Knovitz and D'Haese's Narva veterans. Thomas Müller would continue as divisional commander back in Soltau, but the Flemings' combat leader at the front would once again be Conrad Schellong, this time as head of Kampfgruppe Schellong.

Order of battle and command roster for KG Schellong

The most experienced and combat-ready men were concentrated in the 1st Battalions of both SS-Grenadier Regiments 66 and 67, Wangemann's panzerjäger battalion and in the divisional headquarters attached units. It was these sub-units that were detached from the division and put under Schellong's command.

The official order of battle for Kampfgruppe Schellong, also confusingly called KG Langemarck throughout its brief history, was as follows:

- Stab der Kampfgruppe (Battlegroup Headquarters)

Kamfgruppe Commander   SS-Obersturmbannführer Conrad Schellong (German)

Adjutant   SS-Obersturmführer Wilhelm Teichert (German, ex-Adjutant from the Sturmbrigade Langemarck)

- Stab Kompanie (headquarters company)

Commander   SS-Untersturmführer Rudolf Six (German, ex-Sturmbrigade – killed in action May 1945)

Motorcycle dispatch rider platoon   SS-Oberscharführer Fritz Taktasch (German, ex-Sturmbrigade)

- I./SS-Frw.-Grenadier Regiment 67   1st Battalion 'Rehmann'

Battalion Commander   SS-Hauptsturmführer Wilhelm Rehmann (German, of Narva infamy, wounded on 17 February 1945 in Pomerania and didn't return to the Langemarck)

Adjutant   SS-Untersturmfuhrer Jack Delbaere
                                 (Flemish, ex-platoon commander 4th
                                 Heavy Weapons Company SS-Legion
                                 Flandern and Company Commander 9th
                                 Company, 2nd Battalion SS-Sturmbrigade)

• 1. Kompanie   (1st Company -infantry)
Company Commander   SS-Untersturmführer Bauwens (German,
                                 later replaced by the Flemish
                                 SS-Unterstürmfuhrer Ferdinand Ghijssen)
1st Platoon Commander   SS-Untersturmführer Paul Verhaegen
                                 (Flemish)
2nd Platoon Commander   unknown
3rd Platoon Commander   unknown

• 2. Kompanie   (2nd Company - infantry)
Company Commander   SS-Untersturmführer Frank Goyvaerts
                                 (Flemish, later replaced by a fellow

   Fleming
                                 SS-Untersturmführer Ferdinand Jacobs)
1st Platoon Commander   SS-Untersturmführer Flor van Eeckhout
                                 (Flemish)
2nd Platoon Commander   unknown
3rd Platoon Commander   unknown

• 3. Kompanie   (3rd Company - infantry)
Company Commander   SS-Untersturmführer Rik de Meester
                                 (Flemish, ex-3rd platoon commander, 3.
                                 Kompanie, Sturmbrigade Langemarck)
1st Platoon Commander   unknown, although there is evidence that
                                 SS-Untersturmführer Paul Verhaegen from
                                 1st Company commanded at some stage)
2nd Platoon Commander   SS-Oberscharführer Korn
3rd Platoon Commander   SS-Oberscharführer Cardoen

• 4. Kompanie   (4th Company - infantry)
Company Commander   SS-Obersturmführer Horst Hinrichs
                                 (German, ex-11th towed artillery

   Company

                                 Sturmbrigade, as an artillery specialist he
                                 was only an interim appointment and was
                                 later replaced by the Flemish Narva
                                 infanty veteran SS-Untersturmführer
                                 Roger Groenvinck)

1st Platoon Commander   unknown
2nd Platoon Commander   unknown
3rd Platoon Commander   unknown

• I./SS-Frw.- Grenadier Regiment 66	2nd Battalion 'Oehms'
Battalion Commander	SS-Sturmbannführer Johannes Oehms (German, newly-promoted, ex-2nd Battalion Commander Sturmbrigade, didn't serve at Narva)
Adjutant	SS-Untersturmführer Ludwig Plabst (German, Oehm's old Adjutant from the Sturmbrigade's 2nd Battalion)
Orderly Officer	SS-Untersturmführer Ferdinand Ghyssen (Flemish, soon moved to command 1st Company of Rehmann's battalion)
• 5. Kompanie	(5th Company – infantry)
Company Commander	SS-Untersturmführer Wilhelm Schaumann (German, originally started with the Flemish as the 10th Marsch Replacement Company Commander before becoming the Commander of the Sturmbrigade's 6th Company, 2nd Battalion)
1st Platoon Commander	SS-Untersturmführer Vik Donkers (Flemish, killed in action, date unknown)
2nd Platoon Commander	SS-Oberscharführer Stadelmann
3rd Platoon Commander	unknown
• 6. Kompanie	(6th Company – infantry)
Company Commander	SS-Untersturmführer Johann Guldentops (Flemish, ex-platoon and company com mander in the Sturmbrigade Langemarck)
1st Platoon Commander	SS-Untersturmführer Ferdinand 'Fons' Jacobs (Flemish, soon moved to command 2nd Company in Rehmann's battalion)
2nd Platoon Commander	SS-Unterscharführer Mannaerts (Flemish)
3rd Platoon Commander	SS-Unterscharführer Winterhaegen (Flemish, later replaced by his fellow Fleming SS-Untersturmfuhrer Claeys)
• 7. Kompanie	(7th Company – infantry)
Company Commander	SS-Untersturmführer Ferdinand 'Nand'

	Laporte (Flemish, ex-Sturmbrigade, killed in action on 17 February 1945, replaced by Frank Goyvaerts from 2nd Company)
1st Platoon Commander	SS-Untersturmführer Jef Marien (Flemish)
2nd Platoon Commander	SS-Oberscharführer Amaat de Vuyst (Flemish)
3rd Platoon Commander	unknown

• 8. Kompanie	(8th Company – infantry)
Company Commander	SS-Obersturmführer Jan Debaere (Flemish)
Platoon Commanders	SS-Untersturmführer Jan Nijs (Flemish, killed in action), SS-Untersturmführer Alfons Bollen (Flemish), SS-Oberscharführer Dingelreiter

• SS-Panzerjäger Abteilung 27	(anti-tank battalion 27)
Commander	SS-Hauptsturmführer Ekkehard Wangemann (German, ex-Nord, Das Reich and 13th SS Handschar Divisions)
Battalion staff	SS-Hauptscharführer Jaus (German), SS-Oberscharführer Jan de Wilde (Flemish),SS-Unterscharführer Igosse (Flemish)

• 1. PAK Kompanie	(anti-tank company)
Commander	SS-Untersturmführer Anton Kotlowski (Austrian, at one point the company was commanded by the German,SS-Obersturmführer, Karl-Heinz Gustavson who was originally a battery commander in the Sturmbrigade's heavy FLAK Company, he later briefly became the Sturmbrigade's 14th Heavy FLAK Company Commander)

Kotlowski's platoon commanders were the German SS-Oberscharführer Dahlhoff and the Flemings SS-Untersturmführers Hugo Mortier and Marcel Laperre.

• 2. FLAK Kompanie	(anti-aircraft company)
Commander	SS-Obersturmführer Xavier Dillinger (German)
Company officer	SS-Untersturmführer Cesar Geerts (Flemish)

- 3. SIG Kompanie   (heavy infantry gun company)
- Commander   SS-Untersturmführer Ernst Fischer (German)
- Company officer   SS-Untersturmführer Meelman (German)

- 4. Stg Kompanie   (Sturmgeschütz tracked self-propelled assault gun company)
- Commander   SS-Obersturmführer Willi Sprenger (German, killed in action on 19 April 1945 and replaced by SS-Untersturmführer August Heyerick)

They numbered just over 2,000 men, equipped with the majority of the heavy weapons the division had managed to get hold of prior to deployment in the Eifel. They were a small minority of the Langemarck's roll call but a clear majority of its combat effectives. These were the *Oostfronters*, the Flemish *frontschwein*, and they still had a chapter to write in the fight in the East.

After several weeks sitting idle in the snow-covered hills of the border it was blindingly clear that the Ardennes attack was not going to create a breakthrough and with the rest of the division now back at Soltau undergoing further training, the decision was made at the end of January by OKW to send the kampfgruppe, along with the rest of Dietrich's Sixth SS Panzer Army, to Hungary to try and relieve Budapest and its besieged defenders. Dutifully, Schellong and his men loaded their kit and vehicles onto the supplied trains and boarded for their anticipated transfer across central Europe and down south to the Hungarian plain. They would never arrive. En route they were diverted north. Their journey would end in the snows of northeastern Germany, on the windswept plains and in the silent forests of Pomerania.

XI
The Ending: Pomerania

By new year 1945 the picture for Nazi Germany's Ostheer was grim. Kursk in 1943 had been where they had finally lost the initiative in the East and 1944 had been Soviet Russia's Year of the Ten Victories, which had seen the Wehrmacht retreat right back across European Russia and Eastern Europe to the very gates of the Third Reich itself. During this time the Ostheer had restructured itself, the three huge Barbarossa invasion formations of Army Groups A, B and C from north to south, had been replaced by Army Groups North, Centre and South. Army Group North had been shunted back from Leningrad and through the Baltic States with most of it, some 25 divisions no less, marooned in the Courland Peninsula, aptly renamed Army Group Courland! But there were still vestiges of the old formation and they survived under the old Army Group North sobriquet defending Pomerania and Germany's other eastern *länder*. To the south, the incredible scale and ferocity of the Red Army's Operation Bagration had resulted in Nazi Germany's greatest ever defeat, measured in casualties, as the old Army Group Centre was effectively wiped out. Incredibly, the Germans had patched some sort of defence together and Army Group Centre became the 'new' Army Group North Ukraine. Army Group South, now desperately trying to cover the Balkans and their raging partisan wars as well, stayed pretty much as it was with Army Groups E and F trying to flee north, fend off Tito and reach the relative safety of Austria. Meanwhile, the Red Army was preparing itself for a final push that would see it end the war in Europe victorious. In all, the battered Ostheer could field just 2,000,000 men, 4,785 panzers and assault guns and 29,000 artillery pieces against a Soviet behemoth of 11,850,000 men (including 350,000 Poles, Bulgarians and Rumanians), 15,000 tanks and assault guns, plus an eardrum-shattering 110,000 artillery pieces. The Wehrmacht in the East was massively outnumbered and outgunned and soon the Flemish would be in the teeth of the storm.

The black guard splits

The Waffen-SS was now at its zenith in terms of size, though its combat power was past its 1943–44 peak, and it was at this stage that Hitler decided to split his praetorians, the majority of its tried and tested formations sent south to fight in Hungary and defend Austria. Their slogan was to be 'Vienna remains German!' The remainder, including a very large proportion of non-German Waffen-SS units, were sent north to protect eastern Germany and guard the gateway to Berlin itself. The 5th SS Panzer Division Wiking, as the premier freiwillige formation, was down south attempting to relieve Budapest as part of 4th SS Panzer Corps, but in the north was almost every other foreign volunteer unit. Among the foreign Waffen-SS formations being mustered in the north to try and fend off the Soviet giant were the Scandinavians of the 11th Nordland, the Latvians of the 15th and 19th, the Estonians of the 20th, the Dutchmen of the newly-formed 23rd Nederland, Degrelle's Walloons of the 28th Wallonien, the Frenchmen of the 33rd Charlemagne; and now it was the turn of the Flemings from the Langemarck, or more precisely, the 2,000 men from Kampfgruppe Schellong.

Diffusion of the Flemish

The last months of the war in Europe would be chaotic and bloody for most, none more so than for the Flemings. The creation of the 27th SS-Freiwilligen Grenadier Division Langemarck had been intended to bring together all the Flemings fighting with the Germans so that they could enter battle in the East as a cohesive whole. It did not happen. The creaming off of the best of the Flemish soldiers into Kampfgruppe Schellong was just the start. Still others who were considered to have significant combat value, such as the recently recovered Remy Schrijnen, were placed in sub-units directly at the disposal of Felix Steiner and his newly-created Eleventh SS Panzer Army, while the majority of the Division under Thomas Müller's command were moved around the battlefield in an almost haphazard manner. Sometimes these different elements fought together but more often not, and the picture was further confused by hastily trained Flemish reinforcements being rushed from their assembly areas to wherever they were needed the most, thereby representing the Langemarck at different places. What makes matters infinitely more difficult for the student of the formation to untangle was that nearly every single one of these different units went under the name of 'Langemarck'. Even Kampfgruppe Schellong, called this owing to the long standing tradition of a KG being named after its commander, was sometimes called KG Langemarck in the reports and war diaries of the time. Whilst this was symptomatic of the chaos of the time, it leads to bewilderment about the story of the Flemings' last campaign in particular. Each segment of the Langemarck must be tracked individually to get an accurate picture of what happened and why. For instance, it was clear that the hardbitten veterans of both KG Schellong, and Steiner's directly controlled Flemish units, would perform completely differently from the inadequately trained ex-Vlaamsche Wacht men pressed into service back in Soltau. The mass of the new division would make little real impact at the front, but the seasoned core would make the Soviets pay for every yard right until the bitter end. So it was with many of the 'new' Waffen-SS divisions. While most of the Frenchmen in the Charlemagne would be prettily easily obliterated in Pomerania by the Russian steamroller, the 'old hares' of the LVF and SS-Sturmbrigade Frankreich would make their mark at Elsenau and Körlin.

Steiner and the new Russian offensive

Kampfgruppe Schellong was diverted north to rejoin its old Corps, the III (germanisches) SS Panzer, which was now part of the recently established Eleventh SS Panzer Army commanded by the ever-wily Felix Steiner. The Flemings were part of the unofficial 'SS Corps West' reinforcements for Steiner alongside the Frenchmen of Charlemagne, meant to be III Corps reserve, and the Walloons of the 28th Panzergrenadier. Welcome though this influx of new blood was for Steiner, it was a drop in the ocean. The Walloons were a division in name only, in reality being of brigade strength, there were only some 2,000 Flemings and the Charlemagne could field less than 9,000 men all-up.

As Schellong's men themselves disembarked at Stettin and moved up to their position on the upper Oder, the Red Army unleashed their long-awaited New Year offensive on 12 January 1945. Koniev's massive 1st Ukrainian Front smashed into the Wehrmacht's 4th Panzer and 17th Armies tearing them to shreds, and the following day Chernakhovsky's 3rd Belorussian Front to the north attacked into East Prussia. Over the next few days the offensive became a general one as first Rokossovsky's 2nd, and then Zhukov's 1st, Belorussian Fronts swept west between Warsaw in the south and Königsberg on the Baltic coast. The first Russian soldiers to set foot on German soil had been men from the 31st Army back in late July 1944 but they had quickly been pushed back and halted. Now there was no stopping them and waves of Red Army men crossed into East Prussia on 20 January, to be followed by their comrades from the 5th Guards Tank Army, who broke through to the German shores of the Baltic Sea itself, northeast of Elbing, on 26 January. Weiss's Second and Muller's Fourth Armies (Muller having replaced the sacked Hossbach), were now cut off in East Prussia and would be systematically destroyed by the Soviets until the remnants finally surrendered on 9 May. As the Red Army drove west it was progressively splintering the Wehrmacht forces on its northern flank and cutting them off in pocket after pocket, in Courland, Königsberg, Danzig and soon Kolberg.

Schellong and his men had been moved to the Ihna River line to the west of the Madu See, south of Stargard and facing east. To their right was the newly-created 28th Wallonien and one of the 10th SS Panzer Division Frundsberg's panzergrenadier regiments. Although out of the main thrust of the continuing Red Army offensive they were subject to repeated local infantry attacks and heavy artillery bombardment. There was to be no peace in Pomerania for the Flemings.

Operation Sonnenwende

Success, though, brings its own problems, and by early February the Red Army offensive was losing momentum and focus, and a sudden thaw did not help, as much of the ground became boggy and impassable. Colonel-General Heinz Guderian, Chief of the Army General Staff at *Oberkommando des Heeres* (OKH – Army High Command) since late July 1944 and a master tactician, sniffed an opportunity as he saw Zhukov's 1st Belorussian Front spearheads outrun their logistic support and become vulnerable to counter-attack. If the Germans could move fast and concentrate enough combat power there was half a chance of them being able to cut off the lead Soviet formations and severely damage one of the largest Red Army formations aligned against them. Guderian's proposed plan envisaged a double pincer movement with an attack from Stargard in the north breaking through Zhukov's flank and meeting up in the Front's rear with a southern pincer advancing from Frankfurt-an-der-Oder.

Had it worked, the manoeuvre would have been a return to the classic 1940–1942 successes of the Wehrmacht, but those days were long gone. Guderian proposed that the southern pincer of this Operation Sonnenwende (Summer Solstice) offensive was launched by Dietrich's still-powerful Sixth SS Panzer Army. This move from the southern end of the Eastern Front to the fight up north would also mean that the premier Waffen-SS fighting force would be ideally placed to resist the inevitable Red Army assault on Berlin. But such a move had to be sanctioned by Hitler himself and he was still obsessed with the fantasy of retaking Budapest and regaining the lost oilfields of Hungary. He turned Guderian's request down flat, told him the northern pincer would be strong enough, downgraded the offensive from a general counter-attack to a limited one and then went even further by insisting that Heinrich Himmler, as Commander Army Group Vistula (*Weichsel* in German), would be in charge of the offensive. Superb though *der treue Heinrich* ('the loyal Heinrich', Hitler's nickname for Himmler) was at conducting the mass murder of millions of unarmed civilians across an entire continent, he was useless as a military leader. His appointment alone doomed Sonnenwende to failure.

The eve of Sonnenwende

The offensive was to be launched by Steiner's newly-established Eleventh SS Panzer Army, nominally composed of six divisions, all of which were seriously understrength. Arrayed on a 30-mile front the attacking force was split into three columns. The Eastern Group was the weakest, made up of the 163rd and 281st Infantry Divisions and the Führer-Grenadier Division, collectively called the Corps Group Munzel after their commander. Their goals were flank protection and to push out towards Landsberg on the River Warthe. The Flemings of KG Schellong were with III (germanisches) SS Panzer Corps, now commanded by SS-Gruppenführer Decker, in the Central Group with Wangemann's only armoured sub-unit, the self-pro-pelled guns of 4. Sturmgeschütz Kompanie, detached and subordinated direct to Corps. Alongside them in the Corps were the Scandinavians of the SS Nordland and the Dutchmen of the newly-formed SS Panzergrenadier Nederland. The still-strong Führer-Begleit Division was also in the Central Group. The Central Group's mission was to punch south aggressivley and as a first step reach Arnswalde (now Choszno) before exploiting any break-through. Completing the counter-attack force was the Western Group of General Unrein's XXIX Panzer Corps. This Corps contained the Heer's Holstein Panzer Division as well as the elite 10th SS Panzer Division Frundsberg, the 4th SS-Polizei Division and the Walloons of the 28th SS. Their role was flank protection, as with the Eastern Group, but they were also there to exploit and reinforce any success gained by the Central Group. There was no hope of operational surprise as Red Army intelligence was functioning superby well, and so massed against the depleted Germans and their allies were no less than five Armies, including the prime 1st and 2nd Guards Tank Armies, the 3rd Shock, and the infantrymen of the 47th and 61st. With each Soviet Army being roughly equivalent to a German Corps in size, it was clear that even if the attacking divisions had been up to strength they would have been badly outnumbered.

Sonnenwende is launched

The only hope of achieving the necessary three to one ratio generally considered to be needed for an attacker to ensure success against an enemy position, was to concentrate the available forces at key points and maintain momentum. This the Germans failed to do. The staff of Steiner's new Army were not used to working either with each other or with their component divisions, confusion reigned and was not helped by the poor weather, which restricted movement to the major road network. The assaulting formations were desperately slow in assembling their forces ready to begin the offensive and as a result, on 15 February, only the SS Nordland was ready to go. Dutifully they attacked towards Arnswalde but it was hardly the overwhelming punch envisaged by Guderian.

On the following day the rest of Eleventh SS Panzer Army was able to launch itself at the opposing Red Army but only after a series of night marches in drenching rain that left the men exhausted before they had even crossed their start lines. The attack did not go well from the beginning. Resistance was extremely heavy with the well-equipped Soviets contesting every yard of ground and using their massed artillery and air support to pound the advancing units relentlessly. Fighting every inch of the way the SS Nordland did manage to push forward around seven miles and get within sight of the town of Arnswalde, but it was hardly a lightning thrust and casualties were dreadful. In the Western Group the Walloons were providing flank protection for the Frundsberg and were decimated in some of the bitterest fighting they had experienced since Cherkassy.

The Flemings carried out the same role for the Nordland in the centre and were embroiled in similar harsh fighting against vastly superior Soviet forces. The Flemish grenadiers had been shorn of their limited armour support but still had most of Wangemann's anti-tank assets to call on. They struggled forward, coming up against strong Soviet forces in every village and hamlet. Each one had to be cleared in savage hand-to-hand fighting, the Flemings debussing beyond direct fire range and then going in on foot to fight it out with the Russians in the streets. Inevitably, it was slow going and even though the men in KG Schellong were the cream of the Langemarck Division they were not bulletproof and casualties were heavy. At the village of Schwanenbeck the grenadiers of 7. Kompanie were led into the assault by their Flemish commander, SS-Untersturmführer Fernand 'Nand' Laporte. The defending Russians called in artillery, which caused terrible civilian casualties and also threatened to halt the entire attack. Undetterred, Laporte led his men forward through the storm of explosives and shrapnel to kill the Soviet infantrymen and choke off the fire from the guns. The Flemish freiwillige took the last houses in the village at the point of the bayonet, but his heroism cost their commander his life. Laporte, the 23-year-old ex-VNV leader from Blankenberge, was killed in the attack.

He was not the only officer that KG Schellong lost that day. The controversial commander of I./SS-Frw.-Grenadier Regiment 67, Wilhelm Rehmann, was wounded in the fighting and evacuated to the rear for treatment. At least this time there were no questions as to the gravity of his injuries. Rehmann disappeared in the ensuing chaos at the end of the war and never returned to the Langemarck.

Despite the ferocity of the Soviet defence the Waffen-SS did succeed in finally breaking through to the Pomeranian town of Arnswalde. Trapped in the town were several thousand German troops, who had been holding out against continuous Soviet attacks, and many thousands of German civilian refugees.

This was typical of the time, as the Red Army advance of January had been so swift that an orderly withdrawal of both German troops and civilians had not been possible. The situation was not helped by the inefficiency of the local Nazi Party hierarchy who had ignored warnings to begin civilian evacuation and so were caught out. Needless to say, most of these Party functionaries did manage to save their own skins in the end and flee west, abandoning their fellow Germans to their fate. As for the Ostheer, as it fragmented in front of the rampaging Red Army a huge array of units had been left behind and found themselves holed up in cities, towns and villages across East Prussia, Silesia and Pomerania. In the likes of Breslau, Posen and Thorn, tens of thousands of German soldiers were surrounded but still desperately fought on until they were either annihilated or forced to surrender, after taking huge casualties.

As the Flemings and Scandinavians drove into Arnswalde on 17 February they were greeted with unbridled joy and relief by the beleaguered garrison and flocks of civilians. As the Red Army swept into Germany it sought to repay the brutality of the recent German occupation and the result was indiscriminate slaughter of helpless German civilians, looting and rape in particular on an almost industrial scale. Before this tide of vengeance, the people of eastern Germany were literally fleeing for their lives, and now the road to safety in the north was opened in Arnswalde, thousands of them packed their most precious belongings onto hand carts and wagons and swamped the roads. This made it extremely difficult for the advancing units to bring up reinforcements and supplies; but more and more, the Wehrmacht fighting units were seeing their main role not as trying to win a war they all knew was lost, but to save as many civilians as possible from the clutches of the Red Army.

As Arnswalde's population fled north, the Central Group renewed their attack south, but their strength was all but spent. Soviet pressure was so intense that not only did it prove impossible to advance beyond Arnswalde but even keeping the town itself was proving too much for the exhausted SS grenadiers. Against mounting Russian attacks the town was held until all civilians and troops had been evacuated before being abandoned on 23 February. With the loss of Arnswalde it was obvious that Sonnenwende had failed. Steiner had no choice but to call off the offensive after little more than a week and pull back the entire Army to its start lines around Stargard (now Stargard Szczecinski) and Stettin. Back went the dispirited Flemings, harried continuously by the Red Army until they reached their old positions on the Ihna River, and there they stood fending off constant probes by strong Soviet forces.

Following the Langemarck's retreat back to its start line news came through that Conrad Schellong was to be honoured with the Knights Cross. Strangely enough, the award was not for the recent fighting in Pomerania or the relief of Arnswalde, but in recognition of his leadership of the SS-Sturmbrigade Langemarck back in the battles in the Ukraine in 1943–1944, and especially the defence of Yampil. He had been given the German Cross in Gold, one grade down from the Knights Cross, on the back of that campaign, but for some reason it was now decided to 'upgrade' the medal. This was not common practice and several theories have been proposed as to why the decision was made, most peruasively that it was usual for a unit's commander to be awarded a Knights Cross not just for his own courage but in recognition of the bravery of all his men. Whatever the reason, on 28 February 1945 Conrad Schellong became a *Ritterkreuzträger* (Knights Cross winner) and the Sturmbrigade Langemarck's contribution to the savage battles in the Ukraine in the previous year was finally fully acknowledged.

The aftermath of Sonnenwende

Militarily, Sonnenwende had been a conspicuous failure. The Red Army spearheads had not been pinched off, there had been no follow-up break-through to the line of encircled pockets on the Baltic coast, and the partici-pating units of Army Group Vistula had taken terrible casualties in both men and material, which were not going to be replaced. It was also the end of the short-lived Eleventh SS Panzer Army, which was disbanded and renamed the Third Panzer Army on 24 February.

The Russians hadn't got off scot-free. Rokossovsky's 2nd Belorussian Front alone had started January with a massive strength of some 881,000 men and over 2,000 tanks and self-propelled guns, but come the end of Sonnenwende, the Front had lost more than 36,000 men killed and a tremendous 123,000 wounded. Tank attrition rates had been very high and Rokossovsky could only muster some 300 tanks left operational. Nevertheless, the STAVKA was determined to press on and give the depleted Heer and Waffen-SS formations no respite. The initial goal of the Red Army January offensive was to take Berlin and end the war in no more than 45 days. That had not been achieved, but they had made huge strides in conquering all of Poland and taking large swathes of the Third Reich itself.

The Red Army March offensive

What Sonnenwende had also achieved was to convince the STAVKA that its northern flank was vulnerable to a possible German counter-offensive. Their view was that this could threaten their push towards Berlin and in consequence it was necessary to 'tidy up' the front by severely reducing the number of German-held pockets and shattering the Wehrmacht formations in the area, especially Second Army and the rest of Army Group Vistula. With the reinforcement of the 2nd Belorussian Front by the addition of 19th Army, an offensive was launched on 24 February that advanced more than 30 miles in a single day and ripped a huge hole in the crumbling Wehrmacht front. Moving to the east of Lauenburg and its old Wehrmacht NCO School where many Waffen-SS men had received their training, the Soviets soon threatened the encirclement of the entire Second Army. With this accomplished they could then shift their focus onto the depleted remnants of the overstretched Vistula Army Group, which now stood at less than 250,000 men all told. On the River Oder line stood the 150,000 men of Hube's Ninth Army, which included the Langemarck's old stablemate the 11th SS Nordland plus the 10th SS Frundsberg transferred across from Steiner. To the north around Stettin was the newly-renamed Third Panzer Army and its 100,000 men, including the Flemings of KG Schellong and other Flemish sub-units attached directly to III (germanisches) SS Panzer Corps alongside the SS Nederland and SS Wallonien.

On 1 March, after the usual pounding from Russian artillery and air assets, the 1st Belorussian Front crashed into Steiner's men with six whole Armies including the elite 1st and 2nd Guards Tank Armies. Attacking northwest towards Stettin from around Arnswalde the Soviets hit the sparse defenders very hard indeed. The front began to fracture almost immediately as the massed attackers swept towards Belgard, Kolberg and the Isle of Wollin. On the River Ihna the Soviets began to envelop Stargard and Schellong brought up his only reserve, the SS-Panzerjäger Abteilung 27, to try and hold off the assaulting waves of Russians. Wangemann was now commanding Rehmann's old battalion as well as his own, with Rehmann out wounded. The main weight of the attack in the sector fell on the neighbouring Dutchmen of the SS Nederland Division, who were soon reduced to just two battalions a piece in both SS Panzergrenadier Regiments 48 General Seyffardt and 49 De Ruiter. The Walloons too were hit very hard and their casualties were crippling.

Rearguard at Zachan

By only the second day of the Red Army offensive it was clear to Schellong and all his commanders that the line could not be held and the Kampfgruppe would have to retreat or be destroyed. Leaving a small rearguard of 100 men in the village of Zachan, the rest of the Flemish began to move back towards Stargard. Shortly after the main body left Zachan, the first Russian patrols appeared and tried to force a way through. The rearguard put up a stiff defence, pouring fire into the adjacent fields as Soviet infantry tried to work their way into the village, and when the Flemish were pushed back from the outskirts by sheer weight of numbers they concentrated their fire on the lanes and alleys between the houses. Soviet infantry went down everywhere and their response was brutal if predictable; a storm of artillery fire hit the village, smashing in roofs and setting fire to buildings. The Flemings were veterans though and had expected just such a reaction, and on seeing the Russians move back awaiting artillery support they moved back as well, into the far corner of the village, away from where the Russians would concentrate their fire. The result was that though much of Zachan was destroyed its defenders suffered very few casualties and were able to run back into position when the bombardment stopped and again bring down withering machine-gun fire on the surprised Russians confidently advancing towards the burning village.

With Zachan holding throughout the afternoon, Wangemann, who by this time had taken his battalion back to the tiny hamlets of Gross and Klein Schlatik, decided to stop retreating and try to return and link up with the stubborn rearguard and even launch a limited local counter-attack. The move was ambitious and aggressive, but unfortunately for Wangemann it was spotted by Soviet artillery observers who poured indirect fire onto the advancing grenadiers. With casualties mounting the relief attempt was given up and the retreat back to Stargard began again that night of 2–3 March. Only a handful of the rearguard made it out of Zachan alive to rejoin their comrades.

Stargard is lost

The town of Stargard was the hinge of the German defensive line on the Ihna River and to lose it would mean losing the last natural barrier of any real sort east of the Oder River itself. If the Wehrmacht could hold it, the Russian offensive would be seriously hampered. Schellong and the Flemish fought a dogged rearguard defence all the way back to the town from Zachan. They would dig in around a village or hamlet and wait for the Russians to appear before hitting them with everything they had. The advancing Soviets would be forced to deploy and mount a full attack, giving the Flemish time to scramble to their vehicles and get away. It was the same philosophy later nicknamed 'shoot and scoot' by NATO forces and adopted for use against the descendants of the same Red Army men on the plains of northern Germany in the Cold War. It may sound simple, but it was tremendously hard to carry out. After some 36 hours the remnants of the Kampfgruppe arrived in Stargard itself to find the town defended by a mixed Walloon-German force. Schellong now had only 500 men left from his original 2,000 veterans, the rest were now either wounded or lying dead in between Zachan and Stargard. As for equipment, the KG had always been woefully short of heavy weapons, especially as Sprenger's Sturmgeschütz Company was on permanent loan to Corps Headquarters, but now it was in dire straits, being down to just three PAK guns from the original nine in Kotlowski's Company. For the rest of the grenadiers, their hopes of stopping a Russian tank lay with their panzerfäusts or home-made Molotov cocktails.

The Flemings had barely been in position a few hours before the Red Army launched a very heavy attack on the town on the afternoon of 4 March, with waves of infantry following behind lines of tanks driving almost side by side. With so few heavy weapons and no reinforcements the town's defenders held on for as long as they could, but the Soviets were soon in the town itself and the fighting was house-to-house. After Stalingrad and dozens of other city battles, the Red Army veterans had become past masters at urban fighting and in Stargard the experienced troops of the assaulting 61st Army could also bring their huge superiority in numbers and equipment to bear. Any building from where the Flemish and Walloon grenadiers were firing from was marked as a target and a tank was called up to stand off and blast it to rubble. The town had to be abandoned and by 4pm there was not a live Fleming in Stargard.

Alongside the Walloons, the Flemish retreated first to the village of Grimme and then further west, as they were pulled back to Stettin on the west bank of the Oder for a much-needed rest at the end of the first week of March. The spring weather had turned and the heavens had opened, and with rain pouring down the ground had become a morass. The Soviets could not deploy off-road in such conditions and the offensive had slowed, allowing KG Schellong to recover and the rest of Army Group Vistula to establish a new defensive line anchored on the town of Altdamm on the east bank of the Oder, a few miles to the south and east of Stettin itself.

Altdamm – the last redoubt

Northeastern Germany had effectively been lost in that first week of March 1945. East and West Prussia had been overrun as well as most of Pomerania and Silesia, and although surrounded Wehrmacht garrisons were still fighting on in several northern ports, the truth was that most of Germany's Baltic coastline was in Soviet hands too. The new frontline at Stettin was now only some 60-odd miles northeast of the outskirts of

Berlin itself. If the Oder River was crossed and Stettin fell, then all of Pomerania would be under Red Army control and the roads would be open not only to Berlin but to all of Mecklenburg through to Rostock and even Hamburg.

The Oder and its tributaries presented a major obstacle to the Red Army. Stettin itself was an inland sea port at the southern end of the vast Oderhaff, a huge lake leading to the sea with the port of Swinemüde at its northern edge. This lake was connected to Stettin by a part of the Oderhaff called the Dammscher See and was fed by the mighty Oder itself which formed two major branches as it flowed into the lake. (The name Stettin would reach a wider audience on 5 March 1946: 'From Stettin in the Baltic to Trieste in the Adriatic, an Iron Curtain has descended across the continent...' Winston Churchill, Fulton, Missouri.) The main road, with its vital bridges, ran from Stargard through the town of Altdamm on the east bank of the main Oder line and to Stettin and beyond. To further aid a defender there was another major lake to the southeast, now called the Jezioro Miedwie, that would restrict the manoeuvres of any attacking force and more or less confine it to a frontal assault on Altdamm to smash its way through. All in all, the Altdamm bridgehead would be a tough nut to crack so long as the Germans had the strength to man its defences. That job was given to General Hasso von Manteuffel's Third Panzer Army. The diminiutive German panzer commander had carefully husbanded his forces since the beginning of the Soviet spring offensive and so, although not flush with troops, he had at least a chance to hold Altdamm and delay the Red Army advance into Germany. Transferred over to the Third Panzer Army and specifically earmarked for that defence were the remnants of several of the best of the old Waffen-SS freiwillige formations, including the 650 or so Walloons still determined to fight on, a handful of Danes from the Nordland's Danmark Regiment, and Schellong's surviving Flemish companies, which were down to no more than 30 to 40 men each. The volksdeutsche and Reichsdeutsche of SS Panzer Regiment 10 from the Frundsberg were already there, with their scattering of tanks to support the grenadiers when they were called up. There would be no help though from the third Western European SS formation sent to Pomerania at the beginning of January as part of the unofficial 'SS Corps West', the Frenchmen of the 33rd SS Charlemagne, as they were scattered over much of northern Germany with thousands dead or wounded at Elsenau and Belgard and the survivors fighting for their lives in Körlin and Kolberg.

Hold the east bank

After several days of relative inaction because of the weather and some logistics issues Zhukov ordered the 47th Army to begin the assault on

Altdamm in earnest on 14 March. With Soviet pressure building on the bridgehead, both KG Schellong and the Wallonien were called forward from their rest areas to the Stettin docks ready for transporting down to Altdamm to join the defence on 16 March. On arrival in the bridgehead the Flemish were ordered to dig in a few kilometres out of the town to the east to act as the first line of defence against the advancing Russians. Specifically, the 1st and 2nd Companies, I./SS-Frw.-Grenadier Regiment 67 (the battalion now led by Wangemann with Rehmann wounded), commanded by SS-Untersturmführer's Ferdinand Ghyssens and Ferdinand 'Fons' Jacobs respectively, relieved the 50 remaining Danes of the SS Panzergrenadier Regiment 24 Danmark. The aim for the defenders was to maintain the bridgehead on the eastern bank, thus denying the Red Army its use as an assembly area to cross the Oder in force, and also to allow the small Altdamm river port to stay open for supplies, reinforcement and evacuation if necessary.

As for KG Schellong, the men had got some much needed rest in Stettin after nearly two months of continuous combat, but they had not received either any reinforcements or any new heavy weapons and were now down to Kotlowski's three remaining PAKs and boxes of panzerfäusts as their only anti-tank capability. Even their artillery support was minimal.

While Schellong and his few remaining men dug in outside Altdamm the bulk of the Flemish division were trying to continue training and get hold of equipment to become combat effective, but their efforts were constantly frustrated by the spiralling chaos that was descending on the Third Reich. Small arms were forthcoming but there was little in the way of heavy weaponry, particularly now Silesia and its war industries had been seized, and even training areas were hard to come by as Poland and Bohemia-Moravia were lost, and Germany was overrun. With the loss of Romania and Hungary, fuel was in desperately short supply as well, but somehow Müller, as the divisional commander, maintained some sort of training schedule. Sooner rather than later there would be several thousand Flemish reinforcements ready for the front; but they would not be in time to fight at Altdamm.

Hold Altdamm!

As soon as the Flemings were in position they were hit by intense artillery bombardments followed by massed infantry assaults supported by tanks. To try and stabilise the line a counter-attack was mounted by the last few tanks of the SS Frundsberg's Panzer Regiment (during which its commander SS-Sturmbannführer Otto Pätsch was killed), which threw the Soviets back with dreadful casualties. Pätsch was posthumously promoted to SS-Standartenführer and awarded the *Eichenlauben*, the Oak

Leaves, to his Knights Cross for his bravery during the counter-attack. As the Russians pulled back to lick their wounds the fields and hamlets in the Altdamm bridgehead were lit up that night by the burning hulks of Soviet tanks lying strewn across the battlefield.

The next day, 17 March, was not quite so frantic; even though the Soviets pushed forward, their attacks lacked conviction. It was clear that they were massing for another all-out assault but it would not come that day. What did come were tonnes of high explosive as the Soviets sought to grind down the defenders with sheer weight of fire.

The massed attack came the next morning. More than 200 Soviet tanks from the 2nd Guards Tank Army and thousands of infantry from the 47th Army hit the Flemish and their fellow defenders head on. Kotlowski's PAKs fired until their barrels glowed red and the air rang thick with the guttural coughs of panzerfäusts. Tank after tank was brewed up or blown to pieces and rows of Soviet infantry were mown down by machine-gun fire, but the immense pressure soon began to tell. The village and hamlet outposts in the bridgehead fell one by one and the surviving Flemings, Walloons and Germans were squeezed back into a small strip of land around the town of Altdamm itself and its bridge. The fighting was hand-to-hand and came down to men grappling in the bottom of slit trenches with bayonets, pistols and entrenching tools. The dead of both sides lay entwined in clumps across the east bank of the Oder; but somehow, at the end of the day, Schellong's men were still holding onto Altdamm.

The bridgehead is lost

The Russians had been stopped on the Oder but on Hitler's orders Manteuffel had to send some of his remaining formations to help defend Küstrin to the south from yet another Soviet thrust. With no reserves it was obvious to Manteuffel that the bridgehead was untenable, he literally had no more men to send in. The order was given the following day on 19 March – Altdamm was to be abandoned! Schellong's men withdrew in groups in the afternoon and evening, as did the Walloons. The last defenders crossed over to the western bank of the Oder early the following day before the bridge was blown. The defence of Altdamm was over. The fighting on the east bank of the Oder had cost the Third Panzer Army 40,000 men killed with the Russians capturing another 12,000. As a combat force it was crippled. The Walloons had lost 110 men, about 1 in 6, but the Flemings had lost even more. Schellong took just over 500 men into the bridgehead but came out with only 200 men alive and unwounded. Many others had been wounded during the battle and evacuated out of the bridgehead, but without more bodies KG Schellong was finished.

Reinforcements arrive

At first the Kampfgruppe was sent into reserve to the Politz sector, north of Stettin, where it helped to build fortifications, before going southwest to the villages of Brüssow and Retzin to the west of the Randow River to be rebuilt. It now became clear that the 27th SS-Freiwilligen Grenadier Division Langemarck would never fight as a cohesive unit. Many of its troops were lukewarm at best towards the idea of fighting the advancing Red Army, and overall the level of training was poor, with the mass of recruits having had only four months or so of disrupted training time. Müller and Schellong conferred and divided up the bulk of the Division between the two of them so that Müller would continue to be in over-all command, concentrating on the support units, logistics and training replacements, while Schellong would lead the combat element of the Langemarck in a newly-reinforced KG Schellong. Under this arrangement a host of new troops came from the divisional training camp including the bulk of the hitherto incomplete SS-Freiwilligen Grenadier Regiment 68 (two battalions in total with the regimental staff), of which the 1st Battalion was made up of the idealistic Flemish youths 'persuaded' to enlist in the *Wehrertüchtigungslager* and led by the Dane, SS-Sturmbannführer Oluf von Krabbe. Soldiers from KG Schellong's original three battalions who had been wounded and had now recovered also came back to swell the ranks, and they were joined by comrades from the other two battalions each of SS-Regiments 66 and 67. This influx took the strength of KG Schellong on 1 April 1945 up to 167 officers, 408 NCOs and 3,537 other ranks, totalling 4,102 men. Equipment was scarce to say the least, but somehow Müller had scraped together 102 light machine-guns, 20 heavy machine-guns, 4 medium mortars, 4 light infantry guns, 2 heavy infantry guns, 6 light field howitzers and 2 heavy field howitzers. Transport was also provided: 22 motorcycles, 26 assorted cars/kubelwagens, 41 trucks and some 380 horses.

The Flemings spent the next fortnight and more shaking themselves out into their new combat sub-units and carrying on desperately needed training in the local area. As this went on, Müller kept on feeding more men forward as they were passed fit and ready for active duty with Schellong's fighting troops, so that by mid-April KG Schellong was almost 6,000 men strong and was more commonly referred to as KG Langemarck since the majority of Flemings from the Division were now in it. To give some idea of individual sub-unit strengths, SS-Untersturmführer Johann Guldentops 1. Kompanie of I. 66 Regiment had grown from 80 men at the beginning of April to 120 on 18 April.

This fortnight was to be the very last period of relative calm the Flemings were to enjoy during the War. There was some patrol activity from both sides and sporadic firefights, but casualties were very few and although the rumble of artillery was omnipresent, peace more or less reigned in the division's area. On 15 April Kotlowski's reconstituted PAK Kompanie, including Schrijnen, left the control of III Corps headquarters and finally rejoined the division for the very last act of the War in Europe. This move considerably beefed up the KG's anti-tank capability, and the entire formation was ordered to move south to Schwedt-Freienwalde and hold itself ready to help block the anticipated Red Army offensive on Berlin. This prompted another reorganisation as the non-combatant Walloons and Flemings were brought together under Thomas Müller's command and entitled *SS-Divisionsgruppe Müller*, while Conrad Schellong remained in overall command of the division's combat elements but detached one battalion, under SS-Hauptsturmführer Jan De Mulder, to join a combined separate kampfgruppe of three battalions under the command of the Walloon officer, SS-Sturmbannführer Frans Hellebaut. This KG was to be the point unit for both the Walloons and Flemings, and in effect the first combined 'Belgian' Waffen-SS unit. Alongside De Mulder's Flemings there was a Walloon battalion commanded by SS-Sturmbannführer Henri Derricks and an alarm battalion of Pomeranians, the so-called Kolberg Battalion.

Counter-attacks

On 20 April the Red Army's 2nd Belorussian Front launched a new offensive between Kürow and Schillersdorf, to the south of Stettin, aimed at reaching Berlin from the north and finally ending the war in Europe. A kampfgruppe from the 4th Panzergrenadier Division SS-Polizei, supported in part by the few remaining Sturmgeschütze from the Langemarck Division that had been permanently detached from their parent unit since being formed, were holding the bridges over the Oder where the autobahn, then as now, crossed over the Oder's two main branches. This was the axis of the Soviet attack from their 47th Army. The weight of the assault was immense and the Waffen-SS defenders were wiped out to a man. The Red Army then swept over the Oder River and into the flatlands beyond, causing general panic.

The attack had to be contained before the Soviets could build up large forces on the west bank of the river and then break out towards Berlin. A counter-attack was launched to the south of the autobahn by Hellebaut's KG with De Mulder's Flemish tasked with retaking the hamlet of Hühneberg right on the banks of the Oder, Derrick's Walloons were to recapture Neu-Rosow to the west of Hühneberg, and the Kolberg Battalion was to secure the village of Schöningen just south of the two other objectives. The idea was to attack from west to east and pin the Russians back to the sand dunes on the banks of the river. Initially the counter-attack went well and both Neu-Rosow and Schöningen were taken with heavy Russian casualties. The Flemings also pushed aggressively towards their objective and were soon within sight of the river. Hühneberg proved a hard target though as the Russians threw troops over the bridges to go straight into the battle and hold off the Flemish. The Walloons tried to go a step further themselves and push the Soviets out of Schillersdorf and reach the Oder, but their attack crumbled in the face of terrific fire that left their dead and wounded strewn over the approaches to the town.

Back at Army Headquarters Manteuffel knew that if the Red Army established a viable bridgehead it was all over and so he was determined to continue the counter-attack. Reinforcements were called forward and a further three of Schellong's grenadier battalions were sent into the sector to renew the assault.

H-hour for the new counter-attack was set for 4am on the morning of 21 April, with Hellebaut coordinating the Flemish on the left, the Walloons in the middle, and the Kolberg men on the right. A preparatory two-hour artillery bombardment actually turned out to be a few desultory shots from a battery of 88mm guns that lasted no more than 10 minutes. Rather than disrupting the Soviets and causing them grievous losses the fire only succeeded in alerting them to the coming attack so that when the grenadiers moved off they were met by a storm of defensive fire, including massed artillery. Men fell everywhere and within minutes the assault was bogged down amid a welter of blood and screams from dying grenadiers. Some sub-units struggled on valiantly, losing man after man, but it was clear within the first hour that the operation was a disaster. All contact between the assaulting battalions was lost and neither Schillersdorf nor Hühneberg were retaken. By dawn the attack was called off and the decimated battalions were pulled back to their start lines having accomplished nothing but the loss of several hundred men.

The rest of 21 April passed quietly as the freiwillige licked their wounds back in Neu-Rosow, but as dawn broke the next day the Red Army launched an attack from its expanding bridgehead. The Flemings now made up the bulk of the defenders and they resisted desperately, holding onto the town throughout the day. Later on that night the Walloon survivors were withdrawn to the village of Pomelen, north of the autobahn, with the Flemish tasked with taking over their positions in the line. Schellong insisted that a small rearguard of 20 Walloon volunteers be left in situ until his men had time to move up. By 4pm the next day only four men from that rearguard were left in the line alive.

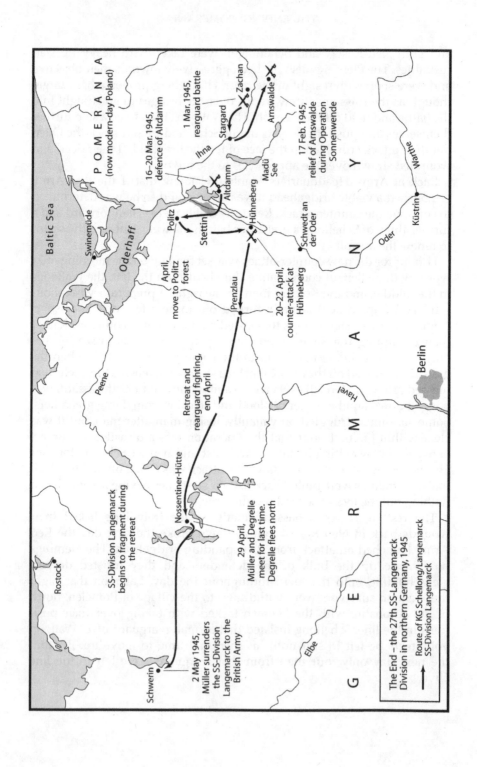

The End – the 27th SS-Langemarck
Division in northern Germany, 1945

→ Route of KG Schellong/Langemarck
SS-Division Langemarck

Schwerin

2 May 1945,
Müller surrenders
the SS-Division
Langemarck to the
British Army

Rostock

SS-Division Langemarck
begins to fragment during
the retreat

Nossentiner-Hütte

29 April,
Müller and Degrelle
meet for last time.
Degrelle flees north

Peene

Swinemünde

Baltic Sea

Oderhaff

P O M E R A N I A
(now modern-day Poland)

Zachan

1 Mar. 1945,
rearguard battle

Stargard

Ihna

16–20 Mar. 1945,
defence of Altdamm

Arnswalde

17 Feb. 1945,
relief of Arnswalde
during Operation
Sonnenwende

Madü
See

Altdamm

Politz

Stettin

Hühneberg

April,
move to Politz
forest

Schwedt
an der Oder

Warthe

20–22 April,
counter-attack at
Hühneberg

Prenzlau

Retreat and
rearguard fighting,
end April

Havel

Berlin

Oder

Küstrin

G E R M A N Y

Elbe

Retreat to the west

Now retreat was all that was left. The Wehrmacht had been unable to hold the west bank of the Oder and the Red Army now had nothing to stop it charging forward and encircling Berlin. The Flemings were unceremoniously shoved out of the way by the victorious Russians and were forced to fight an attritional rearguard battle as they withdrew back northwest from the Oder to Prenzlau, 30 miles west of the river. Having faced the Russians for over three-and-a-half years of gruelling combat on the Eastern Front the Flemings knew that falling into Soviet hands was to be avoided at all costs. Their only chance to avoid summary execution or the long march to the salt mines or work camps of the gulag was to get west as fast as possible and surrender to the Anglo-Americans. Over the next week the unit began to lose some of its cohesion, unsurprisingly, and contact was lost with several platoons and companies, as well as individuals, who were separated from the straggling division by constant Russian attacks.

The Red Army launched its last great offensive of the war on 26 April aimed at conquering Berlin, and a few individual Flemings got caught up in that final conflagration; but the rest were still fighting to survive as Manteuffel's Third Panzer Army finally disintegrated under the continuous pressure of Rokossovsky's Front storming into Mecklenburg.

By 27 April the main body of the Langemarck was at Seehausen just south of Prenzlau even as the lead elements of the Soviet's 70th Army took the town. SS-Hauptsturmführer Stange's SS-Regiment 68 was tasked with holding the new line with its youthful I. Battalion grouped around and between the two lakes of the Uecker See. To their front and north were the understrength companies of the divisional combat engineer battalion, the SS-Pioneer Battalion 27, which was overwhelmingly Flemish in composition (90% overall) but mainly made up of ex-factory workers from the Reich who had only joined up en masse in early November 1944. Tasked with defending a huge area against Soviet paratroop drops or infiltrators they were spread out all over a triangular area from Penkun to Kasekan to the Randow River. Luckily for them, with the fall of Prenzlau the line could not be held and they were not called upon to fight and die, so after a day or so in position they followed the rest of the division as it continued its hasty retreat towards the distant city of Schwerin in the northwest.

The end

As the Flemings pushed northwest away from the main thrust of the Red Army they carried on fighting whenever necessary, especially to assist the desperately pathetic columns of German civilian refugees fleeing from the Soviets. They continued to take casualties from rampaging Soviet tank forces and swarming infantry as they were chased by the 49th, 70th and 65th Armies. Of course by now the Red Airforce was completely unchallenged in the skies and could bomb and strafe at will. With no fuel or spare parts getting through it was not long before all the divisional transport was gone and most of the heavy weapons were abandoned because of lack of ammunition. Kotlowski's PAKs, however, fought on and on, fending off Soviet tanks, until with their one remaining gun the crew blew up one last T-34, before spiking the PAK and heading west on a few bicycles they had found. Kotlowski's platoon commanders did not fare well, as both Kassberger and Marcel Laperre, of Narva fame, were captured by the Russians. While Kassberger managed to escape from Soviet imprisonment two years later and somehow get to the Netherlands, young Laperre was shot out of hand after surrendering. Reports state that he had just killed a Russian soldier before being captured and it was pure rage on the part of one of the Russian's comrades that sealed his fate; or it may have been when the sig runes of the SS were seen on his jacket, no-one can know.

Müller and Degrelle

On 29 April Thomas Müller met Degrelle at the village of Nossentiner-Hütte (Degrelle was on his way to Lübeck some 50 miles to the northwest) where they discussed what would happen now the war was lost and what were the chances of re-establishing contact between the scattered Flemish and Walloon sub-units. It would be their last ever conversation. By this time, nothing could be done and the two men parted having achieved nothing. Degrelle had decided to leave his men and was to escape retribution by fleeing to Franco's Spain, whereas Müller would stay with his men and go into captivity with them.

Surrender at Schwerin

By 1 May there were Flemings stretched all over northern central Germany. Luckily, most had managed to avoid the advancing Red Army and were now congregated between Schwerin in the south, along the western shore of the Schwertner See and up through Bad Kleinen to Wismar on the Baltic coast. This was pretty much the line where the advancing British Army met the Soviets. On Schwerin's outskirts Thomas Müller had managed to gather most of the Flemish Langemarck survivors and issued his last set of orders. He released the men from their oaths and gave them the choice of trying to evade capture and making their own way west back to Flanders or staying with him and going into captivity. Exhausted, footsore and dispirited, the majority chose to stay with their divisional commander.

He then burnt most of the division's records to try and hide as many men's identities as possible before surrendering the vast bulk of the 27th SS-Freiwilligen Grenadier Division Langemarck (flämische Nr.1) to the British on 2 May 1945. The Flemish war was all but over, now would come the peace.

Names to remember

With his back wound flaring up during his propaganda tour in Germany and Flanders, Schrijnen spent the beginning of 1945 in hospital having lumps of metal removed from his body. It was not until late February that he returned to the front, but even then he was not to reunite with his old comrades in the new Langemarck Division. Instead he was placed in an anti-tank gun company at the direct disposal of III (germanisches) SS Panzer Corps. The unit was multi-national and drawn from veterans from across the Corps, but the mainstay of the unit were Flemings, including Schrijnen's old fellow-crew-member from Narva, Kamiel Horre. Back behind the gun sight of a 75mm PAK Schrijnen did what he did best for the rest of the War and destroyed Soviet tanks. March found him and his unit defending the route to Kösslin and desperately trying to hold the roads open for fleeing refugees. Rejoining the Langemarck on 15 April, Schrijnen continued to fight his war until the very end. Retreating westwards he and his crew were still killing Russians until 10 May, two days after the official capitulation, before finally spiking their gun and surrendering to the oncoming British. Having assumed the identity of a dead German mountain trooper, he was promptly handed over to the Americans, and then on discovery of his real identity he was sent back to Belgium and imprisonment.

As for Georg D'Haese, Narva was to be the end of his war. Injured in a motorbike accident in early 1945 he was in hospital recovering during the battles in Pomerania and never served with the Langemarck again. With the War ending he discharged himself and, along with his German girlfriend, went underground to avoid the inevitable post-war retribution. He would stay out of sight for some years to come.

XII

Retribution

I consider the treatment I got as a prisoner of war to have been absolutely bestial, both from the British and the Americans, but I have to say that this treatment was not at the hands of frontline soldiers. Interned as an SS man and as a 'foreigner', I had no POW status and thus was denied the protection this brings. Later, in Belgium, I was badly beaten by the gendarmes with clubs and rifle butts, and kicked in the testicles – anything was permitted. Even Red Cross nurses who had served with Germany were given up to 20 years in prison. (From Gordon Williamson, *Loyalty is my Honor*, Brown, 1995)

Like many survivors from the 27th SS-Freiwilligen Grenadier Division Langemarck, Remy Schrijnen was interned at Beverloo Camp back in Belgium. This was the same complex where the youngsters of the 12th SS Panzer Division Hitlerjugend were first mustered and trained prior to combat in Normandy. Rations were extremely poor, services were non-existent and overall treatment was bad. As with all the people of the previously occupied nations of Western Europe, the Belgians (and that definitely meant both those of Flanders and Walloonia) were struggling to come to terms with what had happened to them. How had they fallen to invasion so quickly, why had there been so little active resistance for so long? And then there was the issue of collaboration.

Thousands of young Flemings had voluntarily joined the Wehrmacht, and the Waffen-SS in particular, and had served with incredible bravery and fortitude for a country that was not their own. The key driver without doubt had been nationalism, the overwhelming desire to break away from a Belgian state they saw as morally bankrupt and to determine their own destiny. Allied to this patriotism was a general anti-communist feeling that viewed the threat from the Bolshevik East as real and recognised Nazi Germany's leadership in challenging that threat. So for many young Flemings, particularly from nationalist backgrounds, what the Waffen-SS offered was the ability to combat communism and earn their place as a 'free' nation in Nazi Germany's New European Order. Besides these lofty ideals the Waffen-SS also offered good pay and benefits, welfare for volunteers' families, and the undoubted glamour that went with being a member of an elite fighting brotherhood. Such factors will always have a pull on adventurous young men.

One of the freiwillige, Jan Vincx from Herentals, who was a 22-year-old teacher and reserve army officer when he volunteered for the SS-Legion Flandern in 1942, said after the War that as a staunch Catholic he joined out of a sense of anti-communism. He soon learned that politics was never discussed by his German comrades and very soon all he and his fellow Flemings talked about was fighting and the usual pre-occupations of soldiers – wine, women and song.

Trials, convictions and executions

After the War, 100,000 suspected Belgian collaborators were arrested – one in every hundred of the population! Of that total some 87,000 were actually charged and taken to trial. Special courts, consisting of two civilian and three military judges, were established in November 1945 to deal with this flood of proceedings, and eventually over 57,000 Belgians, both Flemings and Walloons, were convicted of collaboration. Per capita this was the highest number anywhere in Western Europe except Norway. The vast majority of those convicted served short prison terms and suffered various other penalties such as loss of civil rights, but 16,000 were handed down long terms of imprisonment and 4,170 were sentenced to death. Of those, 3,193 death sentences were for military collaboration, many in the SS-Legion Flandern, Sturmbrigade Langemarck or the SS Langemarck Division. Many survivors did try to hide the level of their involvement, as can be seen from this extract from a G-2 Intelligence report from US 99th Infantry Division from 29 April 1945, concerning prisoners taken from the last ever Waffen-SS division formed, the 38th SS-Panzergrenadier Division Nibelungen, made up of boys from the Hitler Youth and cadets from the elite Bad Tölz officer academy. The interview was with a Flemish Bad Tölz officer cadet from the 4th Company, 2nd Battalion, 95th Regiment SS Nibelungen, captured in the vicinity of Neustadt.

...the case of the PW was similar to that of the Dutchman of the 6th Company. A Belgian by birth, and a student of engineering in Vienna, the PW was forced to volunteer for the Belgian Legion Flandern, which was later absorbed into the SS Division Langemarck. He disliked the Germans intensely, partly because of what they did to his home city, Antwerp. He arrived at Bad Tölz at the end of February 1945, and was eventually expelled because he dared to talk back to the Germans.

This smacks of falsehood. Individuals were not sent to Bad Tölz on a whim, only the most able and dedicated were selected for entry. However, no-one can blame this unnamed prisoner for trying to save himself when post-war retribution was rife. Back in the East Flemish POWs were kept in the gulags for years and as mentioned earlier, it was not until 1962 that the last 4 survivors from Kampfgruppe D'Haese, captured at Narva, were released by the Soviet authorities.

After the judicial marathon in Belgium most of the death sentences handed down were actually commuted to long prison terms, but about 230 were carried out, including several dozen Flemish Waffen-SS Oostfronter veterans and the aged World War I collaborator August Borms, who had been reprieved following his conviction 20 years earlier but was not so lucky this time. Along with the official retribution there was also the inevitable unofficial score settling and hundreds of Flemings were on the receiving end of rough justice from the resistance. Months after the end of the War bodies were still being found in towns and villages across Flanders with a bullet through the head and a placard around the neck, proclaiming the victims to be collaborators who had got their just deserts.

Across Western Europe the leaders of the various collaborationist movements were seen as symbols of treason and were to a man tried, convicted and executed. In France it was Laval and Darnand, in Norway Quisling and in the Netherlands it was Mussert. But in Flanders almost every leader of any consequence was dead already by the end of the War. De Clercq had died in his bed back in 1942 and Reimond Tollenaere even earlier on the Russian Front. After that the Flemish had contributed many leaders to the struggle in the East but all had been at a relatively junior level; their senior officers had been Germans like Schellong. Back in Flanders, Dr Hendrik Elias had stepped into De Clercq's shoes but had always been pretty lukewarm towards the occupying authorities and was able to convince the Belgian court that he had obstructed the Germans rather than helped them. This saved him from the firing squad and he was instead sentenced to a long prison term. DeVlag's leader, Jef Van De Wiele, had no such defence, having advocated the annexation of Flanders to Nazi Germany, but by the time of his trial in November 1946 much of the vengeful passion had gone out of the process. Although he was convicted and sentenced to death there was little appetite for more bloodletting and his sentence was commuted to life imprisonment. Seventeen years later he was quietly released, whereupon he moved to West Germany to live out his days.

Aftermath

Having served their sentences, most Flemish veterans went home and tried to pick up their lives. Many started their own businesses and were relatively successful, although there was an undercurrent of bitterness towards the State as the government refused to grant an amnesty to veterans, as happened across most of the rest of Western Europe. This led directly to the establishment in 1951 of a Flemish Waffen-SS veterans organisation, *Sint Maartensfonds*, which is still going strong today, chaired by the old PAK veteran, Toon Pauli.

As for the German veterans from the Flandern and the Langemarck, their stories did not end in May 1945 either. For the SS-Legion Flandern's first commander, Michael Lippert, there was to be no quiet retirement after the War. Arrested (along with Sepp Dietrich, who had already served 10 years and was re-arrested) in 1957 by the West German authorities, he was tried for his role in the Night of the Long Knives in 1934. Both he and Dietrich were found guilty, Lippert specifically for his part in the murder of Ernst Röhm. On 10 May the prosecutor, Dr Weiss, demanded a two-year sentence for Lippert claiming that he represented 'a pitiless police-state system' and that he was actually more culpable than Dietrich as he was the more intelligent of the two! Invited to make a personal statement to the Court on 13 May, Lippert pleaded that he was nothing more than a patriot doing his duty. Dietrich declined the offer. The following day the Court President, Dr Graf, found both men guilty and sentenced them to 18 months in prison each. Dr Graf remarked in his judgement that he found Lippert 'filled with a dangerous and unrepentant fanaticism.'

More remarkable than Lippert's trial was that of the man who commanded the Flemings at the front for almost three years and will be forever associated with them. 'Former Nazi Guard Deported' – this was the headline used by the Associated Press on 24 September 1988, covering a long-running story about an immigrant to the United States who had been fighting since 1982 to keep his US citizenship and not be deported. The immigrant in question was none other than the former Commanding Officer of the Flemings, SS-Standartenführer Conrad Schellong. On 10 September 1982 a Federal judge in Chicago had decreed that Schellong's citizenship was invalid due to 'material misrepresentation' about his past. It was not Schellong's command of the Flemings that so exercised the judiciary – in the form of Federal District Judge Bernard M. Decker – after a 60-day trial, but rather his pre-war service in the infamous Dachau and Sachsenhausen concentration camps. Schellong was not in court that day to hear the verdict in person but he continued to maintain his innocence on the charge of lying on his immigration application. He then took his case to the US Supreme Court. In its judgement in October 1986, Case Number 86-1158 in the matter of Conrad Schellong, Petitioner v. Immigration and Naturalization Service, the Court stated in paragraph 2:

In December 1956, petitioner applied for United States visa. In his visa application, petitioner did not mention his two-year period of service at the

Sachsenhausen Concentration Camp or his three-year service at Dachau. Petitioner obtained a visa the following month, and he entered the United States in February 1957. In 1962, petitioner applied for naturalization. He omitted from his naturalization application any mention of his association with the Brown Shirts in 1932 or with the SS Death's Head Units at Sachsenhausen and Dachau. In addition, petitioner stated that he had been 'only a soldier'...

In its conclusion the Supreme Court stated that on his original visa application Schellong gave his prior history as:

Birth 1910, Dresden, Germany; 1910–1934, Leipzig, Germany; 1934–1939, German Waffen-SS; 1939–1945, Waffen-SS during the war.

It is unsurprising that Schellong did not elaborate on his wartime record. The most damning line in the Supreme Court judgement, which found in favour of the Immigration and Naturalization Service, was undoubtedly the following:

Although there was no evidence that petitioner personally abused any prisoner at Dachau, petitioner admitted that he was aware of the inhumane treatment of prisoners there.

This one line effectively sealed Schellong's fate. The piece in the Associated Press that was headlined 'Former Nazi Guard Deported' reported:

A 78-year-old Chicago man was deported to West Germany for concealing his pre-World War II service as a lieutenant colonel in the Nazi SS at two concentration camps, the Justice Department said today. Conrad Schellong, deported Thursday, had been the target of a 7½-year legal effort by the Justice Department's Office of Special Investigations, which said he served in SS guard companies at the Sachsenhausen and Dachau camps from 1934 to 1939.

Schellong's comment when asked was 'I didn't lie about my application. I'm surprised that I lost.' Conrad Schellong, Knights Cross winner and last field commander of the Flemings on the Eastern Front, died on his birthday, 7 February 1992, at the age of 82.

Remarkably (maybe not), the one commander who did live out his years in relative peace was the disgraced KG commander from Narva, Wilhelm Rehmann, who lived quietly in West Germany until his death on 7 April 1975, aged 63.

The Flemish contribution to the Waffen-SS

The Flemish contribution to the Waffen-SS is complex and the figures can be misleading. The figure most often quoted for the total number of Flemings who served in the Waffen-SS during the War is 23,000. This is a remarkably high number given the size of the pre-war Flemish population. During most of the conflict, however, the Flemings were at no more than a brigade or kampfgruppe strength, with a maximum of 6,000 men serving at any one time. It was only when the War was effectively over in late 1944 and the SS Langemarck Division was formed that there was a huge influx into the Waffen-SS, and most of these latecomers actually did relatively little fighting. It was the hard core of KG Schellong that led from the front at Arnswalde and Altdamm. Even so, casualties were exceptionally heavy, with more than 5,000 Flemings killed in action while serving in the Waffen-SS.

It was not only in the SS-Legion Flandern and the Langemarck, both Sturmbrigade and Division, that the Flemings made their mark on the Eastern Front. Flemings served in the SS Wiking, Das Reich, the Leibstandarte and even in the 15th Waffen-Grenadier Division der SS (lettische Nr.1) where its last commander, SS-Oberführer Adolf Ax, born and brought up in Flanders of German parents, won the Knights Cross on 9 May 1945. About 150 Flemings also served under the German special operations leader, Otto Skorzeny and many even served with the Dutch; the roll of the SS-Legion Niederlande in early January 1942 listed 26 Flemings fighting with the unit on the Volkhov.

Perhaps the best way to assess the impact the Flemish had in supporting the German war effort is to gauge how the Wehrmacht itself judged their contribution. So we must consider and acknowledge the progression of the Flemish from an infantry-heavy SS-Legion entrusted to rear area security and stiffened with a large German command cadre, to a much larger, fully motorised unit with integral armour and heavy weapons, when both were very scarce, and with an overwhelmingly Flemish command structure. For the majority of the War on the Eastern Front the Flemish had an appreciable number of men fighting in some of the bitterest battles of the conflict, where they were respected by friend and foe alike for their qualities of courage and steadfastness. It is a great pity that this courage was in the service of such a terrible cause.

Legacy

Perhaps the longest lasting legacy from the Flemish involvement with the Waffen-SS was the impetus it gave to a renewed and extreme version of Flemish nationalism. Following the War, many veterans became involved in politics and some even participated in the establishment of a new, separatist party in Flanders, the *Vlaams Blok* (Flemish Bloc). An extreme, right-wing party, the Vlaams Bloc enjoyed notoriety and some electoral success but was disbanded and replaced by a new party with much the same platform, the *Vlaams Belang* (Flemish Movement). Spearheaded first by the Bloc and then the Belang, Flemish nationalism has gone from strength to strength. With its slogan *Eigen Volk Eerst* (Our People First), the Vlaams Belang is bent on carving out an independent Flanders and consigning Belgium to history. Their twin policy planks are halting mass immigration from French-speaking North Africa – people likely to gravitate towards fellow French speakers in Walloonia – and stopping the siphoning of taxes from Flanders to Walloonia. Under the existing system the Flemings pay a bigger share of GDP to subsidise their former 'masters' than the West Germans pay towards their economically scelorotic eastern cousins. Belgium now has two regional parliaments for Flanders and Walloonia, with the Vlaams Belang the single largest Flemish party, having polled 24% of the popular vote in regional elections in 2004. They courted controversy when, in 1998, they sponsored a change in the law in the Flemish parliament to pay former convicted collaborators special 'state aid' compensation payments, of around £330 per annum, that were previously only open to those who had suffered directly at the hands of the Nazis, such as members of the Resistance and concentration camp inmates. The announcement was greeted with anger in Walloonia and among former Resistance members. The Walloon politician, Robert Collignon, said that it was 'despicable that war victims be considered as equal to those who had no sense of civic responsibility.'

The Johan Sauwens case

It was not only the Vlaams Belang that inherited something, however indirectly, from the Flemish Waffen-SS. In May 2001 Johan Sauwens, interior minister in the Flemish regional government, attended a reunion of the SS veterans of Sint Maartensfonds. He was caught in a sting by a left-wing newspaper, *De Morgen*, which videoed the event and his participation. During the meeting a speaker called for the creation of a 'greater Germany', at which point Sauwens left, but not before he was caught on camera standing as the anthem of the Flemish SS was sung. Three of the four parties in Flanders' ruling coalition demanded he step down. Sauwens held on for almost a week, saying he would only resign if asked to by his own party, the nationalist *Volksunie* – the People's Union. The Minister's official response to his parliament was: 'I wish to express my apologies over the fault I committed by attending a meeting where international extreme-right elements were gathered.' The Volksunie Party prevaricated before forcing him to resign, only doing so when it came to light that Sauwens had actually been a member of Sint Maartensfonds for 25 years! These relevations caused a political firestorm in Belgium: firstly, because the Volksunie was considered a moderate Flemish party, unlike the extremist Vlaams Belang; secondly, the timing was dreadful, with Belgium just weeks away from its six-month term in the rotating presidency of the European Union, where its stated aim was to lead on combating racism and xenophobia across the Union; and lastly, because it reminded today's Belgium of a past that so many of its citizens so dearly wanted to forget. The Belgian State intelligence service, the *Surete de l'Etat*, has had neo-Nazi Flemish and Walloon groups under surveillance for years, particularly following the waves of bombings and attacks in the 1980s carried out by ultra-right groups such as the *Front de la Jeunesse* and the *Westland New Post*.

The result of the Sauwens incident was a call by many of Belgium's national leaders for a South African-style 'truth and reconciliation commission' to help the nation face its collaborationist past. Although, significantly, attention was only focused on Flanders, with the inconvenient truth of Léon Degrelle, his *Cristus Rex* party and Walloon Waffen-SS involvement quietly forgotten.

The sins of the fathers

In May 2006 20,000 people, many with white armbands, marched through Antwerp to protest at two recent attacks by far-Right extremists in the city. The attacks left three people dead and another seriously injured. The worst incident on May 11 saw 18-year-old Hans Van Themsche, facing expulsion from his agricultural and biotechnological college for smoking, shave his head and buy a Winchester rifle. So armed, he dressed in black and went to the city centre and started firing. He targeted immigrants and shot a Malian nanny and the two-year-old white girl she was minding. He also shot and wounded a Turkish woman, before being wounded and apprehended by a plain clothes policeman. Van Themsche was a supporter of the Vlaams Belang and his father was a founding member of the Vlaams Blok. His aunt Frieda was a Belang MP in the Flemish regional government, while his grandfather had served with the SS Langemarck on the Russian Front in World War II.

What next for Belgium?

In December 2006 in the UK *Times* newspaper, journalist David Charter published a report from Brussels entitled 'It's the end of Belgium as we know it … only joking'. The opening line was 'Thousands of Belgians were thrown into a panic by news that the Flemish half of the country had declared independence.' In an episode reminiscent of Orson Welles' famous 1938 *War of the Worlds* radio broadcast, the French TV channel, RTBF, ran a hoax piece purporting to show the break-up of modern-day Belgium. The show had its host, the well-known TV news reporter Christophe Deborsu, broadcasting live scenes of ecstatic Flemish nationalists waving black lion of Flanders flags, and queues of French-speaking Walloons heading hurriedly towards the new 'border'. The newspaper report went on to say 'Flanders is now the wealthiest of the two halves (of Belgium) but painful memories linger from the 19th Century when the French-speaking aristocracy held sway.'

Hoax though it was, sixty years after the War the few Flemish nationalists still alive who followed their beliefs and fought in the Waffen-SS would have liked it to have been a documentary.

Names to remember

As a civilian, Remy Schrijnen was just as uncompromising as he had been as a soldier. Convicted of collaboration, imprisoned and with his civil rights revoked, he struggled to make a decent living in post-war Flanders. Repeatedly arrested and held for his strident nationalist views he was eventually forced to flee Belgium and, supported by the association of Knights Cross winners, move to West Germany. He and his family settled down to a peaceful life until his death in 2006.

Georg D'Haese and his new German wife remained off the official radar for several years until it was safe enough to come out of hiding. Unlike Schrijnen, who became a totem for the Flemish Waffen-SS, D'Haese preferred to move on from his wartime experience and rarely spoke about it. Although a successful employee working for a publisher, his real love was painting and in 1992 his work was exhibited in a book. He died shortly afterwards.

APPENDIX A

Waffen-SS Organisation

SS Section (Gruppe):
Commanded by a junior NCO such as an SS-Unterscharführer, or a senior NCO such as an SS-Scharführer.
Made up of anywhere between 6 to 12 men depending on casualties, the section, as in all armies, was the smallest building block of the Waffen-SS formations. When a man first joined his unit he would be allocated to a section that would be his home and sanctuary until killed, wounded or told otherwise. If the sections did not work then nothing would. All unit cohesion and performance rested on them. Remy Shrijnen's PAK gun crew were a section.

SS Platoon (Zug):
Commanded by either a junior officer such as an SS-Untersturmführer, an officer candidate such as an SS-Oberjunker or a senior NCO such as an SS-Oberscharführer.
Consisting of usually 3 or 4 sections depending on casualties, the platoon was the most commonly used sub-unit. In panzer formations a platoon would comprise 3 or 4 tanks.

SS Company (Kompanie):
Commanded by a more senior and hopefully experienced, though still very young, officer such as an SS-Obersturmführer or an SS-Hauptsturmführer.
Usually consisting of three platoons the company was the lowest tactical unit that external attachments were made to, including artillery fire observers and forward air controllers. In panzer formations the company would comprise three tank platoons.

SS Battalion (Abteilung):
Commanded by an older and more experienced officer such as an SS-Obersturmbannführer or an SS-Sturmbannführer.

An average battalion would be made up of four companies and could have sections of specialist troops such as engineers attached as necessary for a particular operation. A battalion would be numbered with a Roman numeral in front of its parent regiment's designation, such as II/SS-Panzergrenadier Regiment 6 Theodor Eicke.

SS Regiment (Standarte):
Commanded by a senior and very experienced officer such as an SS-Oberführer or SS-Standartenführer.
Equivalent to a brigade in the British Army, the regiments were a division's major sub-units and as such would have their own integral staff as well as supporting elements including a heavy gun section, an anti-aircraft defence section, a combat engineer section and three infantry battalions, three armoured infantry battalions or two panzer battalions, depending on its designation as an infantry, panzergrenadier or panzer regiment respectively. This was a major difference between Heer and Waffen-SS regiments, with Heer formations having the same number of panzer battalions but crucially only two infantry battalions in each panzergrenadier or infantry regiment. This heavily reduced the unit's combat power and meant that Heer units burned out far more rapidly in the battles of attrition so prevalent on the Russian Front. It was also a major flaw in many Waffen-SS units raised later in the war including the Langemarck and the Charlemagne. The lack of two entire infantry battalions meant the unit's combat effectiveness could be quickly eroded in periods of intense fighting. The regiment would be described by type, Roman numeral if it had one and then honour name if given one, so for example there was SS-Freiwilligen Panzergrenadier Regiment 49 De Ruiter.

SS Division:
Next in the chain came the mainstay of the Waffen-SS system, the division. This was entirely different from the British Army system, where the much smaller regimental formation is the building block of the field army and a soldier's spiritual home. A British soldier would feel loyalty to the Royal Norfolks, the Cameronians or the Irish Guards but in the Waffen-SS it was to the Das Reich or the Hitlerjugend. This 'division as home' concept was a great help in maintaining morale and combat effectiveness during the frequent decimations of the Waffen-SS divisions.

There were three main types of Waffen-SS division, each with its own structure: the Panzer (tank) division, the Panzergrenadier (mixed tanks and infantry) division and the non-mechanized division (either infantry, cavalry or mountain infantry).

All three types were commanded by either an SS-Gruppenführer or SS-Brigadeführer.

Just as with regiments, the division would have a structure of support units and these would typically comprise headquarters staff, military police, transport, medical support, logistics, a signals battalion, an engineer battalion, an artillery battalion and an anti-aircraft battalion (almost all entirely mechanized in panzer and panzergrenadier divisions). The fighting elements of the divisions were as follows:

Panzer division – the armoured fists of the Waffen-SS all had two panzergrenadier regiments of three battalions each and a panzer regiment of two battalions. There were seven full panzer divisions in the Waffen-SS and they comprised the crème de la crème of the Waffen-SS, divisions such as the 1st SS Panzer Division Leibstandarte, SS Adolf Hitler. Of the non-German Waffen-SS formations, only the famous 5th SS Wiking Division was a full panzer formation.

Panzergrenadier division – comprising two panzergrenadier regiments of three battalions each and a single panzer battalion, these were not full panzer divisions but were still very powerful formations with their own integral armour. In the 'combat pecking order' these formations were still an elite within the Waffen-SS. There were six panzergrenadier divisions including the only Waffen-SS division to fight exclusively on the Western Front, the 17th SS Panzergrenadier Division Götz von Berlichingen. Three of the non-Reichsdeutsche Waffen-SS formations attained this status, including the Nordic 11th SS Freiwilligen Panzergrenadier Division Nordland and the Hungarian volksdeutsche 18th SS Freiwilligen Panzergrenadier Division Horst Wessel.

The non-mechanized division (either grenadier, i.e. infantry, cavalry or mountain infantry). These formations formed the bulk of the Waffen-SS order of battle during the war and indeed the vast majority of foreign formations came under this designation. As non-mechanized units they were the least well-equipped of the Waffen-SS formations and were of widely differing organisation, strength and combat effectiveness. A standard grenadier division was meant to comprise two grenadier regiments of three battalions each with supporting arms, as with all the other divisions, but in practice this was chopped and changed to suit the availability of both equipment and manpower. In the French 33rd Waffen-Grenadier-Division der SS Charlemagne (französische Nr.1) for instance, there were only two grenadier battalions in each regiment (for more information see *Hitler's Gauls*). Crucially, these formations lacked any integral armour and the necessary transport to give them the mobility on the battlefield that was increasingly essential. There were eighteen grenadier divisions including the 'twin' designation given to the 29th Waffen Grenadier Divisions der SS of Russiche Nr.1 under Bronislav Kaminski, and Italiensiche Nr.1 under Heldmann, three cavalry (Kavallerie) divisions, not including the defunct 33rd Waffen Kavallerie Division der SS (Ungarische Nr.3) as this unit was overrun before formation and its number reused for the French, and six mountain infantry (Gebirgs) divisions. A few of these formations were worthy of the name elite, including the 27th SS Freiwilligen Grenadier Division Langemarck, and in particular the Baltic formations. Others, though not combat elites, were units with good combat records such as the 6th SS Gebirgs Division Nord. The majority, however, were of lesser quality and many were formed as defeat loomed and were of little value at the front. Some were the lowest of the low and deserve to be remembered with nothing more than horror and contempt at their records, which were brutal beyond belief, the most infamous being the 36th Waffen Grenadier Division der SS under Oskar Dirlewanger: the acceptance of which into the Waffen-SS order of battle will forever stain its reputation.

SS Corps (Korps):
Commanded by either an SS-Obergruppenführer or SS-Gruppenführer.
The Corps was the next level up in organisational terms and consisted of a number of divisions, the minimum of which was two but could rise to three or even four. The Corps was a unit in its own right with a full-time staff comprising complements of headquarters staff, transport, logistics, military police, medical and signalling units of different strengths. Component divisions would then be placed under Corps command but did not 'belong' to that Corps for any longer than the specific campaign the Corps was involved in, or even for no more than a single operation. The Wehrmacht's ability to swiftly regroup formations under differing Corps commands during often complex phases of battle was one of the reasons that the German forces held out for so long. During the latter defensive stages of the Russian campaign formations would often rapidly switch Corps control to face and close off Russian offensive threats. Few armies have ever mastered this art. During the war a total of eighteen Waffen-SS corps were formed, including Felix Steiner's famous 3rd Germanisches SS Panzer Corps and the 1st and 2nd SS Panzer Corps of Kharkov, Normandy and Ardennes fame.

SS Army Group (Armeegruppe):
Commanded by either an SS-Obergruppenführer or SS-Oberstgruppenführer (only Sepp Dietrich ever achieved this rank, see Appendix on Waffen-SS Ranks).
The largest formation ever fielded by the Waffen-SS during the war. This grouping would normally consist of several corps-sized units but was extremely unwieldy to handle even for the well trained Wehrmacht General Staff corps. During the early stages of the war the separate Waffen-SS formations were distributed between the different Wehrmacht Heer Army Groups, such as Army Group A, B or C for the invasion of Soviet Russia, and it was only when to all intents and purposes the war was lost that Waffen-SS formations were brought together in this way (in an interesting volte face, often with Heer formations integral to them).

APPENDIX B

Germaansche SS Vlaanderen, Waffen-SS and comparable Ranks

SS-Maat	SS-Schütze	Private (this was the basic private rank, any speciality would be reflected in the title, e.g. Panzerschütze)
No equivalent	SS-Oberschütze	Senior Private (attained after six months' service)
SS-Stormman	SS-Sturmmann	Lance corporal
SS-Rottenleider	SS-Rottenführer	Corporal
SS-Onderschaarleider	SS-Unterscharführer	Lance Sergeant
No equivalent	SS-Junker	Officer candidate (substantive rank of SS-Unterscharführer)
SS-Schaarleider	SS-Scharführer	Sergeant
No equivalent	SS-Standartenjunker	Officer candidate (substantive rank of SS-Scharführer)
SS-Opperschaarleider	SS-Oberscharführer	Colour/staff Sergeant
SS-Hoofdschaarleider	SS-Hauptscharführer	Warrant Officer Class 2
No equivalent	SS-Standartenoberjunker	Officer candidate (substantive rank of SS-Hauptscharführer)

No equivalent	SS-Sturmscharführer	Warrant Officer Class 1 (after fifteen years' service)
SS-Onderstormleider	SS-Untersturmführer	Second Lieutenant
SS-Opperstormleider	SS-Obersturmführer	Lieutenant
SS-Hoofdstormleider	SS-Hauptsturmführer	Captain
SS-Stormbanleider	SS-Sturmbannführer	Major
SS-Opperstormbanleider	SS-Obersturmbannführer	Lieutenant-Colonel
SS-Standaardleider	SS-Standartenführer	Colonel

(There were no Germaansche SS Vlaanderen ranks above Standaardleider).

SS-Oberführer	Brigadier equivalent
SS-Brigadeführer	Major-General
SS-Gruppenführer	Lieutenant-General
SS-Obergruppenführer	General
SS-Oberstgruppenführer	Colonel-General (only Sepp Dietrich ever attained this rank)

BIBLIOGRAPHY

BOOKS

Ailsby, Christopher, *Hell on the Eastern Front: The Waffen-SS War in Russia 1941–1945*, Spellmount, 1998

Ailsby, Christopher, *Waffen-SS The Unpublished Photographs 1923–945*, Bookmart, 2000

Bauer, Eddy, Lt.Col, *World War II*, Orbis, 1972

Beevor, Antony, *Berlin The Downfall 1945*, Penguin, 2003

Bishop, Chris, *Hell on the Western Front: The Waffen-SS in Europe 1940–45*, Spellmount, 2003

Bishop, Chris, *The Military Atlas of World War II*, Amber, 2005

Brandt, Allen, *The Last Knight of Flanders: Remy Schrijnen and his SS-Legion "Flandern"/Sturmbrigade "Langemarck" Comrades on the Eastern Front 1941–1945*, Schiffer, 1998

Bruyne, Eddy de and Rikmenspoel, Marc, *For Rex and for Belgium – Leon Degrelle and Walloon Political & Military Collaboration 1940–45*, Helion, 2004

Butler, Rupert, *SS-Wiking*, Spellmount, 2002

Butler, Rupert, *The Black Angels*, Arrow, 1989

Butler, Rupert, *Legions of Death*, Hamlyn, 1983

Carell, Paul, *Hitler's War on Russia*, George G. Harrap, 1964

Estes, Kenneth. W, *A European Anabasis – Western European Volunteers in the German Army and SS, 1940–1945*, Columbia University Press, 2003

Graber, G S, *History of the SS*, Diamond, 1994

Hausser, Paul, *Wenn Alle Brüder Schweigen – Grosser Bildband über die Waffen-SS* (When all our brothers are silent), Nation Europa, 1973

Hillbald, Thorolf (edited by), *Twilight of the Gods – A Swedish Waffen-SS Volunteer's Experiences with the 11th SS-Panzergrenadier Division 'Nordland', Eastern Front 1944—45*, Helion, 2004

Jurado, Carlos Caballero, *Resistance Warfare 1940–45*, Osprey Men-at-Arms series, 1985

Keen, Maurice (ed.), *Medieval Warfare: A History*, Oxford University Press, 1999

Le Tissier, Tony, *With our backs to Berlin – The German Army in Retreat 1945*, Sutton, 2001

Littlejohn, David, *The Patriotic Traitors: A History of Collaboration in German-Occupied Europe 1940/1945*, William Heinemann, 1972

Littlejohn, David, *Foreign Legions of the Third Reich Volume 2*, R. James Bender, 1981

Littlejohn, David, *Foreign Legions of the Third Reich Volume 4*, R. James Bender, 1987

Lucas, James, *Das Reich – The Military Role of the 2nd SS Division*, Cassell, 1991

Munoz, Antonio, *Iron Fist: A Combat History of the 17th SS Panzergrenadier Division 'Götz von Berlichingen'*, Europe Books, 1999

Pierik, Perry, *From Leningrad to Berlin – Dutch Volunteers in the Service of the German Waffen-SS 1941–1945*, Aspeckt, 2001

Quarrie, Bruce, *Hitler's Samurai*, Patrick Stephens, 1983

Reitlinger, Gerald, *The SS: Alibi of a Nation, 1939–1945*, Heinemann, 1956

Reynolds, Michael, *The Devil's Adjutant, Jochen Peiper, Panzer Leader*, Spellmount, 1995

Reynolds, Michael, *Sons of the Reich, II SS Panzer Corps*, Spellmount, 2002

Sourd, Jean-Pierre, *True Believers: Spanish Volunteers in the Heer and Waffen-SS, 1944–45*, Europa Books Inc, 2004 (translated by Antonio Munoz)

Taylor, Brian, *Barbarossa to Berlin Volume Two: The Defeat of Germany, 19 November 1942 to 15 May 1945*, Spellmount, 2004

Williamson, Gordon, *The Blood Soaked Soil*, Blitz Editions, 1997

Williamson, Gordon, *Loyalty is my Honor*, Brown, 1995

Williamson, Gordon, *The SS: Hitler's Instrument of Terror*, Spellmount, 2006

Williamson, Gordon, *The Waffen-SS – 24. to 38. Divisions, & Volunteer Legions*, Osprey Men-at-Arms series, 2004

PERIODICALS

Landwehr, Richard, 'The European Volunteer Movement of World War II', Journal of Historical Review

Landwehr, Richard, 'Siegrunen', Volume numbers 41, 54 and 62

Index

Abbeville, massacre of, 36-7
Altdamm, battle of, 191-94, 208
Alte Hasen (old hares - Wehrmacht
    slang for combat veterans),94
Alto Adige (see also South Tyrol),19
Anseeuw, Dries,132, 142
Arnswalde, relief of,185-89, 208
Aryan,45-7, 49-50, 53-5, 106, 168;
    Herrenvolk (master race),47
Arys, training ground,57, 63

Bad Tölz, Junkerschule (Waffen-SS
    officer school),50, 57, 107-108,
    132, 139, 163, 171, 204-205
Battle of the European SS (see also
    Narva, battle of), 5, 15, 133, 135,
    137, 161
Belgae, Celtic tribe,17
Berger, Gottlob, SS-Gruppenführer,
    56, 61, 106-107, 109-111, 117, 135,
    141, 168, 170-171
Blue (Azul-Spanish) Division, 78, 80-
    1, 86, 89, 96-7, 131
Borms, August,28, 205
Bottu, Luc,139, 154
Buyse, Jan, 113

Cherkassy Pocket, battle of 84, 107,
    123, 127, 129, 135, 140, 186
Christophersen, Egon, 163
Clercq, Gustave 'Staf' De, 29-30, 37,
    40-41, 56, 88, 100, 118, 205; death
    of, 101, 110, 118, 130, 205
Concentration camps
    Auschwitz, 101
    Treblinka, 101

Coninck, Pieter De, 20-21
Cristus Rex Party, 210
Croatian Legion, 46

Das Schwarze Korps (SS newspaper),
    113
D-Day, 131, 139, 166, 170
Debica, training ground, 150-51, 99,
    105, 110-11, 128, 131, 135-6, 140
Degrelle, Léon, 15, 23, 28, 30, 36, 79,
    84, 93, 118, 123, 130-131, 172, 182,
    200, 210
Dersmenshceck, Anton, 132
D'Haese, Georg, 32-3, 44, 62-3, 72, 92,
    103, 132, 136, 142, 146, 150, 152,
    154-7, 159-62, 165, 168-9, 175, 201,
    205, 211
D'Hollander, Bert, 142, 147, 150, 156
DeVlag, 31, 41, 43, 88, 100-101, 110,
    138, 163, 166-7, 170, 205
Dietrich, Josep 'Sepp', SS-
    Oberstgruppenführer, 174, 179,
    184, 206, 216, 218
Dinaso, 29-31, 37, 41-2, 52, 58, 170
Doriot, Jacques, death of, 101

Eicke, Theodor 'Papa', SS-
    Gruppenführer, 60, 75, 90, 214
Elias, Hendrik Dr, 101, 138, 170, 205
Erika, clearing, battle of, 80, 82, 85-7,
    89, 94

Fitzhum, Joseph, SS-
    Obersturmbannführer, 88-91
François, Jozef 'Jef', 31, 42-3, 52, 58, 166
Freikorps Danmark, 45, 51, 88, 105

Galicia, 107, 128, 140
Germany,
Army groups,
Army Group A (later North), 66-7, 216
Army Group B (later Centre) 66-7, 75, 119, 139-140, 161, 165, 181
Army Group C (later South), 66
Army Group Courland, 181
Army Group North Ukraine, 128, 161, 181
Army Group Vistula, 184, 188-189, 191
Armies,
4th Panzer Army,183
11th Army, 94
16th Army, 74-5
18th Army, 74, 77, 81, 87, 93, 95-6, 131
Corps,
I Corps, 75
XXVIII Corps, 80, 93
L Corps, 94
Divisions
2nd Panzer, 84
58th Infantry, 79-81
126th Infantry, 77-8, 81
254th Infantry, 97
9th Luftwaffe Field Division, 133
10th Luftwaffe Field Division, 133
Units (Waffen-SS)
Armies
6th SS Panzer Army, 174, 179, 184
Corps
3rd Germanisches SS Panzer Corps, 216
Divisions,
1st SS-Panzer Division Leibstandarte50, 68, 110, 122-123, 127-129, 131, 171, 208, 215
2nd SS-Panzer Division Das Reich, 122-123, 125-127, 129, 141, 171-172, 178, 208, 214, 220
3rd SS-Panzer Division Totenkopf, 66, 68, 75, 90, 109
4th SS-Panzergrenadier Division; Polizei, 68, 80, 82, 85, 96, 185, 196
5th SS-Panzer Division Wiking, 45, 49-50, 55, 68, 84, 87-8, 107, 117, 123, 127, 129, 171-72, 182, 208, 215, 219
9th SS-Panzer Division Frundsberg, 61, 108, 127-28, 169, 184-86, 189, 192-93
10th SS-Panzer Division

Hohenstaufen, 108, 127, 168-69,
11th SS-Freiwilligen Panzergrenadier Division Nordland, 49-51, 106, 134, 144-45, 149, 155, 160-61, 182, 185-86, 189, 192, 215
12th SS-Panzer Division Hitlerjugend 203, 214
15th Waffen Grenadier Division der SS (lettishe Nr.1), 134, 208
17th SS-Panzergrenadier Division Götz von Berlichingen, 169, 215
18th SS-Freiwilligen Panzergrenadier Division Horst Wessel, 107, 215
19th Waffen Grenadier Division der SS (lettishe Nr.2), 135
20th Waffen Grenadier Division der SS (estnische Nr.1), 135
23rd SS-Freiwilligen Panzergrenadier Division Nederland, 159, 182, 185, 189
28th SS-Freiwilligen Panzergrenadier Division Wallonien, 168, 172, 174, 182, 184, 189, 193
33rd SS-Freiwilligen Grenadier Division Charlemagne, 101, 108, 182-3, 192, 214-5
34th SS-Freiwilligen Division Landstorm Nederland, 61, 166
38th SS-Grenadier Division Nibelungen, 204
Brigades,
2. SS-Infanterie Brigade (mot.), 68, 71, 86, 88, 90, 109, 134
SS-Sturmbrigade Frankreich, 107-8, 140, 183
SS-Sturmbrigade Wallonien, 84, 107, 127
4th SS-Freiwilligen Panzergrenadier Brigade Nederland, 134
Regiments,
Danmark, 145, 192-92; Der Führer, 50; De Ruiter, 144, 189, 214
General Seyffardt, 59, 143, 151, 189
Germania, 50
Kriegsberichter-Kurt Eggers, 113
Norge, 145
Geurts, Jules, 92-3, 99-100, 102, 161
Goths,
Ostrogoths, 18; Visigoths, 18
Grenadier Hill, 144, 146, 154-5, 158-61
Grootaer, Jef, 142, 147, 150, 152, 154, 156
Gullik, Willem Van, 20

Hallman, Gerhard, SS-
    Hauptsturmführer, 90
Hausser, Paul, SS-Obergruppenführer,
    50, 97
Hermans, Ward, 42
Hilfspolizei, 90
Himmler, Heinrich, Reichsführer-SS,
    46-50, 52, 54-6, 61-2, 68, 70, 90,
    106-107, 109, 111, 135, 163, 167-68,
    171; command of Army Group;
    Vistula, 184-85
Hitler, Adolf, 38, 119
Hitler Youth, 101, 107, 170, 173, 204
Hulse, Raf Van, 43, 113
Holocaust, 47

Joseph Stalin Tank, 157-8

Kamenets-Podolsk Pocket, 127, 135,
    169
Katyushas (Stalin's Organs), 148, 159
Kausch, Paul-Albert, SS-
    Obersturmbannführer, 160-1
Klykov, Red Army General, 75, 77, 83
Koniev, Red Army Marshal, 82, 127, 183
Kopfstellung, PAK position, 132, 147-
    8, 157
Kotlowski, Anton, 115, 137, 178, 191,
    193-4, 196, 200
Kortrijk, battle of (in French Courtrai,
    aka Battle of the Golden Spurs),
    14-5, 19-21, 53, 89-90, 92, 110, 127
Krasny-Bor, battle of, 96-7, 99, 101,
    103, 110, 112, 132, 135, 172
Kriegsmarine, 47, 75, 84

Lagrou, René, 42-3, 52, 54
Langhe, Jef De, 43
Laperre, Marcel, 137-39, 141-2, 147-8,
    154, 156-7, 159, 178, 200
Laporte, Fernand 'Nand', 178, 186
Leeb, Wilhelm Ritter von, Heer Field
    Marshal, 66-7, 74-5, 77
Leemputten, Walther Van, 136, 139,
    141, 154, 159
Légion des Volontaires Français
    contre le bolchevisme (LVF), 51,
    139, 183
Legion Niederlande, 45, 53, 57-8, 86,
    88, 90-91, 143, 208
Legion Norwegen, 45
Legion Wallonie, 46, 51, 58
Lehembre, Edgar Dr, 101
Leopold III, King of the Belgians, 38
Lettow-Vorbeck, Hans-Albert, SS-
    Obersturmbannführer, 87-8

Lindekens, Hugo, 113
Lindemann, Georg, Heer General of
    Cavalry, 77, 87, 93, 161
Lippert, Michael, 58, 60-61, 80, 86-7,
    166, 206
Luftwaffe, 47, 75, 84, 134, 141, 155, 170

Maginot, André, 35
Maginot Line, 35-7
Manstein, Erich von, Field Marshal,
    94-5, 120, 128-9, 144
Mol, Henri Van, 136, 142, 146, 149
Mooyman, Gerardus, 93, 163
Müller, Thomas, SS-Standartenführer,
    168-9, 172, 175, 182, 193, 195-6,
    200
Mussert, Anton, 28, 30, 106, 205

Namen, Gwidje Van, 20, 168,
Narva, battle of, 15, 133-163
Nationalsozialistisches Kraftfahrkorps
    (NSKK), 100, 170
Nazi-Soviet Non-Agression Pact, 44,
    130
Normandy, battle of, 131, 169, 203
Nugiseks, Haralt, 163

Oberkommando der Wehrmacht
    (OKW), 75, 127, 165, 174, 179
Oostfronters (slang for Flemish
    Eastern Front veterans), 92, 179
Operation Bagration (Soviet summer
    offensive 1944), 139-140, 161, 165,
    181
Operation Barbarossa (German
    invasion of Soviet Union), 50-51,
    62, 66, 130, 139, 181
Operation Citadel (German Kursk
    offensive 1943), 65, 119-121, 135,
    181
Operation Market Garden (Allied
    airborne Arnhem offensive 1944),
    169
Operation Sonnenwende (German
    Summer Solstice offensive 1945),
    184-5, 187-9
Operation Typhoon (German
    offensive on Moscow 1941), 67, 73
Operation Watch on the Rhine
    (German Ardennes Offensive
    1944-45), 174, 179, 216
Organization Todt, 100-101, 170
Orphanage Hill, 144-9, 151, 154, 159,
    161
Ostheer (German Army in the East),
    89, 94, 120, 133, 161, 181, 187

Panzerfäusts, 160, 173, 191, 193-94
Pauli, Toon, 132, 206
Puaud, Edgar-Joseph-Alexandre, 51

Quisling, Vidkun, 28-9, 37, 205

Reeb, Eduard, 142, 147, 149-51, 156
Rehmann, Wilhelm, 136, 141, 144-7, 149-
, 162, 175, 177, 186-7, 189, 193, 207
Rosenberg, Alfred, 47
Röhm, Ernst, 60, 206

Schellong, Conrad, 90, 92, 94, 99, 112,
117, 120, 125-6, 136, 141, 168-9, 173,
175, 179, 182-6, 188-97, 205, 208;
court case and deportation, 206-7
Schrijnen, Remy, 9, 32-3, 44, 61-2, 72,
92-3, 101-103, 111, 117, 122, 131-2,
142, 147-8, 150, 156-8, 160-3, 171,
182, 196, 201, 203, 211
Severen, Joris Van, 29-31, 37; murder
of, 29, 37, 42, 79, 101
sig (runes), 53-4, 117, 169, 200
69.9 Hill, 144-146, 151, 155, 159, 161
South Tyrol (see aso Alto Adige), 19
Soviet Russian Red Army,
Units,
1st Ukrainian ,183
1st Belorussian (White Russian),
183-4, 189
2nd Belorussian (White Russian),
183, 188-9, 196
3rd Belorussian (White Russian), 183
Armies,
2nd Guards Tank Army, 185, 189, 194
2nd Shock Army, 75, 79, 82, 84, 87,
89, 93
Reconstitution of, 133, 145
5th Guards Tank Army, 183
52nd Army, 75
54th Army, 75
59th Army, 75
STAVKA (Soviet High Command),
73, 77, 83, 85, 89, 96, 128, 140, 188
Steenlandt, Joris Van, 42
Steiner, Felix, SS-Obergruppenführer,
160-2, 165, 182-3, 185, 187, 189, 216
Sturmabteilung (SA) see also
Brownshirts, 60, 90
Suys, Paul, 53, 56, 59, 172
Swinnen, Frans, 136, 141, 146, 149, 154

T34 tank, 86, 122, 134, 150-51, 187

Teutonic Knights, 152, 160
Tollenaere, Dr Reimond, 42, 52, 92,
100; death in action, 29, 78-9, 101,
131, 205
Tollenaere, Leo, 79, 142, 157
Totenkopf, organisation, 60, 68, 90,
109-110, 118
Treblinka, 101

Vandals,
Asdings,18
Gepids,18
Versailles, Treaty of, terms of, 40
Vlaams Blok, 15, 209-210
Vlaams Belang, 15, 209-210
Vlaamsche SS - organisation, 43
1. Standarten der Germaansche SS
in Vlaanderen comprising, 43;
Stormbaan I Antwerpen, 43;
Stormbaan II Oost-Vlaanderen,
43; Stormbaan III West-
Vlaanderen, 43; Stormbaan
IV Braband, 43; Stormbaan V
Limburg , 43
Vlaamsch Nationaal Verbond (VNV)
29-33, 39-43, 52-4, 56, 58-9, 78-9,
88, 92, 100-101, 110, 118, 138, 154,
162-3, 167, 170, 186
Vlaanderen die Leu, 21
Vlasov, Andrei, Red Army General,
73, 83-5, 87, 93
Volga Germans, 48
Volk en Staat (VNV newspaper), 30
Volkhov Pocket, 93-4, 103, 109-110,
112, 131, 135, 145, 172, 208
Volksdeutsche (racial Germans), 15,
48, 54, 61, 106, 117, 123, 127, 138,
192, 215

Wiele, Jef Van De, 29, 31, 43, 88, 100,
138, 163, 166-7, 170, 205

Yampil, battle of, 122-3, 125–6, 128,
131, 188

Year of the Ten Victories, 181

Zachan, rearguard action at, 187, 191
Zhukov, Grigory, Red Army Marshal,
83, 127, 183-84, 192
Zwarte Brigade (Black Brigade), 29,
41-2, 52, 58-9, 78-9, 92, 100-101